Southern Miscellany:

Essays in History in Honor of Glover Moore

Southern Miscellany:

Essays in History in Honor of Glover Moore

• • •

EDITED BY
Frank Allen Dennis

Preface by Roy V. Scott

CONTRIBUTORS:
John Ray Skates, Jr.
Richard C. Ethridge
James W. McKee, Jr.
Frank Allen Dennis
Fabian Val Husley
Lee E. Williams, II
William M. Simpson

UNIVERSITY PRESS OF MISSISSIPPI
Jackson

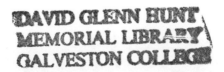

LIBRARY OF CONGRESS CATALOGING IN PUBLICATION DATA

Main entry under title:
Southern miscellany.
    CONTENTS: Skates, J. R. In defense of Owsley's
Yeoman.—Ethridge, R.C. Southern attitudes toward
slavery and secession in 1860 and early 1861 as
reflected by De Bow's review.—McKee, J. W. Congressman
William Barksdale of Mississippi. [etc.]
    1. Southern States—History—Addresses, essays,
lectures. 2. Moore, Glover, 1911-   . I. Moore,
Glover, 1911-   II. Dennis, Frank Allen. III.
Skates, John Ray.
F209.5.S68   975   80–20373
ISBN 0–87805–129–5

Contents

Editor's Note

Frank Allen Dennis

The party certainly had an inauspicious beginning. It was much like other Mississippi State alumni parties I had attended over the years at various historical conventions around the country. Most of the guests had their pretzels and bourbon; I and a few others had our potato chips and Seven-Up. The talk moved aimlessly from this to that as night turned into early morning.

Sometime around 1:00 A.M. Jim Shoalmire and I drifted out to the balcony overlooking the starlit beach of the Mississippi Gulf Coast and began to reminisce about our days in the carrels in Starkville, the snooker games in the Union, and the good fortune we had in being products of Mississippi State University. Eventually, our discussion turned to Glover Moore and the prospect that the day would come when he would no longer be an active member of the Mississippi State history department. As we continued to talk, an idea evolved; we would plan and execute a festschrift in his honor sometime soon after his retirement, which was scheduled for 1977. We would ask several of his former students to prepare a fresh piece of work for inclusion in this book of essays (no warmed-over dissertation chapters, please).

It was decided early that I would oversee the logistics for the proposed book. Almost every person contacted expressed deep interest in contributing to the volume. Some, under the press of other duties, were unable to fulfill their wishes. Even Jim Shoalmire, busy with the Stennis Collection at Mississippi State, was unable to write an essay; yet he takes pride in being the project's cofounder.

The seven authors of the essays contained in this volume teach at seven different universities from Louisiana to West Virginia. We are indeed a varied lot—including two former preachers and a Green Beret Vietnam veteran. Our historical interests range from the Civil War to civil rights and from yeomen to yahooism. Yet we share one thing in common: our professional respect and our deep affection for the slender gentleman from Birmingham, without whom we would not be where we are today.

It is to this master teacher and prince among men that we affectionately dedicate this volume. Each contributor is alone responsible for his own essay; each takes full blame for any mistakes of fact or interpretation therein. And each credits Glover Moore for the good that may be found in these short tomes.

I don't think I have ever heard anyone say anything derogatory about Glover Moore. And I'm really glad; I've never cared much for violence.

Preface

Roy V. Scott

In a recently published pictorial history of Mississippi State University, the authors referred to Glover Moore as a southern gentleman. As something of a carpetbagger I am not quite certain what the term implies, but its application to Moore is appropriate if the authors meant one who is courteous, considerate, and always proper in his relationships with others.

I first met Glover Moore in the spring of 1960 in a bar in Louisville, Kentucky. I was there, recently awarded Ph.D. degree in hand, looking for a job. Moore was there for whatever reasons people attend historical conventions, and when I encountered him he was consuming his limit of one drink a day. In the ensuing conversation, fortunately for me, it appeared that Mississippi State University had a vacancy in its history department that I was reasonably qualified to fill. Thus began a professional and personal association with Moore that has continued to the present.

Glover Moore, Jr., was born on September 22, 1911, in Birmingham, Alabama, to Glover and Maud Mims Moore. After attending local schools, he enrolled at Birmingham-Southern College, where in 1932 he earned his bachelor's degree in history and the distinction of being valedictorian of his class. For his graduate training, Moore chose Vanderbilt. There he studied under Frank L. Owsley, absorbing his illustrious mentor's views on southern agrarianism, independent yeomen, and Confederate diplomacy. Moore received his M.A. degree in 1933 and his Ph.D. in 1936, making him a contemporary of such distinguished historians as Lewis Atherton and T. Harry Williams.

With time out for military service during World War II, Moore spent his entire career at Mississippi State University. When he arrived in Starkville in the summer of 1936, prospects were less than encouraging. Moore was the first Ph.D. recipient in history employed by the institution; Mississippi State College, as it was known then, was a struggling agricultural and mechanical college with an enrollment of 1,900; and Starkville's chief connection with the outside world was a rail line to Artesia. Nevertheless, Moore went to work, progressed through the ranks from instructor, and earned a full professorship in 1953. Although Moore had the good sense to avoid the disease of academic administration, which all too often destroys the usefulness of academicians, he served two brief tours of duty as department head.

The subject of Moore's doctoral dissertation at Vanderbilt was that complex of issues that was resolved, at least temporarily, in the famous Missouri Compromise. The dissertation became his first book, published by the University of Kentucky Press in 1953. Writing in the *Mississippi Valley Historical Review*, Bernard Mayo labeled *The Missouri Controversy* a "distinguished monograph" and the "first comprehensive treatment of that fateful sectional struggle." He went on to say that Moore "has done an admirable job. He is thorough in research, clear and readable in style, and skillful and judicious in his analysis of personalities and complex issues."

If the value of a scholarly book is best measured by its longevity, as Fred Shannon argued in my graduate school days, Moore's *The Missouri Controversy* deserved the praise that Mayo and other reviewers heaped on it. In 1966 the University of Kentucky Press issued a paperback version, and the next year Peter Smith offered a reprint edition. More than a quarter of a century after the appearance of *The Missouri Controversy*, the volume remains the standard treatment of the subject.

Although Moore's scholarly reputation rests largely upon his *Missouri Controversy*, his other writings have substantial merit. In addition to a number of articles, book reviews, and miscellaneous items, Moore published two books dealing with members of his family. *William Jemison Mims, Soldier and Squire* (1966) is the account of the career of Moore's grandfather, an Alabamian who served in the Confederate army and later was a politician in Jefferson County. *A Calhoun County, Alabama, Boy in the 1860s* (1978), which Moore edited, is the autobiographical account by Moore's father of his childhood. These works display the same meticulous scholarship that had earned the praise of reviewers of *The Missouri Controversy*.

It has been as a teacher, however, that Glover Moore has made his greatest contribution. In fact, Moore can be described as a great teacher, in the best sense of that phrase. When he came to Mississippi State, he was one-half of a two-man department, so he taught practically every course in the catalog. Later, as the department grew and especially after it began to offer graduate training, Moore concentrated on the Old and New South and the West. These courses were always popular, and students flocked to them in droves. His lectures were models of clarity and organization, delivered at a pace that permitted students to record in their notes almost every word while devoting some attention to those things that young men and women generally find more interesting than historical details. For twenty years Moore also taught the department's historiography and historical methods course, in which he introduced scores of graduate students to the mysteries of bibliographies, sources, and footnotes.

Perhaps more than any other person, Moore built the graduate program in history at Mississippi State, although at the outset he questioned the wisdom of offering doctoral training in his discipline at what was essentially an agricultural and mechanical college. Not only did he play a leading role in recruiting those staff members who gave the department the stature it now enjoys, but he also directed more theses and dissertations than any other faculty member. Of the fifty-seven doctoral dissertations written in the department up to the time of Moore's retirement, he signed sixteen.

Moore's doctoral candidates wrote on a wide range of topics, generally in southern history. One dissertation dealt with the West, and another examined a nationwide phenomenon. As a group, they surveyed the careers of politicians, soldiers, and journalists, studied political developments since World War II, recounted the evolution of such divergent movements as Methodism and prohibitionism, and discussed Creek Indians in Georgia, Italian immigrants in Louisiana's Tangipahoa Parish, early nineteenth-century travelers and explorers in the American West, race riots after World War I, and aspects of Civil War diplomacy and strategy. To a remarkable degree, these dissertations reflected Moore himself. Always well researched and written, several of them were models of the historical craft. The quality of the training that Moore provided is indicated by the publication of excellent books by several of his students.

The regard Moore's former doctoral students have for him is remarkable. All of them have stories of their experiences to relate, and legends abound, but the consistent themes are affection, loyalty, and respect.

To his colleagues, Moore was a congenial and supportive associate. Certainly such past and present faculty members at Mississippi State as John K. Bettersworth, Harold S. Snellgrove, Warren F. Kuehl, Thomas L. Connelly, D. Clayton James, Janos Radvanyi, J. G. Shoalmire, E. Stanly Godbold, and I have benefited from association with him. Always willing to give freely of his time, Moore listened to our plans, helped us solve the problems that all historians encounter in their teaching and research, and, on occasion, corrected our spelling and grammar. The extent of our esteem for him is suggested by the number of times his name appears among the acknowledgments in our books. His retirement was thus as much of a loss to us as it was to the university he served so well for forty-one years.

The measure of a man, of course, is not found solely in the books he wrote, the students he trained, or the colleagues he aided and encouraged. Glover Moore is a most unusual person. Among his more notable qualities are the old-fashioned ones of loyalty, integrity, and unquestionable honesty. A humble man, little given to conspicuous displays of learning, Moore possesses a remarkable stock of knowledge. With his seemingly total recall of facts and bibliographical details, it was often a source of some chagrin to his associates to discover that he knew more about their specialties than they did. Gentle and compassionate, Moore saw no need to humiliate students or colleagues, regardless of how sophomoric or vacuous their opinions might have been. Arrogance, duplicity, and stupidity disgusted him, but rarely did he give vent to his disgust. Only the most asinine performance in departmental meetings would arouse him to display the anger the circumstance warranted.

Moore has his convictions, strongly held, but he was always able to adjust to changing conditions. A one-time New Dealer who argued for Franklin Roosevelt's court-packing plan, Moore had become a Republican by 1960. In company with the great majority of white southerners, he defended southern traditions, but not many years after 1954 he recognized that the second Reconstruction would produce a better America. In his youth, Moore had been something of a Nashville Agrarian, but as the evidence mounted to disprove the assumptions of that school of thought, he shifted his ground, although I was never able to convince him of the validity of my views of the New South.

In some ways, however, Moore has changed little over time. In physical appearance, he seems to be ageless. At the time of his retirement, he resembled very much the man I had met nineteen years earlier in that bar in Louisville. And he is just as sober now as he was then.

Southern Miscellany:

Essays in History in Honor of
Glover Moore

In Defense of
Owsley's Yeomen

John Ray Skates, Jr.

For generations the antebellum South has been thought in the popular mind to be a land of plantations and mansions, great planters and slaves, and endless cotton fields. That illusion has had amazing persistence both inside the South and out. Southerners have romanticized their past for a variety of reasons, the most important of which stemmed from the Civil War. Soon after the war the Lost Cause took a powerful hold on the southern mind, and the plantation myth developed as a necessary corollary. In great tragedy people must lose something of momentous and distinctive value. After the war a shattered sectional ego was salved by the belief in an antebellum time of greatness, when cavaliers and ladies, attended by devoted slaves, ruled the South. The pangs of postwar poverty could be eased, at least emotionally, by glorying in past riches.

Northern politicians blamed the Civil War on southern planters and, hence, imprinted early on the nonsouthern mind the idea of a planter-dominated southern society. In the twentieth century the powerful appeal of movies like *Gone with the Wind* and television spectaculars like "Roots" planted the plantation South even more firmly in the northern mind. In neither of these was there a role for anyone but the great planter, the poor white, or the slave.

If the plantation myth has persisted in the popular fancy, it has proved hardly less durable in the historical mind, resuscitated when it lagged first by southern apologists and more recently by civil rights advocates and Marxist historians. The idea of a dominant, nonslaveholding, landowning small-farmer class fits neither the ideologies of the economic determinist nor the southern romantic.

At various times three groups have dominated the debate over the makeup of southern society. At the risk of gross simplification one might characterize them in chronological order as the traditionalists, the neo-traditionalists, and the new economic historians or econometricians. The traditionalists held the rostrum until the Second World War. Slightly romantic in their views of southern society, they founded among historians the myth that the South was primarily a land of planters and slaves balanced only by a few yeomen and a large mass of degraded and ignorant poor whites. Some of their patron saints, like Frederick Law Olmsted, observed firsthand the society that they described. In the 1850s Olmsted, a traveler from New York, depicted the plantation South in his book *A Journey Through the Back Country*, and he saw only planters, slaves, and poor whites. In the early twentieth century the greatest traditionalist name of all rose to prominence. Ulrich B. Phillips wrote two books that became catechisms for traditionalist historians, *American Negro Slavery* (1918) and *Life and Labor in the Old South* (1929). In *Life and Labor in the Old South* Phillips found little place for any life except that of the planter or any labor other than that of the slave.

A generation apart in time and a world away in ideology were Phillips and neo-traditionalist Eugene D. Genovese. Yet their views of the structure of antebellum southern society are amazingly alike. Phillips might be accused of ignoring the small farmer for romantic reasons. Genovese ignores him because, in his Marxist model for society, an agricultural middle class is not supposed to exist.

A third group arose from an unexpected quarter. In the 1960s and 1970s the antebellum cotton South became a historical battleground with statistics and computers used as weapons. Styling themselves self-consciously the "new economic historians," economists trained in the esoteric arts of quantification invaded traditionalist and neo-traditionalist terrain. These "econometricians" based their conclusions on much wider and more diverse source material than the traditionalists and neo-traditionalists. Unfortunately, however, most of their work was limited socially and economically to slave conditions and to the profitability of slavery and the cotton economy.[1] They too, by exception more than design, promoted the planters and ignored the yeomen. Historians, no less than the man in the street, have proved resistant to any view of southern society that fails to place the planter at the top.

Although the plantation myth hardly fit the experiences of many southerners, the first serious challenge to it did not come until the 1940s. The traditionalist view reigned supreme when Frank L. Owsley, professor of history at Vanderbilt University, assigned students to study the social structures of antebellum Mississippi and Louisiana. Owsley worked with his wife on Tennessee and Alabama. Together, the group began to construct a new picture of pre–Civil War southern society. They used new sources, the census schedules of 1850 and 1860. These long-neglected sources contained such valuable information as size and value of individual landholdings and slave ownership. Owsley and his students selected sample counties from Tennessee, Alabama, Mississippi, and Louisiana; and, after establishing criteria for distinguishing between planters and small farmers, they began to count agricultural operations. They published their findings piecemeal throughout the 1940s, capped in 1949 with the appearance of Professor Owsley's *Plain Folk of the Old South*.

1. See Robert L. Fogel and Stanley L. Engerman, *Time on the Cross: The Economics of American Negro Slavery* (Boston: Little, Brown and Company, 1974); and Gavin Wright, *The Political Economy of the Cotton South* (New York: Norton Press, 1978)

Owsley stated the issue clearly and unequivocally. The antebellum South was a land of yeomen,[2] not planters, and these yeomen dominated the South numerically, economically, socially, and politically. From that central thesis flowed a number of corollaries.

First, he claimed, historians had overemphasized cotton as a staple crop. The southern yeomen depended more on livestock and corn than on cotton. Even the settlers in the pine barrens, though many might be landless, were hardly poor whites as the traditionalists charged. The first settlers on the southern frontier were herdsmen, Owsley countered, who grazed their herds on public lands and therefore had little need or desire to own the land. As settled agriculturalists filled up the lowlands, the herdsmen retreated to the highlands in the interior South and into the piney woods along the Gulf Coast. Thus, Owsley argued, they were driven to the infertile highlands and forest areas not by the planters and slavery as traditional historians claimed, but by settled agriculture in general. The thrust of Owsley's claim was maintained nearly three decades later by Professors Forrest McDonald and Grady McWhiney. Although critical of Owsley's implication that the southern herdsmen were below the yeomen on the social and economic ladder, these authors essentially extended his argument for the yeomen's importance by claiming that hog drovers were far more numerous than hitherto suspected and, further, that they constituted a permanent and prosperous group in the southern economy. Herdsmen were not, as some argued, in a state of transition to settled agriculture or on their way to the West, but were themselves yeomen in all but landownership.[3] So, Owsley noted, the plantation system hardly existed at all in vast areas of the South—the Appalachian highlands of Tennessee and northern Alabama and the pine barrens of the coastal

---

2. Owsley chose the term "yeomen" to describe the small, independent, freeholding farmers who might or might not own slaves.
3. Forrest McDonald and Grady McWhiney, "The Antebellum Southern Herdsman: A Reinterpretation," *Journal of Southern History*, XLI (May, 1975), 147–66 *passim*.

plain. Here the numerous inhabitants were yeomen or herdsmen, not poor whites.

Furthermore, Owsley claimed, even in "plantation areas" like the Delta-loess section of western Mississippi, small farmers were more numerous than anyone had suspected, oftentimes composing a majority of the agricultural operators. Moreover, the yeomen were not driven from the most fertile lands by the planters but on the contrary lived side by side with them. Owsley found no significant differences in land value per acre or in production per acre between small farmers and planters. He argued, too, that no great social gulf separated the life-styles and values of planters and small farmers.

Owsley suspected that many of his colleagues would be reluctant to accept his conclusions. Charging in his introduction to *Plain Folk* that the small freeholders of southern agriculture had been "relegated either to obscurity or oblivion" only to be "historically exhumed" by him and his students, he warned that the yeomen were yet "in danger of being reinterred."[4]

Immediate reactions proved noncommittal. Rupert Vance, reviewing *Plain Folk* in the *Journal of Southern History*, wondered if Owsley's thesis would be accepted. Vance admitted that "the most extreme myth of the poor white today carries little weight." But, he warned, "history is a tough and stubborn discipline, and the plain folk left few records and fewer apologists—probably because few survivors now wish to establish descent from this group."[5]

Indeed, as early as 1946, when Owsley's conclusions were still tentative, a spirited attack already had been launched. Owsley's *Plain Folk* was still three years in the future, but he had published articles in the *Journal of Southern History* on Alabama and Tennessee yeomen. One of his students, Harry L. Coles, had published a similar article on Louisiana, and another student, Herbert Weaver, had published a thin vol-

4. Frank L. Owsley, *Plain Folk of the Old South* (Baton Rouge: Louisiana State University Press, 1949), vii.
5. *Journal of Southern History*, XVI (Nov., 1950), 546.

ume called *Mississippi Farmers, 1850–1860.* Fabian Linden,
writing in the *Journal of Negro History*, challenged the emerg-
ing Owsley thesis on two fundamentals. First, he disagreed
with the statistical methods used by Owsley and his students.
The Owsley group's methods were faulty on at least one major
ground, Linden maintained. In his book on Mississippi farmers, Weaver should have given statistics based on total population, Linden argued. By dealing only with landowning farmers, Weaver left open to question the status of perhaps 20
percent of Mississippians.

Even when he admitted that the Owsley group's conclusions
were correct, Linden picked at the methodology, charging
that, though some conclusions might be accurate, the reasoning that supported them was faulty. For example, he conceded
Owsley's claim that the small farmers in the 1850s were
increasing their holdings at a more rapid rate than the planters but not, as asserted by Owsley, because they were prosper-
ing as much as the planters. According to Linden, the yeomen
were adding to their holdings because they were closer to the
frontier and "further removed from the size of optimum productive efficiency."[6] Presumably he meant that the holdings of
small farmers were smaller than those of planters.

But Linden's main point, to which he returned time and
again, was that the planters, despite their relatively small
percentage in the farming population, owned the greatest
share of the land and the slaves. Once again he seemed to argue
that the holdings of the planters were larger than those of
farmers—a point hard to deny. Yet it hardly proved that the
yeomen were propertyless or powerless, only that the holdings
of the planters were larger. Despite its exclusion of all but
economic factors, this criticism would remain the central
argument of those who opposed Owsley's conclusions. A generation later the "econometricians" would make essentially
the same attack.

In the 1960s a new national interest arose in the economic

6. Fabian Linden, "Economic Democracy in the Slave South: An Appraisal
of Some Recent Views," *Journal of Negro History*, XXXI (April, 1946), 183.

and social structure of the Old South. Led by young historians like Eugene D. Genovese, the plantation myth resurfaced in a new form. Now antebellum society must fit a Marxist model, and no place existed in that model for the yeomanry. Owsley was brushed aside with a few lines of contempt. Other, non-Marxist historians simply continued to use their traditional methods and sources, taking only occasional notice of Owsley.

Those who wrote the history books before Owsley's studies may be forgiven their myopic views of southern society. Those who continued after Owsley to portray the South as a land of plantations can only be assumed to have some ideological or methodological territory to protect. One need not look far to find numerous examples of indifference or hostility toward the Owsley thesis. A few examples, especially from the historiography of Mississippi, one of the states central to the Owsley studies, will serve to illustrate the point.

In 1958 Professor John Hebron Moore published *Agriculture in Antebellum Mississippi*. Frequently cited, it soon became a widely known study of one of the most important cotton-producing states of the Old South. Moore's book was not primarily a socioeconomic study but a technical history of crops and agricultural methods. Yet his illustrations, examples, and research materials all concerned the large planter class. In the brief space allotted to the small farmers, they emerge simply as miniature planters. "The small Mississippi farm," Moore claimed, "was essentially a cotton plantation, lacking only the Negro slaves."[7]

Another expert in antebellum southern agriculture is William K. Scarborough. In his chapter "Heartland of the Cotton Kingdom," which appeared in Richard McLemore's *A History of Mississippi*, Scarborough wrote largely of planters and plantations. His opening sentence, "Cotton, slavery, and the plantation system—these were the dominant elements in Mississippi's agricultural economy from the time of statehood

7. John H. Moore, *Agriculture in Antebellum Mississippi* (New York: Bookman Associates, 1958), 65.

until the Civil War,"[8] appropriately introduced a chapter in
which Mississippi farmers played little role.

In *Mississippi: Conflict and Change* authors Charles Sallis
and James Loewen set about correcting some of the myths and
omissions of earlier books on Mississippi. But, like the others,
they paid homage to the plantation myth. "Under the slavery
system, social distinctions were clear cut," they observed. "At
one end of the scale were the wealthy planters; next came
merchants, independent farmers, poor whites. . . . Political
and social events were dominated by the planter elite, an elite
that eventually led the state into war."[9] Whether the authors'
motives were to show a rigid social-economic class system as a
foil for the historical persecution of blacks or simply to repeat
the old pre-Owsley interpretation of southern society is unclear. Sallis and Loewen included two paragraphs pointing
out that only about 5 percent of Mississippi's planters owned
more than 30 slaves and that perhaps 60 percent of Mississippians owned none at all. Yet for the next nine pages they
discussed at length slavery and plantation life.

One of the most widely known authorities on the Old South,
Eugene D. Genovese, stated unequivocally that "the
hegemony of the slaveholders, presupposing the social and
economic preponderance of great slave plantations, determined the character of the South."[10] Furthermore, "the concentration of landholding and slaveholding prevented the rise
of a prosperous yeomanry and of urban centers."[11] Genovese
buried Owsley in an explanatory footnote and, as if brushing
away a fly, asserted, "An attempt was made by Frank L.
Owsley and his students to prove that the Southern yeomanry
was strong and prosperous. . . . This view was convincingly
refuted by Fabian Linden."[12]

8. Richard A. McLemore (ed.), *A History of Mississippi* (2 vols., Hattiesburg:
University and College Press of Mississippi, 1973), I, 310.
9. Charles Sallis and James Loewen, *Mississippi: Conflict and Change* (New
York: Random House, 1974), 93.
10. Eugene D. Genovese, *The Political Economy of Slavery: Studies in the
Economy and Society of the Slave South* (New York: Random House, 1965), 13.
11. *Ibid.*, 34.
12. *Ibid.*, 37.

Authors of textbooks still repeat the plantation myth as developed in the late nineteenth century or, in the case of younger writers, wipe the yeomen aside with the statistics, the charts, and the graphs of the "new economic historians." In his recent book called *The South: A History*, Idus Newby devoted some space to a summary of the Owsley thesis but concluded by asking, "Was this rosy picture accurate?" He answered bluntly, "Alas, no."[13] Newby argued that slave ownership, not the ownership of land, determined economic and social status. Thus the planters dominated. He acknowledged, however, an intellectual contradiction, in that democracy among whites seemed to be growing at the same time that planter power was increasing. He resolved that anomaly by implying that the planters allowed democracy to the masses of whites only so long as it promoted white racial solidarity and never threatened the planters' economic position by promoting increased taxes, social services, and active government.

Newby's is a strained and questionable interpretation. The nonslaveholders were racists because they feared the prospect of a large free black population more than they suspected the planters. Even then race overrode class. Furthermore, anyone who has lived in the rural South should know that resistance to taxation and support for frugality in government are perhaps stronger among the lower middle class than among the rich. One suspects that the yeomen held similar attitudes.

As Newby's argument indicates, ignoring the yeomen nowadays is a more subtle matter than it once was. When pressed, most historians will admit that the yeomen dominated numerically, and a few will even speculate that they formed a powerful economic force. Almost none will credit the small farmers with much political power. But the life of the yeoman is yet ignored while reams of data, stacks of computer printouts, articles, and books about plantations and plantation slavery inundate the historian. By writing only about planters and slaves, historians subtly imply that those two groups were all that mattered in southern society. The popular mind is led

13. Idus A. Newby, *The South: A History* (New York, 1978), 157.

to a similar conclusion by television phenomena like "Roots."
The question remains—why have so many proved so resistant
to the Owsley thesis for so long?

Owsley and his students cited two reasons. First, the yeoman
has been ignored, they said, because he was "conventional
and prosaic."[14] They were right. The yeomen hardly furnished
the kind of image needed for nineteenth-century romantic
novels. *Gone with the Wind* could no more have focused on
small farmers than *Oedipus* on a common laborer. Second,
Owsley also recognized that plantation records—letters, journals, diaries, and account books—were abundant and readily
accessible to historians. Such records were vigorously collected over the South, cataloged and organized by librarians,
and located in great university libraries. Both the archivists
who collected them and the scholars who used them obviously
developed proprietary interests in these papers. Yet, over the
next generation, forces that Owsley could hardly have conceived aligned against his thesis.

It is axiomatic that each generation rewrites history to suit
its own tastes. Certainly the post–Civil War romantics had a
vested interest in portraying the antebellum South as a land of
plantations and in describing slavery as a system of kindly
paternalism. It is equally certain that black people in the
1970s, inheritors of the most successful civil rights struggle in
American history, have a stake in the plantation South. Their
heritage, they say, lies on the plantation, and on the plantation
their culture was formed. Similarly, black apologists have an
interest in portraying the plantations as holding large numbers of slaves, as being impersonal places, brutal and coldly
economic. Where the southern romantic saw the paternalistic
planter, today's blacks see only an overseer with a whip and a
planter moved only by considerations of profit. Where the
southern romantic sees only loyal house servants, modern
blacks see only Nat Turner. Recently, at a conference on
slavery, a professor charged that the benign picture of slavery

14. Herbert Weaver, *Mississippi Farmers*, 1850—1860 (Nashville: Vanderbilt University Press, 1945), 13.

contained in *Time on the Cross* was warped. Even if it were true, he said, it should be suppressed, for it might harm the progress of black Americans.

But plantation slavery is certainly not the heritage of all blacks. Not enough attention has been given to the proportion of the slave population that belonged to small farmers. Lewis C. Gray in his *History of Agriculture in the Southern United States* included some information on this point. He listed the percentage distribution of slaves by state and by size of slaveholding in 1850 and 1860. According to his totals, 47.2 percent of southern slaves in 1860 were the property of men who owned fewer than twenty slaves. In the border states that percentage rose to 61.7. In the Lower South the figure fell to 38 percent.[15] One can as reasonably speak of slavery on the farm as about plantation slavery. Few have.

Small-farmer states like North Carolina, Tennessee, and Virginia have seldom been mentioned either in the writings of the traditional defenders of the plantation thesis or in the statistical analyses of the more recent econometricians. A disproportionate emphasis has always been put on the social and economic characteristics of states like South Carolina and Louisiana, states in which the Owsley thesis is easiest to refute. Furthermore, the new economic historians limit the argument by investigating only the cotton South, ignoring almost wholly those portions of the section in which tobacco or livestock was the principal crop. The deck is stacked by geographic selection.

Perhaps the most important reason that Owsley's studies have been treated with indifference stems from the tacit (sometimes overt) acceptance of a Marxist world view by modern historians. Marxists find no place in their ideology for an agrarian middle class. Such people are not supposed to exist, and, if they do, revolutionary Marxists look upon them as a greater threat than capitalist factory owners. Hence, an antebellum social order dominated by the yeomen does not fit

15. Lewis C. Gray, *History of Agriculture in the Southern United States to 1860* (2 vols., Washington, D.C.: Carnegie Institution, 1933), I, 530.

the Marxist model. But planters do, and, although they may be branded "precapitalist, quasi-aristocratic landowners" who "represented the antithesis of capitalism,"[16] they still occupy a place in the Marxist world, as do the Russian boyars or the Prussian Junkers.

The current debate over southern society is almost wholly economic. Many historians, especially the econometricians, start from a premise of raw economic determinism—that nothing matters but wealth, that wealth is always power. They recognize neither the numerical power of the yeomen nor anything so sentimental as the democratic impulse. If one accepts that premise, then the division of southern society into the haves and the have-nots, the planters and the oppressed (white and black), naturally follows. Marxist theology is neat, logical, and symmetrical. In the writings of historians like Genovese and economists like Gavin Wright, the southern planters emerge as a highly unified and self-conscious social and economic class. That picture may fit the symmetry of Marxism, but it leaves many unanswered questions.

Was southern society that neat? Few historians deal convincingly with a fundamental contradiction—that as this supposed planter dominance was growing so was Jacksonian Democracy, an egalitarianism unparalleled in America until our own day. Still fewer have dealt with the social fear that may have motivated the masses of yeomen to side with the planters on the issue of slavery, even though they had little economic interest in it. Nor must it be accepted without argument that the southern planters were a highly unified, self-conscious social and economic class. In Mississippi the planters were overwhelmed numerically by the yeomen, did not control politics, and in the vast majority of cases had risen to the planter ranks in their own lifetimes. Thus they had, except perhaps in Natchez, the manners and values of yeomen. Nor does anyone who grew up among planters believe that any great social distance separated the planter from his yeoman neighbor. A lifetime in the Yazoo Delta proves, to me at least,

16. Genovese, *Political Economy of Slavery*, 23.

that it wasn't like Genovese and the econometricians tell it. Something about the work of the neo-traditionalists and the econometricians is unsatisfying. For all the argumentative brilliance of Genovese or the statistical creativity of the econometricians, something is lacking. There is about much of their work a cold and logical quality, a lack of humanism if not humanity. Somehow they create in their work the idea that the Old South was not a land of people but a collection of abstract political and economic forces. Historians should be interested more in what men thought and what values and ideals they had, more in their perceptions of themselves, than in what they had or in some neat division of society along economic class lines. It is not how we view antebellum southerners that will resolve the debate over southern society, but how they viewed themselves. After all, the debate is really over how antebellum southerners *were*, not how we now perceive them to have been.

Southern Attitudes Toward Slavery and Secession in 1860 and Early 1861 as Reflected by *De Bow's Review*

Richard C. Ethridge

J. D. B. De Bow, one of the most successful magazinists of the Old South, lived forty-seven years and most of his adult life espoused the cause of his section while serving in important public positions[1] and by writing prodigiously. His basic aim as an author was to foster the economic, political, and social advancement of the South via *De Bow's Review*. Comprising thirty-odd volumes, this monthly publication was printed in that critical period of southern history surrounding the Civil War.[2] During this era De Bow became convinced that political harmony between the North and South was doomed because of northern hatred of southern institutions. He warned the South of alleged violations of the Constitution by the North that were designed to change the region and repeatedly predicted that the new anti–states' rights, antislavery Republican party would not cease its efforts until it had undermined the

1. Ottis Clark Skipper, *J. D. B. De Bow: Magazinist of the Old South* (Athens: University of Georgia Press, 1958), 69–80. De Bow served as superintendent of the seventh census in the late 1850s. In this position he gained insight into the future of the South in the Union.
2. *Ibid.*, ix.

southern status quo.[3] He solicited articles from a diversity of prominent people on these issues and often printed material about which there was little agreement to expose all sides of an issue.[4] The resulting literature justifies the assertion that no person ever "left so full a record of Southern resources and enterprises and of schemes for betterment and apprehensions of impending dangers" for the South than is to be found in the fifty thousand pages that he personally wrote or edited.[5]

This essay, based on material from *De Bow's Review*, examines the attitudes of southerners toward slavery and secession during the period beginning January, 1860, and extending through the firing on Fort Sumter in April, 1861. No claim is advanced that the findings represent the thinking of the entire white populace of the South on any point considered, but conclusions will be made regarding the effectiveness of the periodical as a propaganda apparatus based on action that it advocated taken in the South.

For some time before 1860, southerners had observed with dismay the steady political and economic ascendancy of the North over the South. In 1860 many southern leaders believed that the time had arrived for definite action if they were to maintain southern traditions.[6] Two important facts led them to this decision. First, the Republican party, which had risen in the Midwest, was fast becoming the majority party of the North. Second, the population of the South had not increased proportionately with that of the North, and southerners were losing any effective voice in Congress. Southern response to these two threats to the section's position in the Union reveals much about the region's attitudes toward slavery and secession.

Because of its impact on the South, the advent of the Republican party deserves serious consideration. Politics was an intriguing subject to antebellum southerners, and the pros-

3. *Ibid.*, 113–20.
4. *Ibid.*, 93–95, 120–21, 134–35, 139, 205–206.
5. *Ibid.*, ix.
6. L. Gibson, "Our Federal Union," *De Bow's Review* (hereinafter cited *DBR*), XXIX (July, 1860), 31–31. Gibson lived in Louisiana.

pect of an antislavery Republican president heightened interest to full capacity in 1860. One writer associated the fall of
constitutional government, the end of civil liberty, and the
beginning of disunion with the party.[7] The men most feared
within its ranks were William Seward and Abraham Lincoln.
Seward openly denounced slavery and declared that "an irrepressible conflict between the institutions of the North and
South" existed that could only end in the liberation of the
slaves.[8] Both he and Lincoln were considered presidential
prospects early in 1860, but Lincoln was viewed with more
contempt since it was thought that he was responsible for
Seward's "irrepressible conflict" idea. Compared with Lincoln, Seward was even considered to be a "virtuous" candidate,[9] although both men were credited with desiring the
subversion of the South. It was further imagined that they
planned ultimately to establish a dictatorship in America if
their party captured the presidency.[10] The possibility of this
happening in 1860 and of the subsequent abolition of slavery
evoked vehement arguments in behalf of the "peculiar institution" embracing myriad approaches to the subject. Some were
rather naive; others were irrational; some were religious;
some purported to be legal; and some defy classification. The
following are samples of them.

One basic southern justification for slavery was the argument that the North, driven by jealousy, wanted to be rid of the
institution merely because it was not economically feasible in
that area. Northern soil was not as fertile as that of the South,
and the expense of maintaining slaves could not be earned by
returns from their labor in agriculture. Heavy immigration to
the region from other countries rendered slavery unacceptable
for industry. Southerners reasoned that their northern
neighbors developed the theory of "equality of the races" to

7. Python (only identification), "The Issues of 1860," *DBR*, XXVIII (March,
1860), 245.
8. S. D. Moore, "The Irrepressible Conflict and Impending Crisis," *DBR*,
XXVIII (May, 1860), 531. Moore lived in Alabama.
9. J. D. B. De Bow, "Presidential Candidates and Aspirants," *DBR*, XXIX
(July, 1860), 100–102. De Bow lived in Louisiana, but he traveled extensively.
10. Python, "Issues of 1860," 269.

deprive the South of a profitable system. The danger in the
philosophy of equality and freedom for blacks, according to
southern logic, was that if fully developed it would lead eventually to a demand for an equal distribution of property. The
second would follow the first as a matter of course. It was
claimed that, in all past societies where the idea of equality of
races was pressed to the fullest, those granted equality then
wanted an equal distribution of property.[11] This could not be
allowed in the South.

Another southerner contended that the concept of the "irrepressible conflict" was "probably" hereditary. The gist of
this supposition was that North America was colonized by two
distinct classes. The Puritans, people of the "lower" classes
usually, settled New England. Being highly intolerant of ideas
differing from their own, they were unfit "for rational freedom, civil or religious." Nor were they capable of self-rule,
because when they had it their intolerance caused them to lose
it. Conversely, the South was settled by "Cavaliers," by people
"almost entirely from the better and more enlightened classes
of Great Britain and France." Southerners were not perfect
because of their origin, it was admitted, but they confessed
their imperfections. New Englanders were equally imperfect
but refused to acknowledge it. The danger to slavery and
southern tradition that they posed and had spread over the
North sprang from their inherited tendency to want to destroy
systems dissimilar to their own.[12]

Negro slavery was further defended by a writer who argued
that there was no real basis for northern criticism of the
institution since "slavery" existed in both regions. Southerners honestly labeled their labor system, but northerners did
not. It was argued that the person "who performs menial
service, no matter what his color, is a slave." Many white
northerners worked as servants for wealthy people, and this
was thought to be unnatural because there was a "natural

11. Gibson, "Federal Union," 33–34. Ancient Rome and France were cited as
examples of where this had occurred.
12. A. Clarkson, "The Basis of Northern Hostility to the South," DBR,
XXVIII (Jan., 1860), 7–11. Clarkson lived in Alabama.

repugnance to live in the condition or to perform the offices of servitude" among whites. The only difference between the wage slaves of the North and those of the South was that northern slaves were "possessed of social and political power." It was suggested that this power caused the "slaves" of the North to desire the eradication of slavery in other areas.[13]

Black bondage was also justified per se by the contention that blacks enjoyed their position of servitude. Blacks were represented as being unwilling to leave their "beloved homes" for the uncertainties of freedom. A typical argument of this sort involved the case of a dozen blacks freed by Young Edwards of Russell County, Alabama. Upon being liberated, they were told that they had thirty days to leave the state under Alabama law. Not choosing to do this, these blacks asked Ben H. Baker, a politician, to arrange for their staying in the area. Baker subsequently secured legislation that returned them to slavery, thus enabling them to remain in Alabama. These blacks, it was asserted, knew that they would be clothed, cared for, and better rewarded for their work in the South than any northern laborer and that they would have security in sickness and old age. Consequently, they did not "choose to go into wretchedness, privation, and squalor of free negro life in the North."[14]

Then a contributor suggested that the peculiar institution was worthwhile and proper because, whatever the condition of southern slaves, the situation of blacks in the North was worse. According to the census of 1850, there were approximately 200,000 free blacks there, most of whom, some 163,000, lived in New York, New Jersey, Pennsylvania, Ohio, and Indiana. About 54,000 lived in Pennsylvania, which had the largest number of any northern state. Indiana, with only 11,000 blacks, had the smallest number of the five listed. New Jersey had 23,810 which was more than all the New England states contained as a whole; only 23,021 lived in the latter

13. Moore, "Irrepressible Conflict," 531–32.
14. "Slave Life Preferred by Negroes," *DBR*, XXVIII (April, 1860), 481.

region. Northerners usually considered free blacks to be "nui-
sances," it was argued, because they were "lazy, vicious, and
licentious." These characteristics prodded some states, such
as Illinois and Indiana, to forbid blacks to enter their boundaries. The formula governing the overall reception of free
blacks in the North was that they were "commonly esteemed,
just in proportion to their scarcity." For this reason, the
argument continued, New England was more favorably disposed toward them than other regions. In the small villages
and hamlets there, their "antics and whims" amused the white
population, and the Negro assumed "a position something
similar to that of the court-fools in bygone days." Areas such as
these, where so few blacks lived, could not understand the
"prejudice" that existed against them in other sections. Only a
few blacks resided in New Hampshire, and here they were
enfranchised. This was not too great a concession, however,
because the total Negro population was only 520 according to
the 1850 census, opposed to a total white population of
317,456. Of the 520 Negroes, only 155 were qualified to vote.
Conversely, in Pennsylvania white people bitterly opposed
blacks. They were not allowed to drive wagons or carts in
Philadelphia and could not be buried in cemeteries used by
whites. This writer sought to strengthen his argument by
relating that "all travellers who have visited both the Northern and Southern States . . . are agreed that the condition of
the free negro in the North is worse than that of the slave in the
South," although "many express their surprise on first observing this fact, it being so opposed to their preconceived notions." Excerpts of the writings of such travelers were given to
illustrate the contention.[15]

Southern slavery was likewise championed by the assertion
that the climate of the North was too harsh for blacks to live
long within it. It was asserted that above forty degrees north
latitude their health deteriorated rapidly. Involved statistics
were produced to verify this contention, illustrative of which

15. W. W. Wright, "Free Negroes in the Northern United States," *DBR*,
XXVIII (May, 1860), 573–76. Wright lived in New Orleans.

was a study of the annual mortality rate of blacks compared with whites in Philadelphia, which revealed that proportionately twice as many blacks died as whites. For every 1,000 of the city's inhabitants of each race, 196 blacks died compared with 100 whites. Negro mortality was even higher in the jails of the area. In the penitentiary 316 blacks died annually to each 100 whites out of each 1,000 for each color incarcerated.[16] The implication of this was that blacks lived longer in the South, even in slavery.

Perhaps the most vehement justifications for slavery were made on assertions of divine sanction of the institution. Multitudinous arguments advanced from this frame of reference generally agreed that the Bible taught that slavery was not inhumane. Any inhumanity connected with it was practiced in years past by the British and New England slave traders, and it was pointed out that this was not the responsibility of the southerner of 1860.[17]

Possibly the most unusual biblical justification for slavery, ostensibly based on a "faithful" interpretation of the original language of the book of Genesis, revealed that it had been the divinely sanctioned state of blacks from the act of Creation. According to this argument, there were two creations of rational beings. The ordinary person, it was asserted, had no knowledge of this because the King James and Douay translators of the Scriptures mistranslated a vital passage revealing it. God actually created an "inferior" man with a soul and intelligence along with His creation of cattle and other forms of animal life. This was done in the work described in the first chapter of Genesis, the twenty-fourth verse. According to this contention the verse should read: "The Lord said, Let the earth bring forth *intellectual creatures with immortal souls* after their kind; cattle, and creeping things, and beast of the earth after his kind, and it was so." It is pointed out that in the English version, instead of "intellectual creatures with immortal souls," there are only the words "living creature" representing

16. *Ibid.*, 578–80.
17. Clarkson, "Basis of Northern Hostility," 12–14.

the Hebrew words *napesh chaiyah.* Then it is noted that the last word means "living *creature,*" and that the word *naphesh,* which invests *chaiyah,* or living creature, with intellectuality and immortality, is not translated. Following this action, God made another "superior" creature with rationality and an immortal soul in His "own image" and after His "own likeness." God decreed that the second man should "have dominion over all things on earth"—including the first man. The record of the creation of the second man was correctly translated.[18]

This unique argument further maintained that the first man God created caused sin to enter the world because he was the "serpent" that tempted Eve in the Garden of Eden. Again, close study of the original language proved this. The word that had been translated "serpent" had connected with it such meanings as: "the charmed—the enchanted—watching closely—prying into designs—muttering and babbling without meaning—hissing—whistling—deceitful—artful—fetters—chains—and a verb formed from the name, which signifies to be or to become *black.*"[19] Understanding that the serpent was a black clarified many mysteries in the Scriptures, among them the origin of Cain's wife; Cain simply intermarried with offspring of the first man. Because this amalgamation of the races displeased God, He eventually flooded the world. But the pure Negro type was preserved, since each species of the original Creation was brought onto Noah's ark.[20]

According to *De Bow's Review,* this theory also explained the Negro's present condition of servitude and at the same time gave him hope. God had sentenced the serpent to traveling on his belly and eating the dust of the earth the remainder of his life for deceiving Eve. When one looked over southern cotton fields and saw blacks at work, picking cotton with their abdomens "parallel with the earth," as if moving over it on their

18. Samuel A. Cartwright, "Unity of the Human Race Disproved by the Hebrew Bible," *DBR,* XXIX (Aug. 1860), 129–30. Cartwright lived in New Orleans.
19. *Ibid.,* 131.
20. *Ibid.,* 134.

stomachs, one could understand that their slavery was of divine origin. Further, blacks preferred "ash-cake" to all other kinds of bread, which necessitated consuming much dust. This fact was simply the unfolding of the second part of the Negro's sentence.[21] In these conditions, however, the Negro was being freed. As the descendant of the creature who introduced sin into the world, the serpent, which through the ages came to represent evil and had been worshiped by blacks in Africa, the Negro needed this help.[22] "The seed of the woman" was "bruising the head of the serpent," and slavery in a Christian environment was liberating the Negro "from that evil spirit, which seizes upon his whenever he gets beyond the hearing of the crack of the white man's whip."[23]

Most theological arguments, though farfetched, were not as irrational as this one, since ministers usually argued for the preservation of slavery because of the alleged economic value of the institution. One maintained that inherent within slavery was the "principle of self preservation."[24] It was the white man's responsibility to act as the guardian of the economic security of blacks because they were a helpless race. In perpetuating slavery, the South would not only be thinking of them and of itself, but would be considering the well-being of the entire world. The economy of the world depended upon slave labor to a large degree; since this was God's plan for the Negro, God, not man, had to be obeyed.[25]

Yet another defense of the institution was offered on grounds

21. *Ibid.*, 135.
22. *Ibid.*, 133.
23. *Ibid.*, 136. De Bow allowed a refutation of this article to be printed by W. D. Scull, "Dr. Cartwright on the Negro Race," *DBR*, XXIX (Dec. 1860), 712–16, which is more rational.
24. "Why We Resist and What We Resist—The Two Opposing Views of the Great Issue Between the North and the South," *DBR*, XXX (Feb., 1861), 328. This article was a mixture of opinions from several sources. The one cited from it comes from B. M. Palmer, "A Thanksgiving Sermon," preached in the First Presbyterian Church of New Orleans, Nov. 29, 1860. The pages should be numbered from 223 through 246. They are incorrectly numbered in the following pattern: 223–24; then a mistake, 325–40; then correct numbering again, 241–46.
25. *Ibid.*, 223–46.

that whites were obligated as humanitarians to civilize blacks. The Baptist Convention offered a prize for the best tract on duties of masters to their slaves, and the winning pamphlet had as its thesis the "humanitarian aspect" of the institution. It admonished masters to keep plenty of work for their slaves, because idleness was bad for man. Masters were further advised to be good to their slaves and not cruel; to clothe them well; to provide them good food and good, clean lodging; to attend to their health needs; to require virtuous relationships between the sexes, with marriage being urged; to instruct them in Christian tenets; and to let them share to a degree in the fruits of their labor.[26] In this connection it was asserted that slavery and the watchful care of the white man "was the only way to civilize the heathen" and thus help "civilize the world" at the same time "by adding to its edible wealth." Abolition would be unhumanitarian because it would "in great measure, defeat, or at least postpone, the very objects it professes to advance. Its mercy is poison to the race it pretends to love, and its embrace death to the black man."[27] This was true, it was argued, because free Africans did not know how to care for themselves and were incapable of making decisions for themselves. The framers of the Constitution had realized this and provided that Negroes, whom they deemed unfit for self-government, be made subject to the white man.[28]

Slavery was also justified on the ground that it relieved the government of the responsibility of maintaining a large standing army or large police force. In countries where the lower classes were given equality or near equality in government, trouble always abounded. The only means of control in such states (France, for example) was a strong central government and strong police force. This was unnecessary in the South because in slavery the responsibility of disciplining the "lower

26. J. D. B. De Bow and H. N. McTyeire, "Plantation Life—Duties and Responsibilities," *DBR*, XXIX (Sept., 1860), 357–68. McTyeire, a Tennessean, later became a bishop of the Methodist Episcopal Church, South.
27. J. T. Wiswall, "Delusions of Fanaticism," *DBR*, XXIX (July, 1860), 44.
28. "The South's Power of Self Protection," *DBR*, XXIX (Nov., 1860), 545–61.

element" devolved upon the owners. If slaves were liberated, a large standing army would be necessitated to protect the rights of the upper classes.[29]

Finally, southern writers most ardently defended slavery out of fear that amalgamation of the races might result if Negroes were freed. Certain antislavery writers advocated liberating blacks and allowing them to be absorbed by the white race. One predicted that if blacks were freed "there would be a gradual admixture of the races, and the negro partly through an infusion of Anglo-Saxon industry, would gradually rise to a very respectable if not superior man."[30] Another expressed similar views when he said, "Amalgamation would be the true means of civilizing the black race. By intermarriage, after a few generations, it would be absorbed by the white race."[31]

De Bow's Review produced statistics from all types and opinions of "experts" to counteract and refute these assertions, telling its readers that mulattoes were the "shortest lived" of any of humankind and that they were more susceptible to disease than others, therefore "less prolific." "Mixed-breeds" also were thought to be less productive economically, more capable of barbarities, and more oriented toward criminality than people of pure blood.[32] It was contended that advocating amalgamation was not a kindness to the black man, but quite the contrary. The assertion was made that when the North's "efforts to make the black and white man amalgamate cease—then, and then only, will the colored man in the North begin to be treated with kindness, as he is in the South."[33]

On the whole, however, slavery appears to have been accepted as a matter of course by most southerners. These arguments advanced in its defense by *De Bow's Review* were

29. Gibson, "Federal Union," 34–35.
30. Stribling, *Letters from the Slave States* (n.p., n.d.), quoted in W. W. Wright, "Amalgamation," *DBR*, XXIX (July, 1860), 1.
31. Ampere, *Promenade en Amerique* (n.p., n.d.), quoted *ibid.*
32. Wright, "Amalgamation," 3–13.
33. *Ibid.*, 20.

obviously for the benefit of northerners. They were designed to help the slave owner keep blacks in bondage and at the same time to justify his doing so. As one Mississippian saw it, the "institution of slavery rests upon so many strong and deep foundations that it seems useless on our part to defend it and madness in our enemies to assail it." He further expressed what a majority of his fellow citizens evidently believed about being coerced in the matter, when he said that "silence and apathy with us may be deemed pusillanimity, and we should be as ready to prove our patriotism by expostulation and argument, as in the bloody crucible of battle."[34] Southerners should be ready to debate the matter and defend slavery through writing and should not rule out the possibility of fighting for it.

The second major factor stirring the South to action must now be dealt with in detail. As statistics clearly revealed, this region had been losing control of the national government for some time before 1860 because of the rapid growth of the North and the South's own proportionate decline in population. In 1790 the North had a population of 1,977,899 compared with 1,852,027 for the South. Both sections had equal representation in the Senate then, although the North had a small majority in the House of Representatives and electoral college (due to the provisions of the three-fifths compromise). By 1850 the North's population had risen to about 13,400,000 while the South's had lagged behind at about 9,600,000. By 1860 there was a northern majority of six votes in the Senate, fifty-seven in the House of Representatives, and sixty-three in the electoral college. Added to this significant change in the power structure was the possibility that three new territories would be added to the Union as free states before 1860 ended, thus increasing the North's majority. Southerners were convinced that the 1860 census would show another substantial increase in the population of the North, gaining it additional seats in the House and votes in the electoral college. This

34. A Mississippian, "Our Country: Its Hopes and Fears," *DBR*, XXIX (July, 1860), 85.

accrual of political power would enable the North to easily effect substantial changes in the structure of the national government by legal processes.[35]

Viewing the situation from another perspective caused equal concern. At the outset of the Union the North had seven states and the South six. Until 1850 new states admitted to the Union were alternately slave and free. At this time, however, the balance was upset in favor of the North through the admission of California, and later the admission of Minnesota and Oregon further strengthened the antislavery states. In 1860 other territories were ready for admission as free states. Only on the Supreme Court, which comprised five justices from the South and four from the North, did the South have a majority. But southerners feared that the North would soon control that branch as she was "already claiming her right, by reason of greater population and larger amount of judicial business, to have the majority" there.[36]

Southerners especially regretted that the losses sustained to the North were strengthening the Republicans in Congress. By 1860 they had made tremendous progress, illustrated by the fact that in 1850 there were only five avowed abolitionist senators and in 1860 there were twenty-four Republican senators. Since the Republican party was synonymous with abolitionism to southerners, its continued growth could do nothing but damage slavery.[37] And because the Republicans might win the presidency in 1860, many southerners began to reveal the action they believed they would be compelled to take if attempts were made to deprive them of their constitutional rights of property. Steadily they embraced the beliefs that mere "argumentative" defense of slavery would not suf-

---

35. Gibson, "Federal Union," 40–41.
36. A. Roane, "The South—In the Union or Out of It?" *DBR*, XXIX (Oct., 1860), 449–50. Roane lived in the District of Columbia. It is instructive to note that *De Bow's Review* gave no detailed analyses of the power of the South in relation to the North in the executive branch of government, for it is likely that such would have been inimical to the case the magazine was trying to make. For the first seventy-two years of the Republic (1789–1861), either a native southerner or a doughface was president for nearly fifty-eight years.
37. *Ibid.*, 450–51.

fice and that more "drastic" action might be required. As difficult as it was, they reasoned, they possibly would have to secede from the Union. There was no lack of apprehension about the problems involved in such extreme action, nor were suggestions lacking to ease these apprehensions and solve the problems.

Suggestions about the courses open to the South were readily available in January, 1860. One writer reminded southerners at this early date that 1860 was a presidential election year and suggested that the South prepare for it by making its central theme a sectional one. A contest should be waged matching issues and candidates of the South against those of the North. Although the South was outnumbered in Congress, northern superiority would not be such that southern representatives would be completely powerless to act for their states in the fray. And if a "black Republican" won the executive office, then the southern minority candidate could proceed as if he had been elected. He could organize a government and completely ignore the majority choice. Southern states desiring to do so could then join under the minority president's administration, and to make the coup more auspicious it was suggested that the minority and majority candidates take the oath of office simultaneously. One would not be inaugurated without the other, and both of them would claim the executive mansion. There would be "two" presidents in Washington.[38]

This argument may or may not have appeared ludicrous to those reading it in January, 1860, but argument after argument was presented until a year later when the following scheme had evolved. After Lincoln had been elected but before he had taken office, another writer suggested that the way to keep the southern states in the Union would be to permanently guarantee their power of self-protection. This could be done by amending the Constitution to require a majority vote of both the slaveholding and nonslaveholding states in both houses of Congress to pass on any law affecting slavery, and it was

38. William Middleton, "Black Republican Success and a Southern Union," *DBR*, XXVIII (Jan., 1860), 16–20. Middleton lived in South Carolina.

suggested that this "provision be placed beyond the reach of future amendment, except by the consent of both sections." Should this plan be deemed untenable, it was reasoned that it might be more acceptable to the North if made to apply to only one chamber, the Senate.[39] Naturally other opinions on what ought to be done in seceding had been formulated by this time. Southerners had thoroughly debated the question between January, 1860, and the beginning of 1861, and the arguments took various lines.

The basic justification for secession was that it was necessary to uphold southern honor, which had been assailed by the North. *De Bow's Review* repeatedly published articles about encroachments by the North upon the rights of the South.[40] Most of the grievances were eventually summarized in an article by ex-Governor Henry A. Wise of Virginia. Starting with a discussion of the drafting of the Constitution, he listed every supposed hostile act of the North against the South down to the Republicans' ascendancy in 1860. His indictments against the North included alleged mistreatment of the South in the distribution of territories, the inciting of abolitionists and blacks, the disregard for national law and Supreme Court decisions, and the disregard for southern property rights as shown by the Underground Railroad. Wise likewise observed that the North would have a substantial power advantage over the South after the 1860 census.[41] In view of these facts, he advocated taking drastic action to protect the South if there proved to be no other alternative.

Not only were there urgings to secede from the Union to maintain the South's honor, but some people advocated fighting for that honor if necessary. One writer lamented that the "sword has been hung up to rust in feudal halls," quickly

39. A. Roane, "A Plan of Present Pacification; or, A Basis for Reconstruction of the Union if It Be Dissolved," *DBR*, XXX (Jan., 1861), 107.
40. Examples of this: J. Quitman Moore, "The Attitude of the South," *DBR*, XXIX (July, 1860), 25–31 (Moore lived in Mississippi); S. D. Moore, "Irrepressible Conflict," 531–50; Python, "Issues of 1860," 245–72; and Python, "The Secession of the South," *DBR*, XXVIII (April, 1860), 367–92.
41. Henry A. Wise, "Overt Acts of Northern Aggression," *DBR*, XXX(Jan., 1861), 116–18.

adding that with "all its attendant evils—with all its tragic horrors—with all its mighty retinue of sorrows . . . war—civil war . . . is not the greatest calamity that can befall a people." The greatest disaster was "forfeiture of honor—abandonment of right—sacrifice of principle:—these shadow a doom more terrible than death."[42] In addition to this reason, secession was urged on the basis of the "pure religion" of southerners. As opposed to their northern neighbors, they stood almost as a unit in religious thinking. The South was largely Protestant, and, according to contemporary observation, "religious persecution and intolerance" were "unknown" and "isms and schisms rankle" not "in our hearts. . . . Mormonism, freeloveism, and higherlawism, with their teachings so sensual in morals and so dangerous in politics, disturb not our harmony."[43] It was also suggested that secession was necessary because it appeared that "Providence" did not intend the country to remain united.[44] George Fitzhugh, Virginia sociologist and proslavery propagandist, opined that the Union had served its purpose and that God wanted its disruption. God's providence allowed the Union to be established to give the colonials freedom from England, but in the absence of a foreign threat to its existence it was no longer necessary. Changing circumstances within the 1860 government such as corruption, tyranny, and unwieldiness demanded that God terminate its existence. This writer believed that "nations have little or no free agency. Their action is controlled by an all-wise and overruling Providence. God wills disunion, and man attempts in vain to oppose his decree."[45] One minister stated that southerners should take the attitude of Abraham when he said to Lot, "Separate thyself, I pray thee, from me" so that there would be no strife.[46]

42. J. Quitman Moore, "National Characteristics—The Issues of the Day," *DBR*,XXX (Jan., 1861), 52.
43. A Mississippian, "Our Country," 84.
44. *Ibid.*, 86.
45. George Fitzhugh, "The Message, the Constitution, and the Times," *DBR*, XXX (Feb., 1861), 163.
46. "Why We Resist and What We Resist," 335.

Perhaps the strongest arguments advanced to justify secession centered on the legality of such action. According to *De
Bow's Review* there was little doubt on the part of the southerners of 1860 that it was the legal right of a state to secede if it
chose to do so. One writer urged that, since Northerners had
disregarded the stipulations of the fugitive slave law, southerners should deal with them as American revolutionaries had
dealt with George III. The North's crimes fell into the same
category as the monarch's: it had refused to obey laws necessary
for the public good; it had obstructed justice; it had refused laws
for the naturalization of foreigners; it had caused riots in the
South; and in doing these things it had consistently violated the
Constitution.[47]

The major legal basis for secession, however, involved the
presumption of the sovereignty of individual states under the
Constitution. It was argued that the states, sovereign at the
conception of the Union, voluntarily entered it by delegating
to the national government certain powers to be exercised on
their behalf and for their mutual benefit. When ascertaining
the powers of the national government, it was contended that
one had to remember that they were granted by the states and
defined in the Constitution. But those powers not expressly
prohibited to individual states by the Constitution were still
theirs to exercise, which was stated specifically by the Tenth
Amendment. This meant that the states had the legal right to
secede from the Union.[48] To bolster this concept, arguments
were advanced that the national government did not have
constitutional power to force a state to remain in the Union
just as it had not had the power to compel one to join the Union
when it was formed. It was also noted that, when any state
failed to abide by the principles of the Constitution, other
states were not bound by the document to have dealings with it
and could through their own initiative pass laws prohibiting
political dealings with such an offender. But it was the responsibility of the national government to see that the states in the
Union were treated fairly under the federal compact. This

47. Python, "Secession of South," 369.
48. P. Finely, "The Right of Secession," *DBR*, XXX (April, 1861), 385–99.

being true, citizens of a state had two legal safeguards against
wrongdoing by other states. They had representation in the
national Congress and the power of their own legislatures to
transact their business. If one of these failed to safeguard their
liberties, the other had to do so. Furthermore, if neither did,
sovereignty in the final analysis lay in the hands of the citizens,
who could assert themselves and secure their rights. If the
voters of a state wanted to secede, they could do so, irrespective of national or state governmental notions.[49]
    An interesting justification of or argument for secession
dealt with economics. Moderation was generally advocated by
most early spokesmen, who reasoned that the North could not
survive without southern produce. If the South applied
economic sanctions against northern states not returning
runaway slaves, this would force the North to abide by the law
of the land. One writer argued that this "disunion within the
Union" would bring the North to terms quickly, without
secession, because it would lead to the establishment of more
direct trade between southern ports and Europe. New Orleans,
Mobile, Savannah, Charleston, and Baltimore would build a
thriving business in no time, according to this contention.
While such trade would directly bolster the South economically, educationally, commercially, and industrially, it would
also terminate extreme abolitionist activities, because it was
believed that the North would realize that it could not exist
long without southern "trade, without slave products, and a
slaveholding market for their commerce and manufactures."[50]
    In time, economic justification of secession became more
important, as southerners became convinced that not only the
North but all of Europe was dependent upon slave labor for

49. "South's Power of Self Protection," 547–48. Other articles of note on the
legality of secession were: William D. Porter, "The Coercion of a Sovereign
State," *DBR*, XXX (Feb., 1861), 249–50; "What Is a Constitution?" *DBR*, XXX
(March, 1861), 303–307; and J. H. Thornwell, "The State of the Country," *DBR*,
XXX (April, 1861), 410–29, a reprint from *Southern Presbyterian Review* (n.d.).
Thornwell was a distinguished South Carolina educator and Presbyterian
minister.
    50. George Fitzhugh, "Disunion within the Union," *DBR*, XXVII (Jan.,
1860), 1–7.

economic security. In November, 1860, one writer contended that the North could be enticed to settle its political differences with the South if all northern goods destined for southern markets were taxed, which would in essence have been a "nonintercourse" tax. Admittedly, this would not work if only one state tried it, but a united effort by all southern states would assuredly obtain favorable results. It was proposed that the tax be set at 30 percent and that in no case should it be less than the national average under federal law. This would be constitutional, according to the writer, because a number of Supreme Court opinions had shown that states could enact taxes of this nature. If only Virginia, South Carolina, Georgia, Alabama, Maryland, and Louisiana passed such a law, the program would be successful; these states had the important seaports. Such action would stop the Republicans once they won office.[51]

By January, 1861, after Lincoln had won the presidency but had not yet taken office, economic arguments became more pronounced and radical. One contributor to *De Bow's Review* argued that the South could do better economically out of the Union than in it. If a confederation of southern states were created, he contended, it could continue to maintain peaceful commercial activities with the western states and certainly with foreign nations such as England and France. European countries would be favorable to such trade, because the South would not charge as high an import tax as the North. In fact, the principle of "free trade" could be adopted, since the South would be a peaceful nation and would not have to maintain an army or navy for defense. It was estimated that the South would enjoy a monopoly of trade with the West and Europe within a six-month period after this was accomplished. Even if the North objected, no army or navy would be needed, because England, France, and other nations, whose economic security would be tied up with cotton produced in the South, would not allow any such interference.[52]

51. "South's Power of Self Protection," 554–60.
52. W. H. Chase, "The Secession of the Southern States," *DBR*, XXX (Jan., 1861), 93–101.

By February, De Bow had synthesized other articles expressing similar sentiments in an editorial. He suggested that if all
the southern states seceded they would have as much territory
as Europe, excluding Russia and Turkey, and a population five
times that of the continental colonies at the outset of the
American Revolution. Their commerce would be substantial,
because they already were responsible for four-fifths of the
nation's exports. And the great benefit to be derived from
secession, in De Bow's thinking, would be the harmony resulting from unifying a people of the same blood. The South, he
claimed, was composed of a "homogeneous population, little
admixed with those of foreign blood"; in addition, "its organized servile labor will be the greatest source of strength
and not of weakness, as in the pauper population of other
countries."[53] De Bow believed that a southern confederacy,
having as its stated goals prosperity and peace, would be
speedily recognized by foreign powers. Should difficulty arise
with the North over secession, the South could successfully
cope—on its own, if necessary—even though it currently
lacked military or naval stores. This would be true, he maintained, because when the federal taxes on imports in the South
were no longer collected, the resultant savings could be used
propitiously by southerners to supply their military needs.[54]

Evidently other uncertainties plagued people contemplat-
ing secession, for articles appeared in De Bow's Review designed to give assurance that all would be well within the
South if it seceded. Questions arose concerning what Negro
slaves would do if the young men of the South went off to war.
In addition, there was concern about the response of
nonslaveholders.

One writer labored to demonstrate that, if the South's de-
serting the Union resulted in war, the slaves left at home would
be faithful. Using illustrations from ancient history of the

53. Editorial, DBR, XXX (Feb., 1861), 251–53.
54. Ibid. See also extract from pamphlet of John Townsend, "The South
Alone Should Govern the South," DBR, XXX (Jan., 1861), 120–21. Townsend
lived in South Carolina. And see George Fitzhugh, "Slavery Aggression,"DBR,
XXVIII (Feb., 1860), 132–39, a forerunner of these articles.

fidelity of slaves to their masters during times of adversity, he
sought to set southern minds at ease. Additionally, the conduct
of slaves during the American Revolution was appealed to as
ample testimony that they would not revolt should war come.
Although British authorities had tried to bribe slaves into
betraying their owners during this era, the slaves had refused
to do so, because it was the natural tendency for Negro slaves
to be obedient. There had been, it was admitted, cases in
antiquity when slaves had rebelled, but they had usually been
captured as prizes of war. Southern blacks in 1860 had not
been taken as prizes of war; they had never been free, so they
lost nothing in their slavery. Also, ancient slaves were white
men in many instances and equal to their masters, which
made their bondage more difficult. This was the reason that
the Romans, for example, had had so much trouble with their
conquered masses near the end of Rome's existence as a
mighty power. There was one other all-important difference
between ancient slaves and Negro slaves; the former were
heathens and served heathen masters, but the latter had Christian masters and were Christians themselves. This contributor
concluded that, with "these guarantees, we may confidently
anticipate the undisturbed continuance of a relation, which,
however beneficial to the master, confers its chief blessings
upon the slave."[55]

Then there was the situation of the nonslaveholder, which
needed clarification. As noted previously, De Bow was a statis-
tician and had been in charge of the national census office for a
time during the 1850s. Here he made a thorough study of the
ratio of slaveholders to nonslaveholders, which indicated that
by 1860 the number of southern families owning slaves would
be about 375,000. He maintained, however, that by multiply-
ing this number by the average number of persons within a
family the *actual* number of slaveholders could be determined,
since all members of a family had an interest in the slaves held
by it. Therefore the number of slave owners would be enlarged
to about 2,250,000. De Bow's study showed that approxi-

55. J. L. Reynolds, "Fidelity of Slaves," *DBR*, XXIX (Nov., 1860), 569–83.

mately one-third of the population of the South held slaves, indicating that slavery was not exclusively an aristocratic institution.[56] De Bow argued that nonslaveholders should be categorized as those who were "unable" to buy slaves or who simply "did not need them" because of their business pursuits. Contending that there was no class of people in the South opposed to slavery *per se*, he argued that when the South formed a separate government the nonslaveholders would remain loyal for several reasons. These were simple: their labor would earn them more in the South (the cost of living being considered) than in the North; their working conditions would be healthier here; they would not be subjected to competing with immigrant labor; they would maintain their superior status as white men; they could become slaveholders themselves when they accumulated the money; and, even if they never owned slaves, they would stay because their children might in the future. Thus, there was no reason to worry about the loyalty of nonslaveholders.[57]

While the preceding arguments were occurring, certain states were seceding, but no confederacy had been formed. Many opinions were expressed on how this ought to be done. Southerners naturally wanted to establish a confederation that would endure and gain the sympathy and goodwill of foreign powers, so there was general agreement that the process must be peaceful if possible.[58] One writer, having urged these things, made the pregnant suggestion that all states inclined to secession upon these bases select delegations and let them assemble at Montgomery, Alabama, where a confederacy could be organized. A convention of this type could "proceed to declare the absolute separation of the States assembled in convention from the Union—the basis upon which the constitution of the new confederacy should be formed, and the policy governing it" and could set forth at the

56. J. D. B. De Bow, "The Non-Slaveholder of the South," *DBR*, XXX (Jan., 1861), 67–68.
57. *Ibid.*, 71–72.
58. Thornwell, "State of the Country," 427.

same time the doctrine of free trade with all nations, "but entangling alliances with none."[59]

Varying ideas of how the government ought to operate had been given by writers by February, 1861. One argued that the current type of government was not what the South needed, because it had failed; a completely new frame of government would be needed. Details could be decided upon by the delegates who met to discuss the situation.[60] The overriding thrust of argumentation was that each state in the South should have a great amount of independence.

De Bow's Review printed the secession ordinances of the various states as they were adopted.[61] De Bow was present at several of the state conventions that voted for secession, kept his readers informed on what was happening, and took part, as much as possible, in the proceedings.[62] South Carolina led the way for the other states by seceding in December, 1860,[63] and they followed one by one until the work of secession was completed.

Upon its departure from the Union, South Carolina set up a military committee to study the changes necessary before a successful defense of the South could be made should secession lead to war. *De Bow's Review* printed the report of the group in February, 1861. Admitting that the South was unprepared for war because it possessed only old firearms, the Carolinians noted that all of its weapon-manufacturing techniques would have to be changed. The committee also warned that improvement in small arms rendered it impossible for artillery to be used as successfully against infantry as it had been in the past. Because rifles were effective at one thousand yards, artillerymen could be killed by sharpshooters before grapeshot could destroy infantrymen. This necessitated the

---

59. Chase, "Secession of Southern States," 93. See also Fitzhugh, "Message, Constitution, Times," 166–67.

60. J. Quitman Moore, "The Past and the Present," *DBR*, XXX (Feb., 1861), 187–98. See also Fitzhugh, "Message, Constitution, and Times," 166–67.

61. "The Southern Confederacy," *DBR*, XXX (March, 1861), 352–60.

62. Editorial, *DBR* (Feb., 1861), 251–53.

63. "Southern Confederacy," 357.

improvement of infantry equipment. The cavalry would also be less effective against infantry than previously, because of the increased range of rifles, and its use would have to be modified considerably. The individual soldier, whether in infantry or cavalry, would need to learn to use efficiently weapons of different varieties. Since there had been so many changes with which the South had not kept abreast, the South Carolina committee considered southerners practically unarmed. It was suggested as a first step toward arming the region that every man should provide "himself with an improved rifle, for military service of long and accurate range," and that he acquire "skill in the use of it."[64] There were no delusions of easy victory for the South should war come.

But secession continued, and it was not long before those states that had met in Montgomery to establish the Confederate States of America under the leadership of Jefferson Davis found themselves at war. Davis concurred with secession and had defended this action by his own state of Mississippi when he resigned from the Senate. He said that the action of Mississippi was "justified upon the basis that the States were sovereign," adding that he anticipated the time "when a better comprehension of the theory of . . . Government" would cause none to deny this, as had been the case once before.[65] After his election to head the Confederacy, Davis clung to the doctrine of states' rights in his inaugural. Here he indicated that, though the southern government had undergone an outward change, the "Constitution formed by our fathers is that of these Confederate States, in their exposition of it; and, in the judicial construction it has received, we have a light which reveals its true meaning."[66]

What may be concluded about southern attitudes toward slavery and secession by a study of these arguments from *De Bow's Review*? Was there any pattern to the development of

64. "Military Defences of the South," *DBR*, **XXX** (Feb., 1861), 248.
65. "Speech of Jefferson Davis on Withdrawing from the Senate, January 21, 1861," *DBR*, **XXX** (April, 1861), 474.
66. "Inaugural Address of Davis, Delivered at the Capitol, Monday, February 18, 1861, at 1 o'clock, P.M." *DBR*, **XXX** (April, 1861), 483–84.

these attitudes? And what was the role of the magazine in shaping the thinking of southerners?

Early in January, 1860, the southern attitude toward slavery was a defensive one. Exactly how long it had been such is impossible to determine, but the defensiveness of 1860 and early 1861 was born of the "irrepressible conflict" theme of the Republican party. When southerners were told that a conflict was raging between their section and the North that could end only in the liberation of the slaves, they evidently were unable to respond in any other way. Their natural reaction was to defend themselves and their positions—however wrong they were—which they did vigorously.

In addition, Republican animosity toward slavery caused southerners to go on the offensive. They pugnaciously defended slavery with every type of argument primarily to attack the North. The institution was an accepted scheme of life with Southerners. When southern writers vented their wrath in defense of slavery, they were supplying the slave owner with good arguments for holding his property, but they were doing more than this. However misguided, they were condemning what they considered to be the intolerance or the factual "ignorance" of northerners concerning the institution. They believed that slavery was ordained of God for the civilization of Negroes and the betterment of the world. Blacks were happy within it, and northerners were not entitled to tell southerners that it was inhumane, particularly when living conditions of similar classes in the North were equal to or worse than those of southern slaves. Although southerners insisted that they did not have to defend slavery, they did not want "silence and apathy" on their part to "be deemed pusillanimity." Therefore, they lashed out at their accusers, the abolitionists and Republicans. And, as the Republicans gained control of the government, southerners came to believe that they had only one way out of their dilemma—secession.

De Bow's Review helped to shape the thinking of southerners to this end, but unfortunately the degree to which it did this cannot be accurately ascertained. Although the number of subscribers was never large,[67] the magazine went to important people. And its articles were written by people of renown— leading authors, state governors, famous ministers, and well-known people from other professions. This being true, it would not be presumptuous to assume that persons of the stature of Henry A. Wise were heeded when they argued that the North had mistreated the South. Articles by moderates were printed, but there was no encouragement given to compromise. The Republicans would never submit to such, and presumably De Bow knew this at the time. He merely allowed both sides to be heard.

De Bow's Review defended slavery, attacked the Republicans and abolitionists, and justified secession as a means of escape from a political union with a section determined to change the South. Secession, the magazine contended, would unify a people with a common heritage and outlook; it would maintain the South's honor; it was legal; and the South would be better off economically for doing it. A meeting to form the new government was even held at the place suggested by the periodical. A new framework of government was established espousing what the South considered to have been the views of the founding fathers. The new government was built upon the principle of states' rights. De Bow had urged these things, and to this degree his magazine was successful as a propaganda apparatus.

It cannot be claimed that De Bow's Review precipitated secession by itself, nor can it be assumed that it stirred the people of the South to the point of war. But it is sensible to conclude that it played an important part in all these things. And it is even more reasonable to say that it reflected the times during which it was printed as well as, if not better than, other periodicals.

67. Skipper, J. D. B. De Bow, 24, 50–51, 88, 135–36, 202–205. The circulation of the periodical fell with the loss of northern subscribers after the arguments became bitter and secession began. There were approximately 4,000 subscribers in the South during the period under consideration. The major problem was collecting subscription rates from them.

Congressman William Barksdale
of Mississippi

James W. McKee, Jr.

On November 8, 1853, after months of rugged campaigning, William Barksdale was elected as a states' rights Democrat to the U.S. House of Representatives in one of the most bitterly contested elections in the history of antebellum Mississippi. He served as a member of that enigmatic assembly for four consecutive terms, from 1853 to 1861, during which time he was in the center of the political maelstrom that ultimately culminated in a fratricidal civil war between the North and South. The chief question of a sectional character before Congress during this crucial period was the extension of chattel slavery into federal territory, and, as the representative of one of the South's largest slaveholding states, Barksdale was frequently called upon to defend southern rights and institutions. This he did with such enthusiasm and tenacity that he was erroneously regarded by some of his northern contemporaries as a fire-eating secessionist, which, in retrospect at least, is unfortunate because their criticism tends to cast a false and distorted reflection upon the congressional career of a dedicated public servant. "The South," it has been written, "had

no more capable legislative defender than the representative
from the Third Mississippi Congressional District."[1]
Although the role of southern advocate dominated his congressional career, Barksdale did not belong to that select
fraternity of political agitators who so fervently endeavored to
foment secession in the early 1850s. He was prepared to take a
firm stand on any issue that threatened his section's interests,
but, at this stage of his political development, he was far less
extreme in his views than many of his associates in Congress.
His philosophy of government on entering the national arena
in 1853 was basically that moderate leaders of the North and
South could resolve their differences within the framework of
the Constitution. And, despite occasional outbursts of partisan
sectionalism in moments of stress, he remained comparatively
dispassionate in the performance of his legislative duties until
after the intensification of sectional rancor in the House following passage of the Kansas-Nebraska Act of 1854. Even then
he continued to work faithfully through the auspices of the
national Democratic party, adhering to its principles, so far as
possible, in his efforts to maintain the constitutional rights of
the South. Not until the slave insurrection scare of 1859 and
his mounting fear of an imminent Republican victory in the
approaching presidential election was his faith in an enduring
Republic irreparably shaken. So incensed was he at this critical juncture by the adverse turn of political events that he
promptly joined the ranks of that growing phalanx of fire-
eaters in Congress to promote a southern confederacy.

Typical of many who represented the state in national coun-
cils before the Civil War, Barksdale was not a native Missis-

1. Raymond W. Tyson, "William Barksdale and the Brooks-Sumner As-
sault," *Journal of Mississippi History*, XXVI (May, 1964), 140. For contempo-
rary impressions of Barksdale, obviously based on his association with certain
leading fire-eaters, see Mrs. Roger A. Pryor, *Reminiscences of Peace and War*
(New York, 1904), 102–103; Mrs. John A. Logan, *Reminiscences of a Soldier's
Wife* (New York, 1913), 75; John Sherman, *John Sherman's Recollections of
Forty Years in the House, Senate, and Cabinet* (2 vols.; Chicago, 1895), I, 228;
Henry Wilson, *History of the Rise and Fall of the Slave Power in America* (3 vols.:
Boston, 1874), II, 649.

sippian. He was born August 21, 1821, near Smyrna, Rutherford County, Tennessee, the son of Nancy Hervey Lester and William Barksdale, Sr. His parents were each descended from prominent ancestors of southern birth, whose civil and patriotic deeds were sources of both pride and strength in the Barksdale family for many generations. Nathaniel Barksdale, the paternal grandfather of the future congressman, was a member of a highly respected family of slaveholders in Halifax County, Virginia, who had served with distinction in the Revolutionary War. In 1808, to provide more adequately for his growing family, he migrated to central Tennessee, where he settled on a small plantation near the Stones River.[2] During the War of 1812 the elder William Barksdale enlisted as a private in the Second Regiment of Tennessee Mounted Volunteer Gunmen and fought under Andrew Jackson in the battle of New Orleans. Upon his return from the war, he became engaged in agriculture and by the time of his death in 1836 had become successful enough to bequeath his heirs a comfortable estate. He was survived by his second wife Ann Eliza Calhoun and five children, including William, for whom special provision was made to establish a trust fund for his college education.[3]

Although born into a family with aristocratic traditions, Barksdale was a product of the frontier influences of central Tennessee, which was probably a major factor helping to shape his destiny. After attending the public schools of Rutherford County, he pursued a partial course of classical study at

2. John A. Barksdale, *Barksdale Family History and Genealogy* (Richmond, 1940), 42, 56–57, 266–68, 272–75; Sarah D. Hubert, *Genealogy of Part of the Barksdale Family of America* (Atlanta, 1895), 39–44; Wirt J. Carrington, *A History of Halifax County* (Richmond, 1924), 108–10, 156–59; Charlton C. Sims, *A History of Rutherford County* (n.p., 1947), 73; Trust Deed of Nathaniel Barksdale, Deed Book 8, pp. 329–31, Rutherford County Courthouse, Murfreesboro, Tenn.

3. MSS., War of 1812 Records for the State of Tennessee, III, 238–43, IX, 61, 88–93, 138–45, Tennessee State Library and Archives, Nashville; Marriage Record Book, 1804–1837, p. 8, Last Testament of William Barksdale, Sr., in Deed Book 9, p. 212, Property Schedule of William Barksdale, Sr., in Deed Book 9, pp. 433–46, Guardianship Records, in Record Book 10, pp. 114, 475, all in Rutherford County Courthouse.

the University of Nashville. This phase of his formal education continued until 1839, when he moved to Mississippi with his brothers in search of fame and fortune. He proceeded to settle permanently in the newly formed county of Lowndes near Columbus. He soon expressed a keen interest in the study of law and, encouraged by his older brother and guardian, decided to pursue it as a career. Although his training was superficial by today's standards, he labored tirelessly to prepare himself for the legal profession and was admitted to the bar shortly before his twenty-first birthday. He then established his own law firm in Columbus, and despite his obvious youth, soon won distinction as a "successful practitioner" of his profession.[4] As he prospered, he invested his capital wisely in land and slaves, though many of the latter came into his possession as a result of his marriage in 1849 to Narcissa Saunders, an attractive twenty-year-old "belle" from Louisiana.[5] By 1860 he had acquired thirty-six slaves and a cotton plantation valued at $10,000, in addition to several choice parcels of unimproved land in other parts of the country.[6]

In his quest for economic security and respectability, Barksdale also began to harbor political aspirations. No sooner had a career in public service claimed his attention

4. Microfilm MSS., University of Nashville Records, 1785–1885, IV, 28, 41, Tennessee State Library and Archives; Petition of Harrison, Barksdale *et al.* to Circuit Court, Deed Book Y, pp. 58–59, Rutherford County Courthouse; James A. Barksdale, "Address to the William Barksdale Chapter, S.C.V., Columbus, Miss., Feb. 25, 1954, Ethelbert Barksdale Papers, Department of Archives and History, Jackson, Miss.; "Works Progress Administration History of Lowndes County" (2 vols.; n.p., n.d.), II, 373, Columbus Public Library; W. L. Lipscomb, *A History of Columbus, Mississippi, During the Nineteenth Century* (Birmingham, 1909), 19; *The South in the Building of the Nation* (12 vols.; Richmond, 1909), XI, 44–45.

5. Microfilm MSS., Personal Tax Rolls for the State of Mississippi, Lowndes County, Department of Archives and History, Jackson; Schedule of the Property of Mrs. William Barksdale, in Deed Book 21, p. 15, Lowndes County Courthouse, Columbus, Miss.; *Publications of the Southern History Association* (Washington, D.C., 1897), I, 131.

6. Microfilm MSS., 1860 Population Schedules, Mississippi, Free Inhabitants, Lowndes County, Columbus, Third Ward; Petition of Mrs. Narcissa Barksdale for the Probation of William Barksdale's Will, Lowndes County Courthouse.

than he started to explore the feasibility of a judicious invest-
ment in the area's developing field of journalism, which,
together with his law practice, might help him to realize his
political ambitions. On March 23, 1844, he purchased a one-
half interest in one of the town's local newspapers, the Columbus *Democrat.* Like so many periodicals published in the
antebellum South, the *Democrat* was a political organ, and, as
designated by the masthead, it was operated strictly in the
interest of the Democratic party, the philosophy of which
Barksdale had embraced since early manhood. As editor-
proprietor of the *Democrat,* he frequently used its columns to
express his states' rights views of the Constitution and to
sustain "the doctrines of Jefferson and Madison." Evidently,
he was on the threshold of seeking either local or state public
office, but his immediate plans in this area had to be postponed because of the impending conflict with Mexico.[7]

Although his fame has been largely associated with the Civil
War, Barksdale actually received his first military experience
in the Mexican War. In that conflict he served, with the rank of
captain, as assistant commissary in the Second Mississippi
Infantry Regiment. Inspired by a combination of personal
factors ranging from patriotism to martial fever, he was
among the first recruits from the northern district to be enrolled for active duty with the Second Regiment. However,
after the unit was officially organized at Vicksburg on January
12, 1847, he began to discover that the role of the soldier is
more often tedious than glorious. At length, the regiment was
ordered to join Zachary Taylor in northern Mexico, but it
arrived too late to participate in the celebrated battle at Buena
Vista, the last important military engagement in that theater.
Few were more disappointed than Barksdale, for only on the
field of action could one attain a distinguished combat record
and the public acclaim he so ardently desired. It is true that he

7. Trust Deed of William Barksdale, in Deed Book 21, p. 15. Lowndes County
Courthouse; "Works Progress Administration History of Lowndes County," II,
240–42; "The Mississippi Delegation in Congress," *Harper's Weekly,* V (Feb. 2,
1861), 66; *The South in the Building of the Nation,* XI, 44; Jackson *Mississippian,* May 6, 27, 1853.

was praised for the professional manner in which he discharged his duties as commissary officer, but that was small
compensation for the monotony and privation he endured as a
member of Taylor's inactive army. Aside from an occasional
alert, he did not even participate in an insignificant skirmish,
which consequently meant that his share of the honors of war
would be scant. Nevertheless, he steadfastly remained with his
regiment until honorably discharged on September 1, 1848.[8]
After the Mexican War, Barksdale resumed his former
economic and legal pursuits. He also renewed his partisan
interests in state affairs, but his political activities did not
capture public attention until the emergence of that prolonged
struggle within the state over the Compromise of 1850.[9] Although the right of peaceable secession was part of his creed,
he had spoken of it only as a last remedy. He therefore joined
the moderates of the Democratic party and denounced the
"extraordinary course" of its radical faction, whose policy of
resistance was fraught with potential danger.[10] He admitted to
having certain reservations about Henry Clay's plan of adjustment but did not believe that the compromise program
was sufficient cause for the state to hazard a "collision with the
general government."[11] Having declared his opposition to the
disunionists, he then sought to rally the state's population
against secession and was rewarded by being elected a Union
delegate to the convention that was to assemble in Jackson on

8. Dunbar Rowland, *The Official and Statistical Register of the State of
Mississippi* (Nashville, 1908), 415–17; Rowland, "Roll of Mississippi Soldiers
in the War of 1812 and the War with Mexico" (typescript, 1915), 75; Clayton
Rand, *Men of Spine in Mississippi* (Gulfport, Miss., 1940), 174, 187–88; Jackson
Mississippian, May 6, 27, 1853; Natchez *Weekly Courier and Journal*, Dec. 16,
1846, Feb. 10, 1847; Claim of William Barksdale for Bounty Land, Columbus,
Miss., Oct. 24, 1850, National Archives, Washington, D.C. For a brief period,
the Second Regiment was commanded by Colonel Reuben Davis, a noted
jurist from Aberdeen, Miss. and Barksdale's leading opponent in the congressional election of 1853. See Reuben Davis, *Recollections of Mississippi and
Mississippians* (Boston, 1889), 237.
9. Jackson *Mississippian*, March 31, 1849, quoting the Columbus *Democrat*.
10. Columbus *Democrat*, March 29, 1851.
11. Cleo Hearon, "Mississippi and the Compromise of 1850," *Publications of
the Mississippi Historical Society*, XIV (1914), 163–71, 174–78. See also Columbus *Democrat*, March 29, Oct. 27, 1851.

November 10, 1851.[12] This historic assembly, controlled largely by men of moderate persuasion, adopted a set of resolutions that, with certain reservations, advocated that "the people should acquiesce in the compromise measures of 1850 as a permanent adjustment of the national controversy," which at least temporarily ended the threat of secession in Mississippi. Yet the price had been extremely high for the Democrats, for the controversy made shambles out of the traditional political alignment of their party and many months would elapse before the divisiveness abated.[13]

In contrast to some of his contemporaries, Barksdale did not fade into obscurity after the secession crisis of 1851. He avoided the anonymity that beset other "lesser political lights" by embarking upon a rigorous schedule of public-speaking to discuss the turbulent political situation in Mississippi. On these occasions, in an obvious effort to bind up the wounds of his party, he argued that the estrangement between Unionist and states' rights Democrats was inimical to their faltering organization and, more to the point, that future success at the polls depended upon prompt reunification. His performance at these rallies naturally enhanced his reputation.[14] Among other things, his work in behalf of the resurgent

12. The selection of Barksdale as a Union delegate should not be interpreted to mean that he had abandoned his states' rights beliefs. On the contrary, he demonstrated the strength of his convictions, in both word and deed, during the course of the November convention. Among these was his unequivocal refusal to endorse the resolution introduced at the convention declaring secession to be nothing more than civil revolution. *Journal of the Convention of the State of Mississippi, 1851* (Jackson, 1851), 33; Hearon, "Mississippi and the Compromise of 1850," 215–17; Dunbar Rowland, *Mississippi* (3 vols.; Atlanta, 1907), I, 214; Percy L. Rainwater, *Mississippi: Storm Center of Secession, 1856–1861* (Baton Rouge, 1938), 29.

13. Hearon, "Mississippi and the Compromise of 1850," 201, 209, 215–17; Donald M. Rawson, "Party Politics in Mississippi, 1850–1860" (Ph.D. dissertation, Vanderbilt University, 1964), 118–19.

14. Barksdale's growing influence in state politics is partially illustrated by some of his activities during the presidential election of 1852. That year he was chosen as a Union delegate to attend the Democratic National Convention at Baltimore, where he supported both the platform and ticket. Of special interest, prior to accepting this assignment he had been nominated an elector by the party's states' rights wing by acclamation, but, for reasons not fully

movement brought him to the favorable attention of the party's hierarchy, which would soon have a direct bearing on his
quest for public office. Meanwhile, intimate friends urged him
to allow them to nominate him for the state legislature, but his
personal reaction to that entreaty defies proper assessment
because reliable evidence is lacking. To avoid being impolitic,
he may have expressed a tentative desire to stand election for
the general assembly, but his actions suggest that he thought
that he should not seek any elective office until he could be
reasonably assured that his candidacy would be approved by
the electorate in his legislative district, a predisposition
strengthened by the fact that the reunification campaign was
still in an embryonic stage. In any case, he noticeably refrained
from entering into any formal political commitments before
the resurgent party movement was almost completed. In-
terestingly enough, by biding his time, he would be presented
with an opportunity to seek a much more prestigious office
than his associates had envisioned for him.[15]

The chain of events that offered Barksdale his first real
chance for an important political career was set in motion
during the weeks prior to the state convention scheduled to
meet in Jackson on May 2, 1853, to select candidates for the fall
election. On April 11 Barksdale attended a Lowndes County
Democratic meeting in Columbus, where he was named a
member of an uncommitted delegation to attend the Jackson
convention.[16] As indicated, the purpose of the latter assembly
was to nominate both a state and congressional ticket for the
Democratic party, including a candidate from the state at

disclosed, the nomination had been respectfully declined. Columbus *Democrat*, Jan. 31, 1853; Natchez *Courier*, Feb. 3, 1853; Natchez *Mississippi Free
Trader*, June 7, 1853, quoting Columbus *Democrat*; Jackson *Mississippian*, July
29, 1853. See also James L. Harrison, *Biographical Directory of the American
Congress, 1774–1949* (Washington, D.C., 1950), 815.
    15. In the weeks ahead, Barksdale's name was also mentioned in certain
quarters as a possible candidate for the U.S. House of Representatives. For an
interesting newspaper article advancing the public's claim to his services on
the state level, written months after the above reference to Congress, see
Columbus *Southern Standard*, Feb. 12, 19, 1853.
    16. *Ibid.*, April 9, 1853. See also Jackson *Mississippian*, April 22, 1853, which
contains the complete proceedings of the Lowndes meeting.

large for the newly created seat in the U.S. House of Representatives.[17] Insofar as can be determined, Barksdale had his political sights set on the state legislature, but it soon was suggested that he might be able to secure the congressman-at-large nomination. His political enemies later accused him of attending the convention with a plan for obtaining that nomination, but no conclusive evidence was ever produced by them to support the allegation, which appears to be groundless. During the two-day convention, he would receive the nomination, but it should be noted that the highly coveted prize had fallen to him only after an extremely close contest against a field of worthy opponents and some rather adverse conditions. In fact, at one point he was confronted with a situation that might easily have eliminated him as a prospective candidate before the nominations began.[18]

On the first day of the convention, Benjamin H. Kinyon, a Union Democrat from Tishomingo County, introduced a series of resolutions proposing that state offices be divided equally between the Union and states' rights factions of the Democratic party. It was not explicitly stated, but was clearly implied, that half the state offices for the Union Democrats was their price for reconciliation. In strong language, Barksdale objected to the "infamous resolution" on the grounds that such a division would make it appear that the Democrats were still divided in sentiment, just as they had been over the Compromise of 1850. However, this was not the only reason Barksdale was opposed to Kinyon's proposition. By this time he had been approached by John J. McRae, Albert

17. In 1850, according to the census, Mississippi had a population of 606,526, a number that entitled the state to an additional representative to Congress. A revision of the legislative districts thus became necessary, but, because of the failure of the legislators to redistrict the state before the congressional election of 1853, it became manifest that the recipient of the newborn post be elected from the state at large. US Bureau of the Census, _US Census of Population: 1950_, Vol. II, _Characteristics of the Population_, Part 24, Mississippi (Washington, D.C., 1952), 5; Rowland, _The Official and Statistical Register of the State of Mississippi_, 232–33.
18. Columbus, _Democrat_, Jan., 31, 1853; Columbus _Southern Standard_, Feb. 12, 19, April 9, 1853; Jackson _Mississippian_, April 22, 1853; Natchez _Mississippi Free Trader_, June 14, 1853.

G. Brown, and other patriarchs and informed that he would have their support in obtaining the congressman-at-large nomination if he would agree to return to the states' rights faction of the Democratic party. The significance of this offer was not lost on Barksdale, who readily agreed to seek the coveted nomination under the prescribed condition. Thus, if Kinyon's resolutions for the equal division of state offices had been passed, the Union Democrats would have been in a better position to choose the representative to Congress, thereby jeopardizing Barksdale's chances for the nomination.[19]

As forecast by Barksdale, Kinyon's resolutions transformed the convention into a tinderbox of dissension, so much so that the delegates were still in a state of "intense excitement" at the end of the day's proceedings. Ironically, in creating such discord, Kinyon enhanced Barksdale's prospects for a position on the Democratic ticket, because the acrimony engendered by his demand that the "loaves and fishes" be distributed evenly between the two wings of the party allowed Barksdale to deliver a strong protest speech that definitely scored points for him with the delegates. Besides eliciting a modicum of partisan admiration, his stern criticism of the incongruous set of resolutions produced "a little talk" in his favor for the congressman-at-large nomination. More support materialized for him that night at a special strategy session attended by an influential minority of delegates. After examining his qualifications, they conceded that he was probably the best available choice for the office in question. After all, here was a states' rights Democrat "by education, by study, and by practice" who had been on the popular side of the "great contest" of 1851.[20] Hence, on the second day of the convention, his name was placed in nomination along with six others. Three of the

19. Jackson *Mississippian*, May 6, 1853; Yazoo *Democrat*, June 1, 1853. See also Lamar B. Neal, "Chronicles of the Fire-Eaters: A Contemporary Account of the Secession Controversy in Mississippi" (M.A. thesis, Mississippi State University, 1956), 153–54.

20. Jackson *Mississippian*, May 6, 27, 1853; Natchez *Mississippi Free Trader*, June 7, July 19, 1853; Columbus *Southern Standard*, May 14, 1853; Yazoo *Democrat*, June 1, 1853. See also James B. Ranck, *Albert Gallatin Brown, Radical Southern Nationalist* (New York, 1937), 112.

nominees withdrew before the balloting started. Of the three other aspirants, Barksdale's strongest opposition came from Reuben Davis of Monroe County, who received thirty-seven votes to only twenty-five for Barksdale on the first ballot. On the second roll call, however, Barksdale started to gain ground, and he continued to acquire additional support on each subsequent vote, until finally, on the fifth ballot, he received a majority of the votes. Shortly thereafter, on a motion by W. L. Harris of Warren County, he was declared "the unanimous choice of the convention" to be the Democratic candidate from the state at large for Congress.[21]

To the dismay of many states' rights Democrats, Barksdale's nomination provoked an adverse reaction in northern Mississippi. Nowhere was this more true than in the counties of Chickasaw and Monroe, both of which refused to abide by the decision of the convention because their champion Reuben Davis had been "wantonly sacrificed." The state had won its fifth representative to Congress because of the population growth in the northern districts, and the representatives of these counties thought that they should have the privilege of designating the candidate for Congress at large. Impelled by this interpretation, they had remained steadfast in their support of Davis at the convention, and when Barksdale was chosen over the "Aberdeen Lamb" they claimed that an "unmitigable outrage" had been perpetrated upon the Democrats of north Mississippi. Of course, they realized that it was too late to reverse Barksdale's nomination, but they could attempt to discredit him in the eyes of the public with contrived propaganda and thus reduce his chances of winning the election. In pursuit of this objective, they accused him in private and public of resorting to everything from chicanery to base intrigue in obtaining the nomination. The most universal complaint was that, "while he [Barksdale] was the professed friend of Col. Reuben Davis, he connived at the use made of his

21. Jackson *Mississippian*, May 6, 1853; Columbus *Southern Standard*, May 14, 1853; Neal, "Chronicles of the Fire-Eaters," 161; Davis, *Recollections of Mississippi and Mississippians*, 332.

name to defeat Davis." Actually, the truth of the matter was
that Barksdale had agreed to support Davis only if Davis was
nominated, but this relevant fact was conveniently suppressed
by Barksdale's adversaries in northeast Mississippi, which
soon became the scene of a protest movement known as the
"Chickasaw Rebellion."[22]
    Beyond a doubt, the Chickasaw Rebellion created a major
paradox for Barksdale, one that materially altered the contest
from his point of view. The revolt furnished Davis with an
opportunity to enter the congressional campaign as an independent candidate, and, to make matters worse, this indomi-
table opponent was supported by several important news journals in northern Mississippi, all of which employed tactics
designed to convert the popular discontent of that section into
action in behalf of Davis' candidacy.[23] Nor was this all. Additional trouble was being manufactured for Barksdale by the
Whig party, the leadership of which had understandably "re-
joiced" at Davis' decision to announce as an independent. The
Whigs had recently failed to disrupt the reunification campaign of the states' rights Democrats in Mississippi and were
consequently pleased at the prospect that Davis' candidacy
might revive the late division of the Democratic party, in
which case the Whigs might capture some of the top honors in
the fall election.[24] To this end, they induced Major Alexander
Bradford, a Mexican War hero and a prominent Whig politician from Marshall County, to run as an independent candidate for the disputed congressional seat. By comparison, he
was a much more illustrious candidate than either Barksdale

22. Jackson *Mississippian*, May 27, 1853; Vicksburg *Whig*, May 21, 1853;
Aberdeen *Independent*, July 9, 1853; Columbus *Southern Standard*, June 4, July
2, 1853; June 11, 1853, quoting Holly Springs *Guard;* Natchez *Mississippi Free
Trader*, June 7, 1853, quoting Monroe *Democrat;* Davis, *Recollections of Missis-
sippi and Mississippians*, 332; Ranck, *Albert Gallatin Brown*, 111–12; Rawson,
"Party Politics in Mississippi, 1850–1860," 123–26.
    23. Jackson *Mississippian*, May 27, 1853, quoting Vicksburg *Sentinel;* Aber-
deen *Independent*, June 11, 1853, quoting Oxford *Flag;* Natchez *Mississippi
Free Trader*, July 19, 1853; Yazoo *Democrat*, Aug. 24, 1853, quoting Monroe
Democrat.
    24. Jackson *Mississippian*, June 10, 17, 1853; Aberdeen *Independent*, July 30,
1853. See also Rawson, "Party Politics in Mississippi, 1850–1860," 118ff.

or Davis, and it is not surprising that his sponsors were confident that his magnetic name and personality would "enlist a host of warm supporters" from both parties.[25] Having reviewed the exemplary credentials of Bradford, the editor of one out-of-state newspaper asserted that, if Mississippians failed to elect such a distinguished personage as Bradford, they would "deserve to be represented by demagogues and pothouse politicians ever hereafter."[26]

Of the two other candidates, Barksdale regarded Davis as the primary threat to his election. His decision was dictated in part by the expediency of defusing the issues seized upon by Davis to inflame the public against the regular state ticket, so the appearance of Bradford was initially treated as a nominal distraction to the main contest between him and Davis. Barksdale's canvass of the northern counties was underway when Bradford announced his candidacy, and Barksdale noticeably refrained from altering his campaign strategy, which was to curb the Chickasaw Rebellion before it could reach overwhelming proportions. To accomplish this difficult feat, Barksdale engaged Davis in a series of joint rallies during the early weeks of the campaign. On these occasions the two men, who were not on friendly terms, treated their audiences to the inflammatory rhetoric for which both were to be known throughout their political careers. Although national issues were occasionally mentioned, the recurring almost monotonous theme permeating their joint canvass was the probity of the recent Democratic convention at Jackson, with each denying the legitimacy of the other's claim to the disputed congressional seat. This invariably led the embittered rivals into the equally controversial area of the "origin, cause, and grounds" of the Chickasaw Rebellion, and the lively discussions that ensued were often attended by angry emotionalism. In fact, because of the unrestrained criticism that tended to characterize their debates, it became increasingly evident to those

25. Vicksburg *Whig*, Aug. 23, 1853.
26. *Ibid.*, July 19, 1853, quoting Memphis *Enquirer*.

closely associated with the campaign that the disputatious candidates were on a "collision course."[27]

By the end of June, the rancor between Barksdale and Davis had reached dangerous proportions. The caustic remarks they exchanged with such reckless abandon had served only to compound the resentment emanating from the Jackson convention, and in the absence of the moderating influence of impartial audiences it was perhaps inevitable that their joint canvass of the state should culminate in a violent physical encounter. The altercation occurred at Vicksburg on July 1, a few hours before the controversial pair was scheduled to appear at a public rally.[28] Oddly enough, the fracas erupted while the two men were engaged in an abortive attempt to arrange a duel. Although the details are unclear, it seems that after accepting Barksdale's challenge to meet him on the field of honor Davis started to quibble about the time and location for the projected fight and had been denounced in unfavorable terms by Barksdale. One harsh word led to another until Davis, in a fit of anger, struck Barksdale in the face with the back of his hand. Equally agitated, Barksdale responded with a heavy blow, the force of which repelled Davis back across the room. Recovering quickly, Davis drew a knife from his pocket and began to brandish it menacingly in Barksdale's direction. Undaunted, Barksdale charged forward with characteristic belligerency and started to pummel his antagonist with a series of punches to the head and body, using his left arm in a vain effort to fend off repeated knife thrusts by Davis. In the confusion, two of Barksdale's friends finally came forward somewhat belatedly and separated the combatants before serious damage had been inflicted. As it was, Davis was "con-

27. Columbus *Southern Standard*, June 11, 1853; Jackson *Mississippian*, June 24, July 1, 1853; Natchez *Mississippi Free Trader*, July 5, 1853.
28. Regarding the speakers, the *Whig* reported laconically "We do not know that either of them can enlighten our citizens very greatly upon the principles of government, or the powers of Congress, but as we have had no political speeches for some time, and as the discussion promises to be rich in many respects, we are satisfied that there will be a full audience." Vicksburg *Whig*, July 2, 1853.

siderably bruised and blackened," and Barksdale was saturated with his own blood, having sustained nearly a dozen cuts
on his left arm, chest, and side during the melee. His wounds
required medical treatment but were fortunately diagnosed
superficial.[29]

The "unheralded collision" at Vicksburg marked an abrupt
and inglorious conclusion to the joint canvass of Barksdale
and Davis. The remainder of their speaking engagements was
cancelled, and each aspirant went his separate way by mutual
consent.[30] In the case of Davis, however, it proved to be an
exercise in futility. He was described as the villain of the fracas
in Vicksburg because he had been armed, and that kind of
adverse publicity was bound to affect his popular standing.
Importantly, his decline was paralleled by a corresponding
increase in the popularity of his opponent, causing him to
realize, perhaps for the first time, that the nomination of
Barksdale by the state convention was not nearly as odious to
the northern Democrats as he had initially believed. Indeed,
Barksdale seemed to be gaining in public esteem throughout
that section of the state with each passing day, attested by the
fact that some of the journals that had earlier advocated Davis'
independent candidacy were now switching their support to
Barksdale.[31] Even worse, the repudiation movement that
Davis and his associates had so carefully engineered was
beginning to take on the appearance of an "arrested development," and he knew that his election was solely dependent
upon the organization of a sectional party for northern Mississippi, the creation of which now looked like a remote possibility. This realization, coupled with continued evidence of wan-

29. *Ibid.*, July 7, 1853. The account of the fight carried in this issue of the
Whig is based on testimony brought out during a session of the local court,
which was presided over by Mayor J. S. Byrne. Byrne ruled that Davis could be
released on bail but ordered him to appear before the next session of the circuit
court to answer the charge of "aggravated assault." See also Aberdeen *Weekly
Independent*, July 16, 1853.

30. Vicksburg *Whig*, July 9, 1853.

31. Natchez *Mississippi Free Trader*, July 19, 1853; quoting Pontotoc
Sovereign, July 26, 1853, quoting Fulton *Monitor;* Yazoo *Democrat*, July 17, 20,
24, 1853.

ing public interest in his candidacy, soon forced the frustrated
Davis to reassess his prospects for winning the fall election.
The result must have been depressing because on September
27, 1853, he announced that he was withdrawing from the
contest, stating rather feebly that he had been invited to
become an agent for the New Orleans Railroad. Undoubtedly,
he had seized upon this offer as a means to exit gracefully from
the contest and avoid certain defeat at the polls.[32]

With the departure of Davis from the contest, Barksdale's
political fortunes looked brighter, but it would be a grave error
to assume that he had the election locked up. On the contrary,
he still had a formidable Whig opponent. It is true that Bradford was an acknowledged member of the state's minority
party, but he had a "strong hold upon the affections" of many
Mississippians, irrespective of their political affiliations.
Added to that, he possessed a superior military record that
could be counted on to secure additional support. Moreover,
his campaign was being conducted under the tutelage of
Henry S. Foote, who was running against A. G. Brown in the
senatorial contest. By accompanying Foote, Bradford obviously expected to draw heavily upon the governor's current
popularity to override the party loyalty of Union Democrats,
which is understandable since his success at the polls was
dependent upon a coalition of Union-Whig voters. He no doubt
believed that if Union and Whig voting strength could be
united, as it had been in 1851, he had a good chance of winning
in November.[33]

To meet the threat, Barksdale embarked on his second
"grand tour" of north Mississippi, one specifically designed to
contain Bradford's influence to as few counties as possible in
that particular section. The circumstances that caused this
decision can be easily traced to several interrelated factors.

32. Jackson *Mississippian*, Oct. 7, 1853, quoting Monroe *Democrat*; Davis,
Recollections of Mississippi and Mississippians, 332–33. See also Charles D.
Fontaine to Jefferson Davis, July 13, 1853, in Dunbar Rowland (ed.), *Jefferson
Davis, Constitutionalist* (New York, 1923), II, 234–36.
33. Aberdeen *Independent*, July 2, 1853, quoting *Flag of the Union*; Vicksburg
Whig, Aug. 23, 1853.

First, Barksdale's base of popular support was satisfactorily established in the south and central portions of the state, except for certain parts of the Delta, which were Whig strongholds. Second, he knew that Bradford enjoyed his greatest popularity in the northern counties and might successfully use this advantage to rally Union Democrats to his banner. Third, he also knew from bitter experience that it was the disaffection of the electorate in several of the northeastern counties that had induced Davis to boldly challenge the regular state ticket. Evidently, he suspected that the hardcore followers of Davis would either abstain from voting in the forthcoming election or, even worse, throw their support to Bradford as a final gesture of defiance. Finally, he was anxious to reply to the charges levied against him by the Whig press, which was seeking to destroy him in the public confidence by misrepresenting his position on the compromise measures in 1851.[34]

Addressing himself to these problems, Barksdale issued a spirited challenge to his independent-Whig opponent to meet him in a series of public debates. He doubtlessly hoped to lure Bradford away from the Foote organization, but his elusive opponent refused "to leave the wing of his patron."[35] Barksdale therefore was compelled to finish the canvass by himself. Even so, he managed to attract fairly large crowds to his rallies, primarily by carefully timing his visits to correspond with county court sessions. On these occasions he warned his audiences that Bradford was playing a deceptive game to enhance the prospects of the Whig party and to weaken the Democrats. His strategy had obviously undergone only slight modification, for he was still exhorting Democrats to remain loyal to the "old standard." As a reward for his partisanship, his speeches were given favorable coverage by Democratic journals, some of which even began to credit him with "perfecting the harmony of the party."[36] One editor,

34. Jackson *Mississippian*, July 22, 1853, Oct. 7, 1853; Yazoo *Democrat*, Aug. 24, 1853.
35. Jackson *Mississippian*, Aug. 12, 21, quoting Ripley *Advertiser*, Sept. 26, 1853.
36. Jackson *Mississippian*, Aug. 26, Oct. 7, 1853; Natchez *Mississippi Free Trader*, Nov. 8, 1853.

particularly impressed by the "real old-fashioned democratic" speech that Barksdale made at Oxford, assured his
readers that "if the Captain acquits himself elsewhere as he
did here, the Democratic party may well be proud of their
noble standard-bearer."[37]

Indeed, although he had not long played the role of an active
campaigner, Barksdale was proving himself to be not only an
aggressive public speaker but also an astute political
strategist. His canvass of the northern counties centered
primarily on the theme that a divided Democratic party would
assure a Whig victory, and his tactics for encouraging Union
and states' rights Democrats to return to their former al-
legiance were proving effective, attested by the defection of a
sizable number of voters from Bradford's camp in the closing
weeks of the campaign. For example, shortly before the voters
went to the polls, several Democratic journals, including the
Columbus *Southern Standard*, noted confidently that
Barksdale would defeat the "Julius Caesar" of Marshall
County by a substantial margin, probably 5,000 to 8,000
votes.[38] The exact process by which these editors arrived at
this interesting calculation is unclear, but it must have been
based on fairly thorough straw votes because the prediction
was surprisingly accurate by the standards of the day. When
the ballots were officially tabulated after the election on
November 7–8, the returns indicated that Barksdale had in
fact won the hotly contested congressional seat by a popular
plurality of nearly 5,000 votes. His total vote throughout the
state was 32,175 to 27,347 for his opponent.[39]

Barksdale's victory, the result of a massive turnout of Union
and states' rights Democrats, produced mixed reactions across
the state, with commentary varying according to party affilia-
tion.[40] To be sure, each candidate on the Democratic state
ticket was subjected to a certain amount of adverse criticism,
but it would have required more than was published to take

37. Jackson *Mississippian*, Oct. 28, 1853, quoting Oxford *Flag*.
38. Columbus *Southern Standard*, Nov. 8, 12, 1853.
39. For the official vote by counties, see Jackson *Mississippian*, Dec. 2, 1853.
40. Aberdeen *Independent*, Nov. 26, 1853.

the bloom off the victory achieved by Barksdale, who was
understandably jubilant because he had at last risen to leadership in the Democratic party. Of greater significance, he was
now in a position to influence political events beyond the state,
and in the ensuing years he would make every effort to prove
himself worthy of the trust bestowed upon him, as did the
other notables who joined him in Congress. During the 1850s,
the state of Mississippi could not have asked for more ardent
defenders than the individuals who composed its delegation to
the national Congress. Referring to the zeal of these men, the
Natchez *Free Trader* exclaimed: "With such men as Albert
Gallatin Brown and Jefferson Davis in the Senate, and John A.
Quitman, Otho Singleton, William Barksdale, Reuben Davis,
and L.Q.C. Lamar in the House, Mississippi must and will be
heard, and her honor and interests, and those of the entire
South, maintained and vigilantly guarded. There is not one of
these representatives who would not reflect the highest honor
upon this or any other State."[41] If this was an accurate reflection of the consensus of the state's electorate, it is not surprising that Barksdale, who was bound to his section by strong ties
of blood and affection, was enthusiastically returned to Congress by the constituents of the Third Congressional District
until he resigned his post on the eve of the Civil War.[42]

On December 5, 1853, Barksdale took his appointed place in
the House of Representatives of the Thirty-third Congress. It
was an auspicious moment for him because it meant that he
was about to enter the mainstream of national politics. He was
thirty-two years old and in the prime of manhood, mature in
both thought and physical being. His grounding in law and
political science made him a formidable adversary in debate,
and his frank manners and imposing frame added weight to
his "decided remarks." In appearance, he stood about five feet
eleven inches and weighed nearly two hundred pounds. Simply stated, he was the embodiment of robust health, a condi-

41. Natchez *Mississippi Free Trader*, March 1, 1858.
42. Columbus *Democrat*, Sept. 2, 1854, Jan. 20, 1855; Natchez *Mississippi
Free Trader*, Jan. 27, Feb. 25, May 31, 1858; Jackson *Mississippian*, Sept. 27,
Oct. 11, 1859.

tion enabling him to bring the same boundless energy and
enthusiasm to the House that he had exhibited during the
recent election. More important, he also brought with him the
convictions that had been shaped and molded during his life in
the South. Foremost among the fundamental principles of his
creed was his staunch and unyielding belief in the strict interpretation of the Constitution. An ardent disciple of the
doctrines of Thomas Jefferson and James Madison, he believed
strongly that the states had the inherent right to choose and
maintain their own institutions, without any interference
from the national government. He was also a firm advocate of
low tariffs, the institution of slavery, and a social order based
on white supremacy.[43]

Although ideologically prepared to join the struggle to
maintain the constitutional rights of the South, Barksdale did
not begin his congressional career with incendiary displays of
"southernism." Instead he plunged into the arduous task of
drafting legislation for the alleviation of some of his state's
economic problems, which partially reflects his moderate
political philosophy. Less than one week after the session
opened, he announced his plans to introduce the first of several
pieces of important legislation, none of which was designed to
foment sectional discord. Each was specifically designed to
advance the general economic interests of his section and
represented the type of bills that he either sponsored or supported during his first term in Congress. This is not to suggest
that his activities epitomize the true spirit of accommodation,
but rather that they tend to disprove the impression that he
initially undertook his congressional duties as a radical southerner hell-bent on inciting political ferment between the sections, which is the image unintentionally created by some
historians in describing certain episodes involving him during
his last years in Washington. At this juncture, he was mainly
interested in serving the best interests of his section by secur-

---

43. *Congressional Globe,* 33rd Cong.and 1st sess., 2; Harrison, *Biographical
Directory of the American Congress, 1774–1949,* 815; Rowland, *Mississippi,* I,
213; Davis, *Recollections of Mississippi and Mississippians,* 348; "The Mississippi Delegation in Congress," 66.

ing legislation to encourage rail and river improvements, and it seems safe to assume that he probably would have been content to confine his energies to achieving those goals had his attention not been repeatedly diverted by more compelling political considerations.[44]

As fate would have it, Barksdale had barely answered his first roll call when the fires of sectionalism were rekindled in the capital by the introduction of the Kansas-Nebraska Act of 1854. In fact, on the very night that the Mississippi House delegation arrived in Washington, its members had been visited by Senator Stephen Adams. According to one source, Adams had summoned his colleagues together to forewarn them about the probable introduction of a new territorial bill in the Senate and to advise them to be prepared for reopening discussion in the House on the question of territorial slavery. Hence, during this impromptu meeting, a tentative plan of action was devised for the delegation to pursue pending the arrival of official instruction from Mississippi.[45] The exact role played by Barksdale at this strategy session cannot be ascertained from extant records, but he apparently concurred with the plan because he was selected to present the resolutions that were subsequently adopted by the Mississippi legislature endorsing the controversial Kansas-Nebraska bill. While awaiting the official response of the legislature on this matter, he devoted his attention to his official duties, namely, preparing the legislation that he proposed to introduce and getting acquainted with his responsibilities as the newest member of the Committee on Roads and Canals.[46]

In discharging his official obligations, Barksdale soon established a reputation for tenacious devotion to duty. He personally adhered to a strict code of conduct, and two of the basic rules from which he rarely deviated were regular attendance during congressional sessions and constant vigilance for legislation that might adversely affect southern institutions, which

44. *Congressional Globe*, 33rd Cong., 1st Sess., 95, 114, 370.
45. Dunbar Rowland, *Courts, Judges, and Lawyers of Mississippi, 1798–1935* (Jackson, 1935), 302.
46. *Congressional Globe*, 33rd Cong., 1st Sess., 34, 678.

were often under attack during this period. As a consequence, much of his time and energy were spent in safeguarding the political rights of the southern states, especially Mississippi. And, more than once, his alertness called the attention of his colleagues to items within certain bills that if passed could prove costly to the South. In early 1854, for example, Congressman Junius Hillyer of Georgia introduced a bill in the House to change the time for Congress to convene. By this measure, all future sessions of Congress would commence on the first Monday in November instead of the first Monday in December. Representative Rufus W. Peckham of New York moved to amend the bill by striking out "the first Monday in November" and inserting "the first Monday in October." Barksdale hastily pointed out that under Mississippi's existing election laws Peckham's amendment would disfranchise the state for an entire month and, furthermore, that it would involve considerable expense to change the Mississippi constitution to prevent being disfranchised for the period in question. His remarks were well received, and enough opposition was aroused to defeat Peckham's amendment.[47]

Another trademark established by Barksdale early in his congressional career was a singular obsession to improve the economy of the South. During his four terms in Congress, he sought to secure for his constituents federal benefits ranging from post roads to relief for settlers residing on public lands. For example, one of the first bills that he introduced in the House provided for federal assistance to expand interstate rail communication in Mississippi and neighboring states. A few weeks later, he asked Congress to appropriate $55,000 to complete the marine hospital at Vicksburg, and not long thereafter he sponsored a bill to have Columbus constituted "as a port of delivery." These internal improvement measures, like all the others that Barksdale supported during his tenure in the House, were decidedly regional in character. Of course, this sometimes left him open to sarcastic criticism; but seedy language, bristling with caustic denunciations, was the order

47. *Ibid.*, 1446–47.

of the day, especially after the sectional debate was greatly inflamed by the advent of Senator Stephen A. Douglas' territorial bill, to which several highly controversial amendments had been attached.[48]

For all practical purposes, Barksdale's debut in the acrimonious debates engendered by the revised territorial measure of Douglas was March 20, 1854, when he formally introduced the resolutions adopted by the Mississippi legislature. These proposals, concerned primarily with northern opposition to the expansion of slavery, resolved that the organization of a territorial government for Kansas and Nebraska was "in accordance with the principles of the Constitution" and expressed the view that the Mississippi delegation in Congress should be "instructed to support this bill by all honorable means."[49] That injunction no doubt influenced Barksdale's decision to endorse the measure, but personal as well as ideological considerations also figured prominently in determining his stand on the organization of two new western territories with the status of slavery to be decided by popular sovereignty. Above all, he earnestly hoped that the passage of Douglas' measure would bury the slavery controversy, which had proved to be so disruptive to national party unity and sectional tranquillity; and, although he was only a fledgling congressman, he made his presence felt by the great energy and forcefulness with which he defended the bill. Indeed, throughout the prolonged struggle in the House over the Kansas-Nebraska bill, he acquitted himself like a veteran of many congressional battles.[50]

On March 29 Barksdale delivered his maiden address in the House of Representatives. His speech was both argumentative and reflective, but the text of his remarks was prepared with enough tact to discount radicalism. He made it clear at the outset that he did not intend to discuss the general provisions of Douglas' bill. This was primarily because, he said, they were "similar to the details of all bills organizing territorial gov-

48. *Ibid.*, 114, 370, 2nd Sess., 21.
49. *Ibid.*, 1st Sess., 678.
50. *Appendix to the Congressional Globe*, 33rd Cong., 1st Sess., 474–75.

ernments" previously enacted by Congress. Instead he intended to respond to certain loudly articulated complaints
made by the bill's detractors and "to declare my opinions as to
certain amendments which have been incorporated in it." He
assured his colleagues that he also did not "intend to engage in
a discussion of the abstract question of slavery." But, while
managing to confine his arguments mainly to a defense of the
bill, he obviously could not resist the temptation to demonstrate publicly his personal commitment to southern rights
and institutions. For example, in the preamble of his address
he made it evident that he believed that slavery was not only
desirable and necessary for the good of mankind but also that
it was sanctioned by the Constitution. Of course, he would
have much more to say on this subject in the ensuing months,
with the result that he was soon recognized as a leading
spokesman of the proslavery Democrats in Congress.[51]

In his initial address, however, Barksdale was content to
keep his comments on slavery brief and to the point. Ostensibly, he made no attempt to offer a definitive statement on the
subject at this time because it was not germane to the central
theme of his speech, attested by the following statement: "So
far as the argument I design making is concerned, it is not
necessary that I should do so. It is sufficient that I should say,
that whatever, in my opinion, may be the benefits and blessings of slavery to the master and the slave, not only in the
southern States where it exists, but in the nonslaveholding
States, which both manufacture and consume the articles
produced by slave labor, we rest its defense, in this discussion,
upon the Constitution of the country, where it was placed by
the sages and patriots who formed the Government and
moulded our institutions."[52] On the latter point, he left no
room for dubiety, for he quickly added, "Shielded by that
instrument, we may safely bid defiance to those whose business here is to assail it; and whose political existence depends
upon the agitation of this question."[53]

51. *Ibid.*, 471.
52. *Ibid.*
53. *Ibid.*

Barksdale then addressed himself to the main objections against the Kansas-Nebraska bill. He first sought to dispose of the chief complaint of its southern opponents, who contended that the bill was premature and an "anomaly" in legislation. He rejected the allegation that the white population in the territories in question was too small to warrant the immediate attention of Congress. These objections, he said, simply would not "stand the test of facts and scrutiny." He pointed out that "indubitable evidence" had been introduced in the House to show that the territories had been inhabited by American settlers and that, regardless of their actual number, they deserved the protection of the federal government. Furthermore, even if the immigration reports for Kansas and Nebraska were inaccurate and misleading, he maintained that it was only a question of time before Congress would be forced to create a government for these territories because each would soon be occupied by a horde of pioneering farmers. To buttress his argument, he dramatically reviewed the history of westward expansion, emphasizing the adventurous enterprise of the hardy pioneer, and observed that if the lawmakers refused to act decisively in this matter the same courage and determination that enabled these settlers to conquer wildernesses would cause them to "act for themselves." "And it seems to me," he concluded, "that no southern man, with the light which the last few years has shed upon this subject, and the experience which the stormy period of 1850 furnishes, particularly in the admission of California, can hesitate as to the importance of promptly passing this bill."[54]

Having demonstrated the "futility" of postponing official action on the territorial bill, Barksdale then addressed himself to the charge that opening the territories of Kansas and Nebraska to white settlement would be a moral and legal violation of "the most solemn treaty stipulations" to the Indians. To his mind, this was undoubtedly a political maneuver by New England congressmen who hoped to embarrass the bill, not to mention a covert attempt to deny southerners their rights in

54. *Ibid.*, 471–72.

the territories, by creating an issue of the sanctity of federal contracts. They insisted that a portion of the territory in question had been set aside as a reserve for the Indians and that the government's agreement that they could "hold it in fee-simple forever" should be maintained at all hazards. For instance, Congressman James Meacham, an ordained Congregational minister from Vermont, felt that armed force should be employed to protect the rights of the hapless Indians if that was the only way the government could keep its commitments to those tribes transferred to the western reservation. "If that will not do," he averred, "keep your word, and plant a Chinese wall around it, and let a flaming sword gleam over every gateway." Barksdale objected strongly to Meacham's line of reasoning because he was personally satisfied that "full and ample provision" had been made to protect the Indians in the Kansas-Nebraska bill, but, in an effort to silence Meacham and his followers, he proposed an amendment stipulating that "nothing in this act contained shall be construed to impair the rights of persons or property now pertaining to the Indians" residing in the territory so long as such rights remained inextinguished by treaty. He then chided Meacham by saying that, if the wording of his amendment was not strong enough, "let the gentleman offer amendments in good faith, not with the intention of embarrassing the bill or defeating its object, and, for one, I will vote to sustain them."[55]

As might be deduced, Barksdale had a dual motive in devoting a portion of his speech to the Indian question. Deeply resenting the defamatory inferences cast upon his section by Meacham and others in their warnings to the House to "preserve inviolate" its contractual agreements with the Indians, he took this occasion to respond in kind to their indirect allegation that the South was incapable of adhering faithfully to its "compacts." In doing so, he offered a subjective descrip-

---

55. *Ibid.*, 472. In taking up this matter, Barksdale may also have been partially influenced by the fact that some southerners regarded the Kansas-Nebraska bill as a violation of the government's agreements with the western Indians. See Joseph H. Parks, *John Bell of Tennessee* (Baton Rouge, 1950), 289–90.

tion of the way in which certain northern states, especially Vermont, had flagrantly violated the fugitive slave acts of 1793 and 1850, both of which were sanctioned by the Constitution. In a deliberate transgression of this "plain provision," he exclaimed, the Vermont legislature had made it a penal offense for its citizens to assist federal officials in enforcing these national laws. He suggested, therefore, that the above statute ought to be repealed before Meacham undertook to lecture others on the subject of plighted faith. "It comes with bad grace from him," he stated caustically, "when the State he represents treats with contempt the authority of Congress, and tramples upon the plainest provisions of the Constitution. Let the gentleman plant a Chinese wall around the Constitution, and gleam a sword over its every 'gateway,' if he wishes to show his fidelity to compacts."[56]

Following this digression, Barksdale returned to the main theme of his speech by attacking the strongest objection lodged against Douglas' measure in the House. As revised, the bill contained a provision that specifically called for the repeal of the slavery restriction clause in the Missouri Compromise, and that had evoked a storm of indignant protests from the northern members. They not only questioned the "propriety" of repealing the clause barring slavery north of 36°30' in the remainder of the Louisiana Purchase, but also argued that to do so would be a gross violation of a "sacred compact" between the North and South. This interpretation was totally repugnant to Barksdale. Aside from innate proslavery bias, he favored the abrogation of the slavery restriction line because it was incompatible with the implied principle of congressional nonintervention in the Compromise of 1850, and consequently he did not regard its repeal as a violation of a solemn compact between the sections. In fact, he denied that such a compact had ever been formed, for in his opinion the "southern Representatives had no right, and did not, in fact, undertake to make such a compact for the South, and the action of no southern State can be found, pledging the people forever to the Missouri

56. *Appendix to the Congressional Globe*, 33rd Cong., 1st Sess., 472.

restriction." He explained, "The South, when overwhelmed by
superior numbers, acquiesced in, but never indorsed that
compromise. It was accepted as a last resort to preserve the
Union, as an offering upon its altar; but its justice or constitu-
tionality has never been acknowledged by the South."[57]
Like many southern representatives, Barksdale believed
that slavery had to be expanded into the western territories in
order for the South's brand of civilization to be perpetuated
within the Union. He took great pains, therefore, to demonstrate how the Missouri restriction had discriminated against
the South. He agreed with his colleague Alexander Stephens of
Georgia that this part of the compromise was probably unconstitutional, because, by prohibiting slavery north of 36°30' in
the Louisiana territory, the equality of the southern states had
been violated. Moreover, he felt that the North had not only
failed to abide by the terms of the compromise, but also had
"repeatedly rejected it when offered by the South." To illustrate the former point, he cited specific examples of northern
noncompliance with the letter as well as the spirit of the
compromise of 1820. He particularly stressed the delaying
tactics employed by northern congressmen to postpone the
admission of Missouri as a slave state on the grounds that its
constitution discriminated against free Negroes and, even
worse, their subsequent attempts to ban slavery in the Mexican cession by endorsing the controversial Wilmot Proviso. To
support the latter point, he recalled that southern representatives, during the heated debate on the proviso, had offered in
good faith to accept an extension of the Missouri Compromise
line to the Pacific, but that their proposition had been decisively voted down by a northern majority in Congress. It
seemed to him that if certain northerners were sincerely interested in sectional harmony that was the time for them to
have accepted the "olive branch" so often held out by the
South. "But instead of doing so," he declared, "it was indig-
nantly rejected, the institutions of the South angrily assailed,

57. Ibid. Actually neither the North nor the South had hesitated to violate
the spirit of the compromise when in its interest to do so. See Glover Moore,
The Missouri Controversy, 1819–1821 (Lexington, Ky., 1953), 134.

particularly by those who were determined to exclude the South from all participation in Territory we might acquire from Mexico, and appropriate it to themselves."[58]

As far as Barksdale was concerned, the North had no right, constitutional or otherwise, to prevent southerners from carrying their slave property into the territories acquired from Mexico. Believing that the territories were held by the North and South in common, he was highly critical of those who sought to deny the South equal participation in that region. In defense of his section, which had sacrificed so much for the war, he said, "The South had contributed largely of her treasure, and her sons had shed their blood on every field of battle in Mexico, to acquire this territory: yet the edict had gone forth, that every foot of it should be wrested from her and appropriated for the purposes of Free-Soilers and Abolitionists at the North."[59] He charged that it had been the antislavery schemes of these radicals, through either ignorance or design, that had intensified the atmosphere of national distrust in 1850, which nearly caused the disruption of the Union, and he reiterated his argument that much of the dissension between the sections during this critical period would have been repressed if the South's offer to partition the western territories along the line of 36°30' had been accepted. Had this course of action been adopted, he predicted, the country would now be enjoying peace and quiet, for the slavery question, "so fraught with danger to the Union," would have been banished from the halls of Congress.[60]

In describing the events surrounding the Compromise of 1850, Barksdale sought to enshroud the South in a cloak of noble deeds and sacrifices, just as he had done in his analysis of the Missouri Compromise. He discussed, in explicit terms, the objections made by southerners to Clay's omnibus bill, emphasizing their reasons for opposing the admission of California as a free state and the abolition of the slave trade in the District of Columbia. In doing so, he was seeking to demon-

58. *Appendix to the Congressional Globe*, 33rd Cong., 1st Sess., 472–73.
59. *Ibid.*, 473.
60. *Ibid.*

strate the inimicalness of that measure to southern interests and to establish the fact that, with the possible exception of the fugitive slave law, the southern states had derived only one practical benefit from the compromise—the principle of congressional nonintervention with slavery. He also tried to make it plain that many southerners had thought that passage of the compromise measures would set a dangerous precedent and would encourage additional encroachments upon the rights of the South. By making it appear that his section had been compelled to acquiesce in the compromise for the sake of the Union, he evidently hoped to shame the timid members of the opposition into abandoning their claim that the amendments to the Kansas-Nebraska bill were unprecedented and, more important, to dispute the allegation of the more aggressive opponents that the policy of nonintervention was intended to apply only to the Mexican cession and that the South had no right to expect its extension. For example, in concluding this review, he said, "Having, then, forced upon the South the compromise of 1850, we ask the North to adhere to it in good faith, to carry out the spirit, meaning, and purpose of the doctrine of non-intervention of these measures."[61]

Although he clearly favored congressional nonintervention, Barksdale was unsatisfied with the "doctrine" in its present form. As a proslavery Democrat, he was naturally inclined to endorse any concept that would guard against the enactment of hostile legislation concerning slavery in the territories, but not at the risk of encouraging the government to abandon its responsibility to enforce laws protecting slavery in federal territory. He believed that it was the sworn duty of the national government to protect the property of citizens residing in the territories, and he disagreed strongly with the new

---

61. *Ibid.*, 473–74. In regard to Barksdale's accusations, it is certainly true that the fugitive slave provision of the Constitution was widely violated in the North. However, an analysis of the vote in Congress on the adoption of the Missouri Compromise and the Compromise of 1850 does not substantiate Barksdale's contention that the North forced these measures upon the South. See Moore, *Missouri Controversy*, 107–11; Holman Hamilton, *Prologue to Conflict: The Crisis and Compromise of 1850* (Lexington, Ky., 1964), 162.

interpretations that had grown up around the principle of nonintervention. In this context, he said:

> But, sir, I deem it proper just here to declare that if non-intervention means, as some here contend, the abandonment of any duty by the Federal Government to avoid the hazard of performing it, I scorn and utterly reject the doctrine. It is only acceptable to me and those I represent as a principle, which is to confine the action of the Federal Government to the great objects for which it was instituted, not fetter its arm, so that it cannot hold its protecting shield over every citizen of the United States, whether found within the territory subject to the jurisdiction of the Federal Government, or upon the high seas, where Federal protection alone could avail him. Then tell me not this doctrine was for Utah and New Mexico alone; and, above all, tell me not it was there or elsewhere to screen the Federal Government from the performance of the duties for which the citizen pays tax to the Government, the security of political, personal, and property rights. With this interpretation of the doctrine of non-intervention, I accept it, and if it was only intended to apply to this particular Territory, this principle was never designed to be a final settlement of the slavery question. This agitation is to go on; the Halls of Congress are to be the scene of continued strife and contention. The press is still to teem with inflammatory appeals to the lowest passion of the people. Mobs are to be lashed into fury by Abolition orators, and the slavery battle is to be fought over again, whenever a square mile of territory is acquired, or Congress called upon to organize territorial government.[62]

Obviously, Barksdale did not think the Kansas-Nebraska bill was entirely defensible, attested by the pains he took to clarify his political thinking on the question of nonintervention by Congress. He likewise entertained serious reservations about the doctrine of popular sovereignty, the concept of allowing territorial inhabitants to determine the status of slavery, because the bill's phraseology did not clearly distinguish between the northern and southern interpretations of this provision. To Barksdale's mind, such ambiguity could easily hurt the territorial interests of the South unless a consensus could be reached on exact definitions of "popular sovereignty" and "squatter sovereignty." Therefore, in his

62. *Appendix to the Congressional Globe*, 33rd Cong., 1st Sess., 474.

speech, he attempted to expose the doctrine as a source of potential trouble by asking:

Does this Territory belong to the States, as described in the Constitution, or is it the property of those, who in the race of emigration, shall be the first to reach it? Let it not be said that I have asked a question which admits of but one answer, for upon the answer to this question depends the solution of this difficulty which now and for years past has convulsed our country from its center to its circumference. If it be the property of the States, and Congress as the trustee of the States holds it in charge, then we are bound to administer it for the benefit of all the people of all the States—those for whom we hold the trust. . . . But if, on the other hand, the doctrine of squatter sovereignty be the true one, that is to say, if the Territories belong to those few or many who may chance first to reach it, then we have nothing to delegate. The power of legislation is theirs by inherent right, and the duty to administer is theirs, not ours. . . . And to one of these extremes or the other I hold sound logic and a regard for truth compels every man to go. My position is the first; and therefore I hold that Congress, in delegating powers to the territorial government, must have due regard to the limits of the Constitution, measuring out in each case in proportion to the capacity of the inhabitants to receive; and in no case surrendering that supervisory control which, as the agents of the States, they are bound to retain until the States themselves shall in one of the forms established, release them.[63]

At the end of the hour allotted for his speech, Barksdale concluded with a conciliatory appeal to the House. In a refreshing appraisal of his remarks, he said:

I have frankly and freely presented my views and have not withheld those objections which I feel to some amendments which have been incorporated in this bill; and to those who, viewing this subject from a different point, find objections to the measure of a different character from those I have presented, I will say, in that kindness and comity which should animate us all, as the sons of a common ancestry and the recipients of a common inheritance, that I seek no triumph over them, and am willing to make as large sacrifices for the peace and common interests of our country as my duty to those who have honored me with their confidence, and intrusted to me, in part, their interest here, will permit. Had each State and each individual, when our

63. *Ibid.*

fathers met to form this Union, insisted upon every opinion
which was entertained, we should not have lived to enjoy the
blessing, or glory in the triumphs which have resulted from the
different policy and the wise concessions of those great and good
men who founded our political temple.[64]

Notwithstanding the grandiloquence of Barksdale's language, the prudence of his closing admonishment furnishes an
interesting glimpse into the political character of the fledgling
congressman from Mississippi. If nothing else, it shows that he
was not a loud-mouthed demagogue bent on the destruction of
constitutional government. On the contrary, he made it quite
clear that he was not insensible to the pressure being exerted
on the Northern representatives by their constituents and
that he did not expect them "to brave more than every southern man must meet who votes for his bill." In light of this
statement, it is an especially grim historical irony that
Barksdale, soliciting support for the Kansas-Nebraska Act
with guarded optimism, was helping to sow the seeds of a
political whirlwind, the repercussions of which he would
grapple with during his entire tenure in Congress.[65]

Although the antislavery forces had launched a furious attack against it, the Kansas-Nebraska bill became law on May
30, 1854. Efforts to defeat the measure, however, served to
revive the bitter quarrel over the expansion of slavery that had
been settled temporarily by the Compromise of 1850. The
immigration that flowed into Kansas and Nebraska after
passage of the bill was accompanied by the violence and
political turmoil usually found in frontier areas. Rival land
claimants did not hesitate to use violence against each other.
Moreover, an aggressive minority of "political emigrants"
from both the North and South went into Kansas to gain
control of the territory for their respective sections under
Douglas' popular sovereignty provision. Riots broke out, and
before long a bloody civil war was raging in Kansas between
the advocates and opponents of slavery. At first, the slaveholding element was able to maintain control because of an

64. *Ibid.*
65. *Ibid.*, 474–75.

influx of southerners from Missouri, but, as the years passed, it became apparent that the increasing number of emigrants from the North would eventually make Kansas a free state.[66] Meanwhile, another form of intense political ferment, no less ominous, had been set in motion by the Kansas-Nebraska Act—the political realignment of the national parties. The tenuous relationship between northern and southern Democrats was severely strained, as shown by the subsequent defection of the antislavery contingent, and the Whigs ceased to exist as a national political organization because their heterogeneous factions could not adjust to the slavery controversy. The demise of the party caused many former members gradually to find their way into the emergent American and Republican parties, both of which were organized on a competitive basis during the turbulent aftermath of the Kansas-Nebraska Act. A diligent search of extant records has failed to disclose any information concerning Barksdale's private reaction to these events as they unfolded, but, on the basis of his public actions, it seems safe to assume that these interrelated developments forced him to reassess the theoretical "merits" of the Kansas-Nebraska Act. He was clearly incensed by the formation of emigrant aid societies in the North to finance the migration of "good antislavery men" to Kansas, and the ensuing attempt of the free staters to "abolitionize" the territory may well have been the catalyst that stimulated his political metamorphosis. In any event, it was about this time that he assumed a hard, inflexible line against the encroachments of the North, a disposition unquestionably accelerated by the devious political schemes of the American and Republican parties.[67]

66. Paul W. Gates, *Fifty Million Acres: Conflicts over Kansas Land Policy, 1854–1890* (Ithaca, 1954), 59–60; David Potter, *The Impending Crisis, 1848–1861* (New York, 1976), 199–205, 206–10, 216–17; Arthur C. Cole, *The Irrepressible Conflict, 1850–1865* (New York, 1934), 82–87; Roy F. Nichols, *The Disruption of American Democracy* (New York, 1948), 24–27.
67. Arthur C. Cole, *The Whig Party in the South* (Washington, D.C., 1913), 309ff; W. Darrell Overdyke, *The Know-Nothing Party in the South* (Baton Rouge, 1950), 278; Rawson, "Party Politics in Mississippi, 1850–1860," 148; Richard A. McLemore (ed.), *A History of Mississippi* (Hattiesburg, 1973), I, 421–25.

Of the two political parties that sprang forth to rival the Democrats after the Kansas imbroglio, the first to experience Barksdale's wrath was the American party, which had enlisted the active support of many former southern Whigs. The initial volley of his double-barreled attack was fired during his successful bid for reelection in the congressional campaign of 1855, in which he won an impressive victory over his American party opponent, Joseph B. Cobb of Lowndes County. By defeating Cobb at the height of his party's influence, Barksdale thus helped to check the spread of Know-Nothingism in his adopted state, and the ensuing disintegration of the American party as a rival organization assured the supremacy of the Democrats in Mississippi for the remainder of the 1850s. In the 1857 and 1859 elections, Barksdale was returned to Congress without opposition.[68]

After returning to the capital for the opening session of the Thirty-fourth Congress, Barksdale renewed his vendetta against the Know-Nothings. In a major address before the House, he sought to undermine the nativists by exposing the "evil intentions" of their organization, the "midnight" origins of which were almost as repugnant to him as their nativist platform. "In excluding foreigners and Roman Catholics," he declared with conviction, "they are violating the spirit and genius of our institutions, and disregarding the most sacred guarantees of the Constitution."[69] Barksdale made it clear that he considered it his duty to oppose the Know-Nothings with all of his resources. Under different circumstances, he might have become known as one of the more liberal southern congressmen of his day, but, as it was, the times required the services of one who was a sectionalist.

Barksdale also has been erroneously accused of being involved in the celebrated Preston Brooks–Charles Sumner assault by Percy Lee Rainwater in *Mississippi: Storm Center of Secession*, which unequivocally states that Barksdale "made

68. Columbus *Democrat*, Sept. 2, 1854; Jan. 20, 1855; Jackson *Mississippian and State Gazette*, Sept. 19, Oct. 24, 1855. See also McLemore (ed.), *A History of Mississippi*, I, 435–36.
69. *Appendix to the Congressional Globe*, 34th Cong., 1st Sess., 1177.

himself conspicuous by accompanying Brooks to the Senate
Chamber and preventing any interference by others while
Sumner was beaten into insensibility." Another writer notes
that "Brooks, not very chivalrously, took along with him two
other congressmen, William Barksdale of Mississippi and
Lawrence M. Keitt of South Carolina." However, according to
an issue of the New York *Times,* printed the day following the
assault, it was Keitt, not Barksdale, who accompanied Brooks
and, with uplifted cane, prevented anyone from coming to
Sumner's aid.[70] This is also the conclusion of a scholarly
investigation by Raymond W. Tyson, who asserts that
Barksdale has simply been the victim of repeated historical
inaccuracies. In the summation of his findings, Tyson states,
"It is not the purpose of this writer to ferret out all the sources
which have erroneously placed William Barksdale as an ac-
complice to Brooks in the latter's attack on Charles Sumner. It
is clear, however, that this distortion of fact has appeared in a
sufficient number of works and over a long enough period of
time to mar the record of a very gallant man. . . . But for the
sake of the record, his legislative activities did not include as-
sisting Preston S. Brooks in the caning of Charles Sumner."[71]
Barksdale did state later that Sumner had received "merited
chastisement."
    Although he did not participate in the highly publicized
attack on Sumner, Barksdale had definitely hurled the
gauntlet down by this time to all those who shared the northern senator's views on slavery. It is true that he fired some of
his heaviest salvos at the American party because he was
sincerely revolted by its nativist philosophy, but that was not
the only reason. He was unmistakably alarmed by the growth
of this organization into a viable political party because, as
such, it posed a distinct threat to the Democratic party, especially after it started to gain momentum in the South. He was

70. *Ibid.,* 530, 1178; David Donald, *Charles Sumner and the Coming of the
Civil War* (New York, 1960), 280–97, 348–49; Rainwater, *Mississippi: Storm
Center of Secession,* 29; Charles W. Thompson, *The Fiery Epoch, 1830–1877*
(Indianapolis, 1931), 77; New York *Times,* May 23, 1856.
71. Tyson, "William Barksdale and the Brooks-Sumner Assault," 137–40.

equally disturbed by the formation of the Republican party because, even though only a sectional organization at this time, it advocated the congressional prohibition of slavery in the territories. Of course, this helped establish a common bond between the Republicans and the antislavery northern wing of the American party, and the affinity that existed between the northern Republicans and the Know-Nothings had not gone unnoticed by Barksdale. Thus, notwithstanding certain ideological differences among them, he regarded these organizations as a singular menace to the political interests of both his party and section, which largely accounts for his decision to wage an indiscriminate campaign against each of them in the Thirty-fourth Congress.[72]

In attacking the American party in the House, Barksdale made no attempt to disguise the fact that he regarded it as a dangerous political threat. He accused its members of "zealously cooperating with the Black Republican party" and bolstered his contention with an impressive array of data and statistics to show how they had joined the plot to deny the slaveholding states their rights under the Constitution. At one point during the tirade, he was interrupted by Thomas R. Whitney, the Know-Nothing representative from New York, who inquired if Barksdale regarded the Constitution as being sound on the slavery question. After replying that he did, he was then asked by Whitney where the word *slavery* could be found in the Constitution. Without hesitation, Barksdale declared that he considered the term "persons held to service" to be synonymous with slavery. Subsequently, during the same discussion, he was asked if he meant by a previous remark that Congress could legislate in reference to slavery in the states where it already existed. Astonished that his meaning had been so badly misconstrued, Barksdale retorted, "The gentleman did not hear my remark, or he would not have asked me that question. I said no such thing. I was speaking of the powers yielded, tacitly, at least, to Congress, under the Know Nothing platform. I deny the powers of Congress to legislate

72. *Appendix to the Congressional Globe*, 34th Cong., 1st Sess., 1177–83.

upon the subject of slavery anywhere, except to protect. That is my position."[73]

After expressing the opinion that the Know-Nothings were unworthy of the public's trust, Barksdale turned his attention to the Republicans. To him they represented the epitome of northern fanaticism, and he was especially vehement in his denunciation. He described their candidate John C. Frémont, a native of Georgia, as a "traitor to the land of his birth" and denounced the convention that nominated him as a "gathering of the enemies of the South, of those who have no other inscription upon their banner than war upon the South and southern institutions." To prove his point, he plunged into a lengthy spiel about the "unhallowed purposes" of the Republican platform and reinforced it with extracts from speeches previously delivered by some of the party's more "distinguished champions," such as Joshua R. Giddings, Benjamin F. Wade, and Henry Wilson. On the basis of the views reflected by these men, Barksdale predicted the following order of business for the Republicans if they were successful in their first bid for national power: "First, Kansas will be hurried into the Union under the Topeka constitution, in violation of law and every principle of right and justice; next, the Wilmot proviso will be adopted, and thus slavery put under the ban of the Government; it will be abolished in the District of Columbia; the slave trade between the States interdicted; slavery excluded from the dockyards and arsenals, and everywhere else where the Government has jurisdiction. These, sir, are the measures of the Black Republican party. They are not all included in the platform, I know; but should it succeed, and the Union survives, they will be fastened upon the country."[74]

Needless to say, the prospect of the national government being controlled by a sectional organization like the Republican party was completely abhorrent to Barksdale. He no doubt had this possibility in mind when he issued the following stern warning to the Republicans:

73. Ibid., 1177, 1179, 1180.
74. Ibid., 1182.

Sir, I make no threats; but I tell the gentlemen on the other side of this House, plainly, as it is my solemn duty to do, as the representative of a hundred thousand freemen upon this floor, that we submit to no further aggression upon us; "there is a point beyond which forbearance ceases to be a virtue," and for the future "we tread no step backwards." We are done, gentlemen, with compromises. All that have been made you forced upon us; and while we have observed them in good faith, you have shamefully disregarded and trampled them under foot. I hold up before you the Constitution as it came from the hands of its immortal authors, Northern and Southern men—itself a compromise; we claim our rights under that, and we intend to have them.[75]

In this, his second major speech in the House, Barksdale allowed his rhetoric to sweep him toward the brink of disunion, which shows how strongly he felt about the outcome of the impending presidential election. His remarks on this important subject lasted about one hour and were concluded with a forthright endorsement of the Democratic ticket headed by James Buchanan: "I, for one, am proud of the leader we have chosen; and I have every confidence that the banner which he bears in this great conflict, upon which is inscribed, in gilded capitals, 'State rights, State sovereignty, State remedies, and civil and religious liberty,' will proudly float in triumph. But if in this I am mistaken, if these eternal principles of representative liberty and human progress are to be repudiated, if that banner is to sink in defeat, with it the hopes of the country will go down forever."[76]

Because he had been in the forefront of the partisan movement to check the advances of the Know-Nothings as well as the Republicans, Barksdale was invited to speak at several important political rallies during the summer of 1856, most of which were enthusiastically accepted. On August 18, for example, he addressed a mass meeting of Democrats in Baltimore on the forthcoming presidential election. In this message he reiterated many of his previous statements regarding the origins and objectives of the Know-Nothing and Republican parties. His description of the cabalistic nature of the Know-

75. *Ibid.*
76. *Ibid.*, 1183.

Nothings was frequently interrupted by cheers and loud applause, as might be expected in a city largely controlled by members of this organization, but it was his castigation of the Republicans that seems to have evoked the warmest response from the audience. After stating his objections to the Republican party, he declared belligerently, "To oppression like this the South will never submit. I come from a State which has ever been true and loyal to this Union, the State of Mississippi. [Cheers and applause.] The bones of her sons are now bleaching upon your battle fields. But for this Union, hallowed as are the reminiscences that cluster around its history, Mississippi will never wear a northern yoke, or submit to degradation or dishonor. But, fellow citizens, there is still another party in this contest, and in my judgment, it is the only party that can save the country from the storm of sectionalism which is now threatening to burst upon it. It is the Democratic party."[77]

By the end of the campaign, Barksdale's reputation as a leading member of the states' rights wing of the Democratic party was firmly established. As a freshman representative, he had laid the foundation of his record for party regularity by supporting the passage of the Kansas-Nebraska bill, and his adherence to Democratic policies continued unabated throughout most of his congressional career, especially after the presidential election of 1856 resulted in a gratifying victory for Buchanan. In fact, his voting record in the House indicates almost the same preoccupation with sectional interests and party considerations as his public speeches. To the party and its principles he was greatly devoted, believing that in them lay the South's salvation. During his last years in Congress, this was a view that he frequently expressed both in and out of the House. In 1858, for example, during a political rally at the courthouse in DeKalb, Mississippi, he declared, "The Democratic party is the only party organized upon a national basis—it is the only one that pretended to make a

77. William Barksdale, "Address to Democratic Mass Meeting in Baltimore, Aug. 18, 1856," Political Pamphlets, Vol. 44, 1–5, Archives Division, Virginia State Library, Richmond.

fight with enemies of the South upon their own ground. The South should unite as one man in sustaining that party. . . . Should our efforts to preserve our rights in this manner prove fruitless, we can take care of ourselves out of the Union, and control the commerce of the world."[78]

Like most partisan Democrats, Barksdale was also proadministration. As a matter of fact, when not busily engaged in defending slavery and southern rights, he was frequently found defending the administrations of the prosouthern presidents who held office before the election of Abraham Lincoln. He was particularly friendly to Franklin Pierce's administration because of his respect for Jefferson Davis, Pierce's secretary of war. Barksdale had been very much in favor of Davis' appointment, and during Davis' tenure the two men often sought each other's advice. He was also partial to the administration of James Buchanan, whose election he had campaigned so energetically for in 1856. Later, when the Buchanan administration was accused of extravagance, Barksdale came to its defense and showed that its expenses had been necessarily incurred as a result of the country's rapid expansion. Referring to a presidential administration, Barksdale stated that he believed it was his duty "to support it when right, but not to yield it a slavish obedience when he believed it to be wrong." After 1858, however, issues such as government expenditures had for the most part been pushed into the background by the fateful events resulting from passage of the Kansas-Nebraska Act.[79]

Apart from his routine legislative duties and his efforts to see that justice was rendered to the prosouthern administrations, Barksdale spent an inordinate amount of time and energy in the Thirty-fourth and Thirty-fifth Congresses on the vexatious Kansas situation. Having supported the Kansas-Nebraska Act

78. Jackson *Mississippi Semi-Weekly*, Sept. 14, 1858.
79. *Ibid., Congressional Globe*, 33rd Cong., 1st Sess., 1697; J. M. Tabor to Jefferson Davis, Dec. 17, 1853, William Barksdale to Jefferson Davis, Dec. 8, 1855, Jefferson Davis Papers, Manuscripts Division, Library of Congress, Washington, D.C.; Jefferson Davis to William Barksdale, July 11, 1856, cited in Rowland, *Jefferson Davis, Constitutionalist*, III, 53–54.

and hoping for the admission of Kansas as a slave state, he was naturally indignant over the adverse turn of events. He believed that the territories were the common property of all the states and, further, that it was the duty of the government to protect the property of territorial inhabitants until the assumption of statehood. It was his contention, however, that southern interests were not being adequately safeguarded in the Kansas territory because of open defiance of law and order by northern immigrants. In a statement to the House on the fighting in Kansas, which he believed the North's emigrant aid societies had provoked, he said:

> Armed with sharpe's rifles, with cannon and ball, and all the implements and munitions of war, the object of those who were sent into the Territory of Kansas by these emigrant aid societies, was to set at defiance the authority of the Federal Government and the Territorial Legislature, and headed by such miscreants and demagogues as [James Henry] Lane and [Charles] Robinson, they have been but too successful in accomplishing it. They not only refused to obey the law, but property was rendered insecure, and human life itself was put in constant peril. The country was ever and anon shocked with accounts of murders and assassinations committed by the abandoned outcasts who were gathered from the dens and purlieus of northern cities, and transported into that Territory by these emigrant aid societies. Arson, robbery, and murder, and every crime known to the black catalogue of crimes, were committed by these outlaws and traitors.[80]

By early 1858 it should have been evident to Barksdale that the South had lost the battle for Kansas. Nevertheless, he was still hopeful that the territory might be admitted to statehood with a proslavery constitution (the Lecompton Constitution), which actually was unacceptable to a majority of its inhabitants. It is possible that he did not realize that southern settlers were so hopelessly outnumbered in Kansas, but this seems highly unlikely in view of the way he kept abreast of current political events. At any rate, he was certainly convinced that the South was the victim of unfair tactics. To the House, he stated his position and that of the South:

80. *Appendix to the Congressional Globe*, 35th Cong., 1st Sess., 337.

Mr. Chairman, it is time the North and South understood each
other. If this is the position of the North, we of the South desire to
know it. If no more slave States are to be admitted into the Union,
our people should be informed of your determination. In the
language of one of the noble statesmen of the South, (Mr.
Toombs), delivered in the Senate a day or two ago, I, too, have
counted the cost of this Union; and I think I understand something of its value. Sir, this Union was made by slaveholders. The
battles of the Revolution were fought by slaveholders. A
slaveholder headed your armies, and led them on to victory.
Slaveholders laid deep and broad the foundations of this great
Republic. The Declaration of Independence was published to the
world in behalf of thirteen colonies—all of them slaveholding.
The Union which they afterwards formed—"the more perfect
Union"—was a Union of equality, of equal rights, and of equal
privileges. If you intend to deprive the southern States of their
rights, it is well for us that you have so frankly and unreservedly
avowed your purpose. In every period of our history, when
dangers impended over us, the South has been true and loyal to
the Union. When, sir, in the hour of danger, has she ever faltered?
The bones of her sons are bleaching upon the very soil from which
her people are excluded, and the achievements of her heroes
adorn the brightest pages of your history. But, sir, that same
patriotic devotion which inspired them to bare their breasts, and
shed their blood for the Union when it was a glorious Union of
equals, will arouse their hearts and nerve their arms to resist its
aggressions upon their rights and honor.[81]

Obviously, the issue of Kansas statehood was reviving
Barksdale's latent southern nationalism. His public declara-
tions were becoming increasingly belligerent, which is not at
all surprising in view of the hostile atmosphere that per-
meated the House during this period. By the start of the
Thirty-fifth Congress, verbal battles had long since taken the
place of calm deliberation in that chamber, and it was not
altogether uncommon for a congressman of one party to den-
igrate a member of the other party in the course of a formal
address. More often than not these insults were direct and to
the point, but sometimes they were indirect and subtle. Once,
when Barksdale was so insulted, he shouted defiantly, "I
would say to the gentleman that, if he intends by that inter-

rogatory to cast any reflection upon me, either directly or indirectly, I hurl it back with all the scorn, derision, and contempt which its insolence and impudence so justly merits."[82] Inevitably, the lively exchange of abuse and vitriolic name-calling between the proslavery and antislavery members of the House culminated in sporadic outbreaks of fisticuffs. One congressman noted that the "scenes in the House were at times intensely exciting. The country seemed to be bordering on a revolution to be inaugurated in the Hall of Representatives."[83]

The anticipated "revolution" came close to erupting in the House after southern Democrats had pressured Buchanan into forcing a congressional decision on the admission of Kansas to statehood with its proslavery constitution. About two o'clock on the morning of February 6, 1858, during an all-night discussion about whether to refer the president's message on Kansas' Lecompton Constitution to the Democratic Committee on Territories or to a select committee of fifteen, Galusha A. Grow of Pennsylvania left the Republican side of the House chamber to visit the Democratic side. In the meantime, John A. Quitman of Mississippi asked the chairman for permission to enter a motion. When Grow objected to Quitman's request, Lawrence M. Keitt of South Carolina angrily told him to go back to his own side of the House if he wanted to object.[84] Of what followed, the New Orleans *Daily Picayune* gives this rather amusing account:

> Mr. Grow replied that it was a free hall, and that he would object from any point in it which he pleased. The parties exchanged angry words—Keitt calling Grow a black Republican puppy, and the latter retorting that he would not allow any nigger driver to crack whips around his ears. This is the substance of the phrases as related by parties who were near. Mr. Keitt caught Grow by the throat, but they were separated by Mr. Reuben Davis, of Mississippi, who had followed Keitt for the purpose of restraining him and keeping the peace. Immediately afterwards, how-

82. *Congressional Globe*, 34th Cong., 1st Sess., 226.
83. Edward Mayes, *Lucius Q. C. Lamar: His Life, Times, and Speeches* (Nashville, 1895), 300.
84. *Ibid.*, 73–75. See also New York *Times*, Feb. 8, 1858.

ever, he broke loose and again seized Mr. Grow, when the latter (as he himself says) struck him a severe blow, which felled him to the floor. Mr. Keitt denies that he fell from the effects of a blow, but asserts that he stumbled. By this time quite a number of gentlemen (among whom were Barksdale of Mississippi, Craig of North Carolina, and others) rushed forward, some probably for the purpose of getting a better sight of "the ring," and others to separate the contestants. This all occurred on the Democratic side of the chamber; but when the Republicans saw so many rushing toward Grow they thought he was to be badly handled, and quick as thought started *en masse* for the scene of conflict. Potter, of Wisconsin, a stout fellow with a fist like an ox, was foremost, and bounded into the fray like a maddened tiger. Just then Barksdale had hold of Grow, with a view of leading him out of the *melee*. Potter, mistaking his purpose, planted a "sock-dolager" between Barksdale's eyes, which only had the effect of arousing his grit. Looking around, the first man he saw was Elihu Washburne, of Illinois. Supposing it was he who struck him, Barksdale sprang gallantly at him, and they exchanged a handsome little match in less than no time. Potter meantime was striking right and left at Barksdale and anybody else. Cadwalader Washburne also came to the rescue of his brother and attacked Barksdale, who defended himself with coolness, vigor, and skill, saving his face from bruise or scratch.[85]

In vain, the Speaker and the sergeant at arms tried to restore order. Their cries fell upon unheeding ears. During the fracas, Cadwalader Washburne, in his effort to aid his brother, had knocked off Barksdale's hairpiece. No one present knew that Barksdale wore a wig. Now, in his haste to cover his exposed baldness, he restored his hairpiece with the wrong side foremost. As the other congressmen's gaze fell upon Barksdale's undignified countenance, laughter began to drown out the fury of the fight. Perhaps nothing did more to restore order in the chamber than this ludicrous incident involving Barksdale's wig. Gentlemen who had never met before got acquainted and, after shaking hands, returned to their respective seats to resume the business at hand. Nevertheless, one congressman, referring afterward to the

85. New Orleans *Daily Picayune*, Feb. 14, 1858.

fight, said, "Tempers remained ugly, and more Congressmen took to wearing arms."[86]

This disgraceful brawl has been called the "first free fight" to occur in the House of Representatives.[87] Accounts of it were carried in every major newspaper in the country, and it was even reported in such important foreign publications as the London *Punch*. Few journals appear to have found the incident as amusing as the *Picayune* did, however. "Nothing," said the Baltimore *Sun*, "more surely indicates the degradation of congressional character than the effect produced upon the public mind by the fight in the House of Representatives."[88] Most newspapers were highly critical of the ungentlemanly actions of the combatants, not a few of whom were deeply offended by the derisive editorials. In fact, one such account almost led to a duel between Barksdale and John F. Potter, the representative from Wisconsin who had planted the "sockdolager" between Barksdale's eyes.

A few days after the clash in the House, a "sarcastic" editorial had appeared in the Baltimore *Sun* ridiculing the Mississippian for his part in the fight. To say the least, this was more than his sensitive southern honor could bear. Believing that Potter was secretly the author of the article. Barksdale promptly challenged him to a duel. The summons was delivered by Barksdale's friend and second, Lawrence Keitt. In the "note," Potter was requested to select a place somewhere outside the District of Columbia for the confrontation because of the severe penalty affixed to dueling in Washington. Potter,

86. Fawn M. Brodie, *Thaddeus Stevens, Scourge of the South* (New York, 1959), 136. See also Nichols, *The Disruption of American Democracy*, 160; Samuel S. Cox, *Three Decades of Federal Legislation, 1855–1885* (Providence, 1885), 75–76; Ben Perley Poore, *Perley's Reminiscences* (Chicago, 1890), I, 534, 535.

87. Brodie, *Thaddeus Stevens, Scourge of the South*, 136. During the Federalist period, a similar brawl was almost precipitated in the House during an altercation between Matthew Lyon and Roger Griswold. See Claude G. Bowers, *Jefferson and Hamilton: The Struggle for Democracy in America* (Boston, 1953), 360–61; De Alva S. Alexander, *History and Procedure of the House of Representatives* (Boston, 1916), 111–12.

88. Baltimore *Sun*, Feb. 8, 1858.

however, would only agree to meet Barksdale in a closed room inside the capital. Since this was contrary to the code duello, Barksdale was compelled to send his seconds, one of whom was Reuben Davis, to seek a satisfactory reconciliation with Potter. The seconds were instructed to ascertain whether Potter had in fact written the "offending article" and if not to try to effect a settlement. Anxious to end the affair, Potter denied having written the article and further agreed to say that he was in no way connected with the Baltimore *Sun*. This satisfied Barksdale, and the challenge was withdrawn.[89]

Although Barksdale was quick to take offense, he was not one to bear a grudge for any length of time, as is shown by his relationship with Congressman Potter following their near duel. Since the House galleries were filled daily with weapons-carrying "roughs," it was necessary for representatives during this period to leave the Capitol at night in pairs. One evening, several weeks after his misunderstanding with Barksdale, Potter requested Congressman Williamson R. W. Cobb of Alabama to pair with him so that he might go home to dinner, but Cobb's duties would not allow him to leave at that moment. Having overheard Potter's request, Barksdale stepped forward and, holding out his hand in a gesture of friendship, offered to go in Cobb's place. His offer was gracefully accepted by Potter, and, from this time forward, an enduring friendship existed between the two men.[90]

Barksdale continued to be suspicious of northern "designs" in the House. As was his established custom, he scrutinized every piece of major legislation proposed by northern congressmen, searching for provisions harmful to southern interests. Thus, when a new high tariff bill came before the House in 1859, he was among the first to attack it as an attempt to protect special economic interest groups in the North. Instead of increasing the existing rates as was being recommended, Barksdale argued that the custom duties ought to be returned

89. William B. Hesseltine, "The Pryor-Potter Duel," *Wisconsin Magazine of History*, XXVII (Sept., 1943), 404. See also Milwaukee *Evening Wisconsin*, April 28, 1891.
    90. *Ibid.*

to the approximate level of those established in the tariff of
1846. Of course, this brought a sharp rejoinder from the
northern sponsors of the bill, to which the Mississippian replied, "I do not intend offering as a substitute the tariff of 1846.
I merely desired to indicate that I preferred it to the bill which
has been reported. Now, sir, I desire to say that the tariff of
1846 was in force for eleven years; during which period of time
every interest of the country was prosperous. During that time
the war with Mexico was prosecuted, and brought to a successful close; the public debt was paid, and the revenue brought
into the Treasury left still a surplus there. With that tariff, the
country was satisfied; and so far as I am concerned, in many
respects, I regard it as a better, a more judicious, and a wiser
law than that of 1837."[91]

Although Barksdale was joined by other southern congressmen in opposing the tariff bill of 1859, they were unable
to prevent its passage in the House because of the numerical
superiority of the northern delegations. However, Barksdale
fought it at every point in its progress through that chamber,
and, even though his obstructionist tactics were ineffective,
they nonetheless reflected his state of mind. For example, in
opposing an amendment that he considered particularly contrary to southern interests, he said, "I move to strike out the
first section of the bill." After being informed by the chairman
that his motion was not in order, he added, "Well, I move to
strike out all after the first section."[92] In dealing with this
particular tariff and its amendments in such a contemptuous
fashion, Barksdale was not the least bit out of character, for
both houses of Congress were now filled with dominant personalities who were no less adamant than he in the staunch
defense of their respective section's interests. Unfortunately,
the only thing that these extremists had in common was that
they were each convinced of their own righteousness and of the
depravity of their political adversaries.

In keeping with the current trend, Barksdale allowed few

91. *Congressional Globe*, 36th Cong., 1st Sess., 2054.
92. *Ibid.*, 2053.

opportunities to pass to demonstrate his southern creed during his last term in Congress. Justifying the peculiar institution, he declared, "Slavery, in some form, has existed in all ages of the world, and it is sanctioned by Divine authority. We believe it to be right. It is interwoven with our whole social organization, with our very existence as a people; and we are determined, at all hazards, to maintain it."[93] "If there is any society on earth," he added, "where there is the most perfect equality among white men, where labor is respected and the laborer honored, it is in the southern States; and the reason is obvious: there is an inferior race to do the menial service."[94] In his opinion, it was futile for Republicans to broadcast their "infamous and incendiary" propaganda in the southern states expecting to turn the nonslaveholders against the slaveholders. "These appeals," he said, "will fall unheeded upon the ears of the non-slaveholders of the South; they are true and loyal, and loyal to her institutions; and if the struggle between the sections should ever come they will be found rallying around the standard of southern rights."[95]

A slaveholder himself, Barksdale was sensitive to remarks about slavery and more than once lost his temper in the House when the subject was being considered. For example, during the first session of the Thirty-sixth Congress, Owen Lovejoy of Illinois declared that "there is no justification for this practice of slaveholding, from the fact that the enslaved race are an inferior race. No justification from the pretended fact that it imparts Christianity and civilization to them; and none in the guarantees of the Constitution."[96] These were the very arguments that Barksdale had used to defend slavery, and when Lovejoy continued to reject them Barksdale's fiery temper

93. *Appendix to the Congressional Globe*, 36th Cong., 1st Sess., 170.
94. *Ibid.* This seemingly contradictory statement refers to the fact that southerners looked down upon white people who worked as servants and valets (work which they associated with slavery) but regarded all other types of manual labor as respectable. See Gustavus W. Dyer, *Democracy in the South before the Civil War* (Nashville, 1905), 48–49.
95. *Appendix to the Congressional Globe*, 36th Cong., 1st Sess., 170.
96. *Ibid.*, 205.

would not permit him to sit still. He shouted at Lovejoy, "The meanest slave in the South is your superior."[97]

Antislavery agitators were a constant irritant to Barksdale and none more so than Owen Lovejoy. Congressman Lovejoy's brother Elijah, an abolitionist, had been killed by incensed southerners from Missouri in 1837, and Owen let no opportunity pass "to vindicate the principles baptized in his blood." On such occasions, Barksdale called Lovejoy everything from a "black-hearted scoundrel" to a "nigger-stealing thief" and finally refused even to parley with the "perjured villain."[98] In reference to one of Barksdale's verbal attacks on Lovejoy, the New York *Times* commented, "If any person had been taken into the House, on that day, blindfolded, and had merely listened to what was going on around him, he would naturally have supposed himself to have been inveigled into some dismal den of ruffianism in the Five Points. . . . What would have been his surprise at seeing Barksdale—so voluble in the dialect of ruffians—a person in the garb of a gentleman."[99]

Perhaps no war is inevitable, but it is obvious that the total inability of the abolitionists to communicate effectively with southerners like Barksdale made it extremely difficult to avoid a sectional bloodbath in the 1850s and 1860s. The abolitionists were interested in a God of social reform, not the patriarchal Old Testament God that Barksdale worshiped. Both sides professed to believe in democracy, but the Greek democracy favored by Barksdale, with its elite class and slave class, seemed nothing less than farcical to men like Lovejoy. It is small wonder that many close observers of the national political scene began to express their fear that the disruption of the Union was at hand.

Indeed, the sectional conflict was now in its late stages of fermentation. Then, in 1859, John Brown, a militant abolitionist, made his famous raid against Harpers Ferry in an unsuccessful effort to incite a slave insurrection in the South.

97. *Ibid.*
98. Edward Magdol, *Owen Lovejoy: Abolitionist in Congress* (New Brunswick, 1967), 232, 235.
99. New York *Times*, Jan. 1, 1861.

Like most southerners, Barksdale laid the blame for this incident on the doorstep of the Republican party. In a speech to the
Thirty-sixth Congress, he said:

> These are recommendations of this infamous publication [Hin-
> ton R. Helper, *The Impending Crisis*], and they have found their
> proper denouement in the invasion of Virginia by John Brown
> and his traitorous gang, and in the murder of her peaceable and
> unoffending citizens. And, sir, it will not do for the gentlemen on
> the other side to declare, with sanctimonious faces, that they
> condemn the conduct of John Brown. His assault upon Virginia
> was the legitimate result of the philosophy of the Republican
> party, and the doctrine they have indorsed. As was remarked by
> the gentleman from Arkansas the other day, you nerved the arm
> that struck the blow; you taught them that slavery was wrong;
> that it was an injury to the master, and a crime against the
> slave.[100]

After Brown's raid, Congress was more armed camp than
legislative assembly. One senator, in a revealing letter to his
wife, wrote, "The members of both sides are mostly armed
with deadly weapons, and it is said that the friends of each are
armed with deadly weapons, and it is said that the friends of
each are armed in the galleries."[101] The two sides referred to by
the senator almost came to blows following an incendiary
speech by Thaddeus Stevens, an antislavery Republican, in
which he implied that the threats of secession by the southern
members were effective only on the "timid" men of the North.
Infuriated by this remark, Barksdale drew his bowie knife and
sprang toward Stevens. Fortunately, Stevens' friends intervened before Barksdale could test the sharpness of his blade.[102]
In the meantime, Barksdale's friends had followed him to the
Republican side of the House, and for a moment a riot seemed
imminent before the clerk could restore order. Although
bloodshed had been avoided, an air of intense hostility remained in the House. One Democrat observed that "a few

100. *Appendix to the Congressional Globe*, 36th Cong., 1st Sess., 170.
101. Brodie, *Thaddeus Stevens, Scourge of the South*, 135.
102. *Ibid.*; Thomas F. Woodley, *Thaddeus Stevens* (Harrisburg, 1934), 259.

more such scenes and we will hear the crack of the revolver and see the gleam of the brandished blade."[103]

Barksdale believed that it was the North's abolition crusade that had reduced the House to such menacing hostility. In stating what he considered to be the "true cause" of the prevailing disorganization in that chamber, he said, "Disguise it, as gentlemen on the other side may attempt to do, it is the agitation of the slavery question which has caused its non-organization, suspended the business of the country, fired the passions of the people, and imperiled the existence of the Union itself."[104] If there was ever any real doubt about his attitude on the "progress" of the slavery question, he surely dispelled it with the following statement:

> When the Government was formed, the several States of the Confederacy were sovereign and independent, and all of them slaveholding, with, perhaps, the single exception of Massachusetts, and that State was largely engaged in the slave trade. Now, sir, for what purpose was this Government established? I have the Constitution before me. It was, "in order to form a more perfect Union, establish justice, insure domestic tranquillity, provide for the common defense, and secure the blessing of liberty to ourselves and our posterity." This is the language of the Constitution. And have these great ends been attained? Has justice been established? Has domestic tranquillity been secured? Let the answer be found in the existence of a sectional organization, based upon its hostility to the institutions of fifteen States of the Union, upon the never-ending agitation of the slavery question, in the legislation of eight northern States nullifying the plain provision of the Constitution in relation to fugitive slaves, and in efforts which a portion of the northern people are now making to incite our slaves to insurrection and rebellion, and to kindle the fires of servile war in the southern States.[105]

As seen by the recalcitrance in the above declaration, Barksdale's transformation from a moderate defender of

103. Woodley, *Thaddeus Stevens*, 259.
104. *Appendix to the Congressional Globe*, 36th Cong., 1st Sess., 168.
105. *Ibid*.

southern rights to an avowed secessionist was almost complete by 1860. That year, when the Republicans made their second bid for national power, he once again believed that the fate of the Union rested upon the outcome of the impending election. Speaking before the House on January 23, 1860, he declared, "Mr. Clerk, events are rapidly hurrying to a crisis, and we are to-day almost in the midst of a revolution; and I deem it my duty to declare here, what I have repeatedly said before, that in the event of the election of a Black Republican to the Presidency, upon a sectional and hostile platform, I am for stern, unbending resistance to his inauguration as President of the southern States."[106] He demanded constitutional protection of slave property in the federal territories as well as an immediate cessation of slavery agitation, and he scoffed at the Republicans' admonition that the slaveholding states would not be permitted to secede from the Union. "How do they propose to prevent it?" he asked defiantly. "Sir, the army that invades the South to subjugate her will never return; their bodies will enrich southern soil. . . . We plant ourselves upon the right of peaceable secession, and there we intend to stand."[107]

Although personally and politically committed to secession in the event of a Republican victory, Barksdale did not completely shut the door on sectional reconciliation. But he made it clear that, as far as he was concerned, the preservation of the Union was contingent upon Democratic control of the federal government. In his closing remarks, he stated:

> I have never desired a dissolution of this Union, but should the Black Republican party obtain the control of the Government, I shall be for disunion. Heretofore its burdens have been chiefly borne by the South, as the statistics which I have before me will clearly prove; and we have patriotically submitted to it because of our veneration for the Union of our fathers. For the future, I would demand that all the compromises and guarantees of the Constitution shall be rigidly enforced, and I would stake the Union upon the issue. And even in the event of dissolution, I shall

106. *Ibid.*, 171.
107. *Ibid.*

have no fears for the South. With a territory larger than all of Europe; with our cotton now swelling up in value to more than two hundred million dollars; with our rice, and sugar, and tobacco; with a people united in feeling and sentiment, she has within her own borders all the elements of a splendid republic. If, then, we are to have no peace; if these aggressions are still to be continued; if this sectional warfare is never to cease, the South, with the strong arms and brave hearts of her gallant sons, will build up her own eternal destiny.[108]

Barksdale's worst fears were realized on November 6, 1860, when Abraham Lincoln was elected the sixteenth president of the United States. True to his word, he immediately cast his lot with the secessionists.

On November 14 Governor John J. Pettus of Mississippi called a special session of the state legislature to convene on the twenty-sixth to consider the state's relations with the federal Union. To aid him in deciding what action to recommend to the legislature, Pettus invited all of the state's representatives in Congress to meet with him in Jackson on November 22. At this meeting, Barksdale urged immediate secession, a course favored by most of those present.[109] When the legislature convened, Pettus requested that it authorize a convention to consider secession. Following the election of delegates, the convention assembled in Jackson on January 7, and, in compliance with Pettus' stated wishes and by a majority vote, an ordinance of secession was passed on January 9. "The Union is dead," said A. G. Brown, in justification of the ordinance, "and in the process of mortification, and nothing now remains to be done but to bury the rotten carcass."[110]

108. *Ibid.* See also Allan Nevins, *The Emergence of Lincoln* (New York, 1950), II, 206, 216; Murat Halstead, *Three Against Lincoln*, ed. William B. Hesseltine (Baton Rouge, 1960), 15.
  109. Robert W. Dubay, *John Jones Pettus, Mississippi Fire-Eater: His Life and Times, 1813–1867* (Jackson, 1975), 68–69; Wirt A. Cate, *Lucius Q. C. Lamar* (Chapel Hill, 1935), 75, 76; Davis, *Recollections of Mississippi and Mississippians*, 392; Ranck. *Albert Gallatin Brown* 284–85.
  110. J. P. Coleman, "The Mississippi Secession Convention of 1861," paper read to the Mississippi Historical Society, Jackson, March 3, 1961, Department of Archives and History, Jackson: Rainwater, *Mississippi: Storm Center of Secession*, 167–71; John K. Bettersworth, *Confederate Mississippi* (Baton Rouge, 1943), 6–7; McLemore (ed.), *A History of Mississippi*, I, 442–46.

In the meantime, Barksdale had returned to Washington and resumed his legislative duties. By this time, however, there was little inclination by the Mississippi House delegation to preserve the Union and certainly none by Barksdale. In December, believing that constitutional rights and liberties no longer existed for the South within the Union, he joined some of his colleagues in the House in signing a manifesto prepared by two radical southern senators for distribution among their constituents before delegates were elected to the secession conventions. In doing so he agreed with the authors of the manifesto that "the argument is exhausted. All hope of relief in the Union . . . is extinguished, and we trust the South will not be deceived by appearances or the pretense of new guarantees. In our judgment the Republicans are resolute in the purpose to grant nothing that will or ought to satisfy the South. We are satisfied the honor, safety, and independence of the Southern people require the organization of a Southern Confederacy."[111]

For the Mississippians, events were now reaching a climax. Three days after passage of their state's secession ordinance, the following communication was laid before the Speaker of the House of Representatives on January 12, 1861: "Sir: Having received official information that the State of Mississippi, through a convention representing the sovereignty of the State, has passed an ordinance withdrawing from the Federal Government all the powers delegated to it at the time of her admission into the Union, it becomes our duty to lay this fact before you, and to announce that we are no longer members of this body. While we regret the necessity which impels our State to the adoption of this course, we desire to say that it meets our unqualified approval; and we shall return to her bosom to share her fortunes, whatever they may be." This terse proclamation was signed by William Barksdale, Reuben Davis, L. Q. C. Lamar, John J. McRae, and Otho R. Singleton and marks the last official act of these five men as representa-

111. John G. Nicolay and John Hay, *Abraham Lincoln: A History* (New York, 1914), II, 436.

tives of the state of Mississippi in the United States Congress.[112] Hereafter they would serve, in either a civil or a military capacity, the Confederate States of America.

Thus did William Barksdale help to set the stage for the Civil War, the great American tragedy in which he himself was to perish. If the causes of the war be thought of in terms of a breakdown in communication and understanding between leaders of the North and South, Barksdale's career assumes added significance. For Barksdale was not an extremist, although his penchant for dueling and fisticuffs might lead one to think otherwise. After all, he had supported the Compromise of 1850 as a permanent adjustment of the sectional controversy. He did not, like Robert Barnwell Rhett and Louis T. Wigfall, "pant" for a sectional conflict. On the contrary, he was a patriotic American who had happily risked his life on the battlefield in order to expand the boundaries of the United States. In the 1850s he vigorously supported the national Democratic party in the hope that this organization could hold the North and South together. Barksdale became a disunionist only after the election of a Republican president in 1860 convinced him that the South could no longer occupy an honored position within the framework of the American Union. Perhaps he should be called a "fire-eater with reservations" rather than a fire-eater.

112. *Congressional Globe*, 36th Cong., 2nd Sess., 345.

Beauregard and Johnston at Shiloh:
Some Historiographical Aspects

Frank Allen Dennis

Shiloh—even the name reeks of mystery and intrigue. The name of the little church near Pittsburg Landing escapes from the mouth in an ominous half-whisper. Nearly five generations of Civil War historians and buffs have listened as grizzled old-timers reminisced about Gettysburg, Murfreesboro, Sharpsburg, and Chattanooga, as well as the rest of the storied conflicts of the American rebellion. But there was always something special about Shiloh. Mere mention of the word brought wistful gleams to beclouded eyes and animation to palsied hands as generations of grandfathers rocked back in their chairs to enthrall speechless youngsters with tales both true and false of what took place in the meadows and forests during those sad April days in 1862. Men who never saw a picture of Albert Sidney Johnston spoke his name in reverential tones usually reserved only for Robert E. Lee. Armchair warriors who could not even spell his name damned Pierre Gustave Toutant Beauregard to that hell reserved for those who strike only when the iron is cold. And so was born a legend, a legend to be discussed and argued whenever historians wrote for publication or even whenever two feeble veterans clinked glasses of cider. Shiloh was the battle of the people;

it was the one battle about which nearly everyone had an
opinion. So ingrained is it in the American soul that one can
scarcely walk along the Sunken Road or gaze down the bluffs
to the Big Bend Stream without almost smelling burnt gun-
powder. The legacy of Shiloh lives; and so does its controversy.
In the mid-1940s, the legendary iconoclast Otto Eisenschiml
called Shiloh "the most dramatic battle ever fought on American soil, if not the most dramatic battle ever fought anywhere," and observed that the struggle had more "ifs" connected with it than any other Civil War battle.¹ James Lee
McDonough, one of Shiloh's most recent chroniclers, agrees,
noting that Shiloh "probably has more hard questions associated with it" than any other engagement of the Civil War.
In the preface to his study *Shiloh—In Hell before Night*,
McDonough deals in some detail with these issues. He also
criticizes previous works on the battle, calling them "sketchy
and impressionistic."² It is likely, however, that any study of
this battle, including McDonough's, merits at least some such
criticism. The emotions of Shiloh run so deep that anyone who
works with the materials inevitably develops prejudices and
biases. But such is the stuff of which history is made. No one
writes truly objective history, and no subject lends itself less to
objectivity than Shiloh and its controversies.

    This essay deals with three of the major questions of Shiloh:
What was the command responsibility vis-à-vis Albert Sidney
Johnston and P. G. T. Beauregard immediately before and
during the battle? Did the death of Johnston materially affect
the outcome of the battle? Did Beauregard make a mistake in
halting the battle when he did on the afternoon of April 6? It
should be made clear at the beginning that this essay is not a
definitive historiographical study of Shiloh or even of these
three questions among the many that might be considered.
Nearly every Civil War historian who has ever put pen to paper

    1. Otto Eisenschiml, *The Story of Shiloh* (Chicago: Civil War Round Table–
University Club of Chicago, 1946), 10.
    2. James Lee McDonough, *Shiloh—In Hell before Night* (Knoxville: Univer-
sity of Tennessee Press, 1977), vi–vii.

has felt an obligation to opine about Shiloh. Neither is it the purpose of this essay to answer any of these three questions—if indeed they could be answered—for that is not of course the nature of historiographical writing. Instead, it is hoped that these samplings from the rich vein of Shiloh ore will illustrate the insoluble puzzle of what really took place between the forks of Snake and Owl creeks.

WHAT WAS THE COMMAND RESPONSIBILITY?

Any study of the historiography of Shiloh must begin with some consideration of Albert Sidney Johnston and P. G. T. Beauregard, the two Confederate principals. One of the reasons for the continuing debate about these two officers and their roles at Shiloh is simply that both were genuinely charismatic leaders. Both polarized cliques around themselves during and after their lifetimes. Yet they each had a different sort of charisma. Johnston's brand was notably akin to the type Robert E. Lee generated. He, like Lee, was thought to be humble, knightly, chivalrous to women, kind to subordinates, and virtually impervious to sin itself. Like Lee, Johnston was a special favorite of Confederate President Jefferson Davis. Thomas L. Connelly, in a penetrating analysis of the mythology that grew up around Lee after the war, drew this parallel and noted that Johnston even surpassed Lee as the epitome of the "might-have-been"[3] syndrome that flourished at various Confederate reunion meetings and convocations after the war. Jefferson Davis, in an 1878 address accepting honorary membership in the Army of Tennessee, called Johnston "the greatest soldier, the ablest man, civil or military, Confederate or Federal" at the time of the battle of Shiloh.[4] Eisenschiml said Johnston was thought to be "one of

---

3. Thomas L. Connelly, *The Marble Man: Robert E. Lee and His Image in American Society* (New York: Alfred A. Knopf, 1977), 23.
4. Dunbar Rowland (ed), *Jefferson Davis, Constitutionalist: His Letters, Papers, and Speeches* (10 vols.; Jackson: Mississippi Department of Archives and History, 1923), VIII, 231–32.

the ablest military leaders of his time,"[5] and Joseph B. Mitchell labeled him "probably the best known and most admired military figure" in the Confederacy at the war's outset.[6] Both Connelly and McDonough maintain, however, that this image of Johnston had no basis in fact when Johnston's prior military career was considered. As McDonough notes, "Johnston's previous life had not given evidence of any particularly outstanding military ability."[7] Connelly flatly states that "Johnston's past record did not merit such acclaim."[8]

It should be apparent to even the casual student of Shiloh that the tragic circumstances of Johnston's death did much to vitiate any criticism of him. The cases of such people as Abraham Lincoln, the Kennedy brothers, and Martin Luther King, Jr., amply demonstrate this tendency by both historians and the general public. In Johnston's case, most writers were exceedingly kind to him for at least the first fifty or sixty years after the battle. In the wave of nationalistic emotion that washed over the South following the Civil War, ex-Confederates and neo-Confederates brooked little if any criticism of Johnston or Lee. Safe it was to criticize nearly all others, but not these two. Tragic death almost always enshrines men such as Johnston in near-impregnable fortresses.

But Beauregard also possessed charisma. As the hero of Fort Sumter and First Manassas, he wore laurels far more impressive than the thorns Johnston had earned at Mill Springs, Fort Henry, and Fort Donelson. "Old Bory" was the South's first great hero, and Beauregard knew it well.[9] Unlike Johnston, Beauregard was never accused of the virtue of modesty. Indeed, he was arrogant; but, as McDonough notes, "it was arrogance in the best Southern tradition."[10] The swarthy

5. Eisenschiml, *Story of Shiloh*, 12.
6. Joseph B. Mitchell, *Decisive Battles of the Civil War* (Greenwich, Conn.: Fawcett Publications, 1964), 48.
7. McDonough, *In Hell before Night*, 31-32.
8. Thomas L. Connelly, *Army of the Heartland: The Army of Tennessee, 1861-1862* (Baton Rouge: Louisiana State University Press, 1967), 60.
9. Douglas Southall Freeman, *Lee's Lieutenants: A Study in Command* (3 vols.; New York: Charles Scribner's Sons, 1942-44), I, 1-4.
10. McDonough, *In Hell before Night*, 63.

Creole even engendered rumors about his sexual prowess;
southern women engulfed him with gifts and letters.
McDonough calls most of these charges "baseless, [but] they
did help to add spice to his legend."[11]

The sequence of events that led these two unlikely allies to
Shiloh is well known and therefore will be described briefly.
Albert Sidney Johnston, for thirty-five years a close friend of
Jefferson Davis, assumed command of the vast western theater
in September, 1861. He established an ill-manned defensive
line stretching from Columbus, Kentucky, on the west through
Bowling Green in the center to Cumberland Gap on the east.
The collapse of his right wing at the battle of Mill Springs on
January 19, 1862, succeeded in outflanking his position at
Bowling Green, so he took up new headquarters at Nashville.
In less than a month, the Confederate works at Fort Henry on
the Tennessee and Fort Donelson on the Cumberland likewise
fell. The Cumberland River was thus open to Federal invasion
at least to Nashville, and the Tennessee was open potentially
as far upstream as Muscle Shoals. With the Federal army thus
poised to gnaw away huge chunks of Middle Tennessee,
Johnston's positions at Nashville and Columbus were thus
also outflanked, and retreat was again in order.

In the meantime, a new face had arrived in the West. Repercussions from the unconsummated Confederate victory at
First Manassas had led to a rift between Davis and Beauregard
so that it became increasingly evident that Beauregard's days
in Virginia command were numbered. Too, the presence there
of native Virginian Joseph E. Johnston gradually undermined
the Creole's position of authority in the Old Dominion. Accordingly, in January, 1862, Beauregard was ordered to report to
the West, where he ostensibly became Albert Sidney
Johnston's second-in-command.

Almost as soon as he arrived in the West, Beauregard began
to act as though he, not Johnston, was the theater commander.
To McDonough, Beauregard was simply filling a power vac-
uum created by Johnston's apparent inability "to grasp the

11. *Ibid.,* 64.

total command picture of his department" and to develop a comprehensive strategy.[12] After the war, Beauregard noted that Johnston reluctantly "acceded to my views and request" for a concentration of the western Confederate forces at Corinth, Mississippi, while Johnston preferred to make a stand in north Alabama along the Tennessee River line.[13] McDonough notes that the correspondence between Johnston and Beauregard during this period "would leave an unknowing reader with the certain impression that it was Beauregard, rather than Johnston, who was in command."[14]

William Preston Johnston pleaded his dead father's case in the postwar era in *Battles and Leaders of the Civil War* and in a hagiographic biography of the general. Calling Beauregard's assertion that he convinced Johnston to concentrate at Corinth "absurd," the younger Johnston maintained that his father, not Beauregard, conceived not only the Corinthian concentration but all the other aspects of the Shiloh scenario as well, including the battle scheme, the decision to fight, and the tactical execution of the plan.[15] The general's son tartly observed, "General Beauregard considers himself as having inspired General Johnston with the idea of attacking Grant at Shiloh. . . . But he must be mistaken."[16]

There is general agreement among historians that, after arriving at Corinth, Albert Sidney Johnston formally offered command of the assembled Confederate forces to Beauregard. Hamilton Basso, the earliest true biographer of Beauregard, described Johnston as "melancholy and defeated" and maintained that the offer to Beauregard resulted from Johnston's deep depression over his own signal failures as commander. To

12. *Ibid.*, 35.
13. [P.] G. T. Beauregard, "The Campaign of Shiloh," *Battles and Leaders of the Civil War*, ed. Robert Underwood Johnson and Clarence Clough Buel (4 vols.; New York: Thomas Yoseloff, Inc., 1956), I, 574 (hereinafter cited as *Battles and Leaders*).
14. McDonough, *In Hell before Night*, 67.
15. William Preston Johnston, "Albert Sidney Johnston at Shiloh," *Battles and Leaders*, I, 549.
16. William Preston Johnston, *The Life of Albert Sidney Johnston, Embracing His Services in the Armies of the United States, the Republic of Texas, and the Confederate States* (New York: D. Appleton and Company, 1878), 551.

Basso, Johnston thought that "he had lost the confidence of the people . . . and the confidence of his men as well."[17] Alfred Roman, ghostwriter of what essentially were Beauregard's own memoirs, gave the same assessment of Johnston's mental and emotional condition, adding that Johnston thought Beauregard held the confidence of both the army and the Confederate public.[18]

Beauregard, terming Johnston's offer "unselfish," rejected it. Nevertheless he agreed, with Johnston's approval, to "draw up a plan for the organization of our forces, and . . . to supervise the task of organization."[19] To McDonough, the command offer and much of Beauregard's subsequent role in the campaign were results of the Creole's stronger personality, with Beauregard simply capitalizing on this to arrogate to himself more authority than perhaps Johnston himself ever fully realized.[20] Connelly joins in this evaluation of Johnston's personality flaw, calling him "passive" and noting that he "meekly" accepted Beauregard's de facto leadership.[21]

Wiley Sword, whose massive *Shiloh: Bloody April* appeared in 1974, basically concurs with this view, although his work as a whole is more sympathetic to Johnston. Sword argues that Johnston desired to go to Memphis or to Holly Springs, Mississippi, where he would administer the department, relinquishing all field command. Sword admits, however, that Beauregard "functioned much as the army's commander" during preparation for the battle.[22] Thomas Jordan, a Beauregard aide, made especially the same point eighteen years after Shiloh. Writing in the *Southern Historical Society*

17. Hamilton Basso, *Beauregard: The Great Creole* (New York and London: Charles Scribner's Sons, 1933), 176.

18. Alfred Roman, *The Military Operations of General Beauregard in the War Between the States, 1861–1865, Including a Brief Personal Sketch and a Narrative of His Services in the War with Mexico, 1846–48* (2 vols.; New York: Harper and Brothers, 1883), I, 263.

19. Beauregard, "Campaign of Shiloh," I, 578.

20. McDonough, *In Hell before Night,* 74.

21. Thomas L. Connelly, "The Johnston Mystique—A Profile," *Civil War Times Illustrated,* V (Feb., 1967), 21.

22. Wiley Sword, *Shiloh: Bloody April* (New York: William Morrow and Company, 1974), 85.

Papers, he observed that Johnston had offered command of
"the united armies" to Beauregard, limiting "his own func-
tions to those of a department commander."[23] Connelly puts
the matter more bluntly asserting that Johnston's "failure to
stand up to" Beauregard made Johnston a "commander in
name only."[24]
William Preston Johnston, however, bitterly disputed this
version of the situation. Maintaining that Beauregard "evidently misinterpreted . . . [the] spirit and intention" of
Johnston's offer to bequeath command of the army, he claimed
that the offer was made simply because Beauregard was more
familiar with the territory and had been at Corinth longer.
Johnston, said the son, never had the "slightest idea . . . of
abdicating the supreme command" to the Creole.[25] Others
supporting this view include Lloyd Lewis, who observed that
Beauregard was merely along for the trip as a "guest-advisor,"
while Johnston retained full authority and command.[26] But
perhaps Johnston's ablest recent apologist is Charles P. Roland, author of a biography of the general and an article on his
role at Shiloh. Roland lends some credence to parts of William
Preston Johnston's account by intimating that Johnston's offer
to Beauregard was not a truly serious one, that it was merely a
magnanimous gesture to "an esteemed colleague." Roland
bases much of this contention on the fact that Johnston later
authoritatively moved forward with the battle plan when
Beauregard began to vacillate.[27]

Roland also asserts that Johnston was fully aware that U. S.
Grant was about to be reinforced by Don Carlos Buell at
Pittsburg Landing and that Johnston planned to attack Grant

23. Thomas Jordan, "Recollections of General Beauregard's Service in West
Tennessee in the Spring of 1862," *Southern Historical Society Papers*, VII
(Aug.–Sept., 1880), 409.
24. Connelly, *Army of the Heartland*, 151.
25. Johnston, "Albert Sidney Johnston at Shiloh," I, 550–52.
26. Lloyd Lewis, "Rivers of Blood," *American Mercury*, XXIII (May, 1931),
65.
27. Charles P. Roland, *Albert Sidney Johnston: Soldier of Three Republics*
(Austin: University of Texas Press, 1964), 311–12; Charles P. Roland, "Albert
Sidney Johnston and the Shiloh Campaign," *Civil War History*, IV (Dec., 1958),
364.

before this juncture could be effected. Thus, Roland refutes Beauregard's contention that the attack was solely his idea.[28] Samuel Meek Howard, in his audaciously entitled *The Illustrated Comprehensive History of the Great Battle of Shiloh*, also noted that Johnston was "fully informed and knew all about the advance of General Buell" to reinforce Grant.[29] But Nathaniel C. Hughes, biographer of corps commander William J. Hardee, observes that "Beauregard urged Johnston to avail himself of the opportunity and strike Grant's weakened force." He further maintains that Johnston reluctantly approved the attack proposal only when it was endorsed by Braxton Bragg, another corps commander.[30]

The actual marching formation and attack disposition of the Confederate forces as they moved from Corinth toward Pittsburg Landing have likewise long been points of controversy among those who thrive upon the intricacies of military tactics. Although it is not within the scope of this essay fully to dissect this aspect of the Shiloh campaign, some observations are in order. Three of the best Shiloh scholars— McDonough, Roland, and T. Harry Williams—all agree that the tactics actually employed were not those agreed upon earlier by Johnston and Beauregard.[31] McDonough attributes the tactical changes made by Beauregard to his "colossal ego that made him fully capable of scrapping a superior's instructions and writing his own."[32] Roland calls the revised attack formation "awkward" and maintains that the scheme originally decided upon was much more practical.[33]

Williams, the most recent and best biographer of Beauregard, believed that Beauregard assumed he had a cer-

28. Roland, *Soldier of Three Republics*, 312.

29. Samuel Meek Howard, *The Illustrated Comprehensive History of the Great Battle of Shiloh* (Kansas City, Mo.: Franklin Hudson Publishing Company, 1921), 57.

30. Nathaniel Cheairs Hughes, Jr., *General William J. Hardee: Old Reliable* (Baton Rouge: Louisiana State University Press, 1965), 100.

31. For a good description of the complex battle plan, see Connelly, *Army of the Heartland*, 152–56.

32. McDonough, *In Hell before Night*, 74.

33. Roland, "Johnston and the Shiloh Campaign," 369.

tain license in the attack structure and did not intentionally flout Johnston's authority. The Creole, implied Williams, knew that Johnston had entrusted him with executing this phase of the army's preparation and was simply achieving the end by whatever means he deemed best. To Williams, "Johnston did not know what Beauregard was doing."[34] Roland also absolves Beauregard of any deliberate usurpation of authority, maintaining that the confusion was due either to a misunderstanding or to a lack of communication.[35]

As the green Confederate army muddled its way from Corinth toward Pittsburg Landing, all the command problems came into sharp focus at a "council of war" held on the afternoon of April 5. Although a few writers, principally Beauregard and his puppet-biographer Roman, maintained that Johnston called the meeting,[36] most believe that the council developed accidentally. The point upon which all agree is that Beauregard, frustrated at what he thought were unconscionable delays in preparing for the attack, was ready to fall back to Corinth and temporarily abandon plans for an offensive thrust. Johnston, heretofore meekly allowing the Creole wide command latitude, boldly intervened to affirm that the attack would proceed on the morning of April 6.

This curious turn of events has provided ample grist for the historians' mill. Wiley Sword asserts that Beauregard was emotionally unstable at this conference, citing the opinion of Johnston's personal physician to this effect.[37] Although not holding totally to Sword's thesis of Beauregard's alleged mental aberration, Roland does accuse him of having a "virulent case of command 'buck fever,' " possibly brought on by his chronic throat condition.[38] McDonough, on the other hand, is kinder to Beauregard, maintaining that the Creole's pessimis-

34. T. Harry Williams, "Beauregard at Shiloh," *Civil War History*, I (March, 1955), 20.

35. Roland, "Johnston and the Shiloh Campaign," 369.

36. Beauregard, "Campaign of Shiloh," I, 583; Roman, *Military Operations of General Beauregard*, I, 277.

37. Sword, *Bloody April*, 108.

38. Roland, *Soldier of Three Republics*, 323; Roland, "Johnston and the Shiloh Campaign," 370.

tic opinion of the Confederate chances for success would have
been correct if the Federal army had had its eyes and ears open.
According to McDonough, the Confederate approach toward
Pittsburg Landing "had been conducted almost as if the
Rebels were trying to attract the enemy's attention."³⁹ A
somewhat piqued William Preston Johnston observed that
Beauregard's change of heart "freed him from responsibility
in case of a repulse, and compelled General Johnston to take
the hazard" of going ahead with the battle.⁴⁰ Sword concurs,
adding that "Beauregard's late-hour dissent placed the burden of fighting . . . solely on Sidney Johnston."⁴¹

On the morning of April 6, 1862, the battle was joined. The
chief historiographical question regarding the first day's conflict concerns the role Beauregard played in the battle before
Johnston's death in midafternoon. Beauregard claimed that
Johnston rode off to the front at the first sound of the battle,
"leaving me in the general direction, as the exigencies of the
battle might arise."⁴² Sword intimates that Johnston directed
Beauregard to remain at the rear because of grave doubts
about the Creole's mental ability to do any more than shuttle
men and supplies to the front.⁴³

Perhaps the truth of Beauregard's role lies somewhere between these two extremes. Shelby Foote, in the first volume of
his massive Civil War trilogy, notes that Beauregard "performed for [Johnston] the service the other Johnston had
performed for him at Manassas," which was to command the
rear forces and direct reinforcements. This freed Johnston "to
move up and down the line of battle," giving the troops his
personal encouragement.⁴⁴ Sharply disagreeing with this assessment, McDonough notes that this action by Johnston was
an essential abrogation of his authority as the army's commander. To McDonough, "Johnston was playing the role of a

39. McDonough, *In Hell before Night*, 81.
40. Johnston, *Life of Albert Sidney Johnston*, 571.
41. Sword, *Bloody April*, 108.
42. Beauregard, "Campaign of Shiloh," I, 586.
43. Sword, *Bloody April*, 108.
44. Shelby Foote, *The Civil War, a Narrative: Fort Sumter to Perryville* (New
York: Random House, 1958), 336.

gallant combat leader [perhaps acting as a peripatetic regimental commander] rather than acting as supreme commander of an army."[45] Eisenschiml made basically the same point when he noted that Johnston "wanted to be at the front" where he could personally inspire the troops.[46]

Williams took still a different view, asserting that Johnston did not intend for Beauregard "to control the principal movements of troops all over the field," because this would have left "nothing for Johnston to do." Williams concluded, therefore, that Johnston intended to command the troops at the front while Beauregard directed those at the rear.[47] Even Thomas Jordan, Beauregard's aide, said as much when he noted that Johnston said "he would go to the front with the troops engaged, leaving . . . Beauregard to take the proper central position from which to direct the movement as the exigencies of the battle might require."[48]

This Johnstonian bravado would cost him his life and raise other questions that compose the Shiloh mystique. But what really was the command responsibility prior to his death? Although Roland maintains that "every major Confederate decision taken between the departure from Corinth and Johnston's death was made by Johnston,"[49] at least two other interpretations may be offered. Basso, who bluntly said that the "actual truth will probably never be known," made some cogent points about the useless bickering among Shiloh enthusiasts after the war.[50] Perhaps Lewis said it best. Indeed, any who have written on Shiloh might well agree with his pithy analysis: "All that is certain is that Johnston was in command of the West, and Beauregard of the Corinth sector, and that between them they started with their legions for Pittsburg Landing at noon of Thursday, April 3."[51]

45. McDonough, In Hell before Night, 99.
46. Eisenschiml, Story of Shiloh, 29.
47. Williams "Beauregard at Shiloh," 25.
48. Thomas Jordan, "Notes of a Confederate Staff-Officer at Shiloh," Battles and Leaders, I, 599.
49. Roland, "Johnston and the Shiloh Campaign," 375.
50. Basso, The Great Creole, 181.
51. Lewis, "Rivers of Blood," 63.

DID THE DEATH OF JOHNSTON MATERIALLY AFFECT THE OUTCOME?

At approximately 2:30 P.M. April 6, General Albert Sidney Johnston suffered an essentially superficial wound in his right leg. Neither he nor anyone accompanying him paid the injury any attention until he was virtually lifeless in the saddle. Barely able to breathe his immortal "Yes, and I fear seriously" to Governor Isham G. Harris' frantic questions about the possibility of his being wounded, the general died peacefully in one of Shiloh's quiet ravines. Almost overnight, the scapegoat of Mill Springs, Fort Henry, and Fort Donelson became the beloved Shiloh "martyr who succumbed attempting to prove his worth to doubters."[52] In the minds of many, he passed simultaneously into Valhalla and Confederate sainthood.

Among the first to espouse the thesis that Johnston's death cost the Confederates victory at Shiloh were his corps commanders in their Shiloh battle reports. Braxton Bragg stated that nothing contributed more to "loss of success" at Shiloh than "the fall of the commanding general."[53] Leonidas Polk said that Johnston's loss was "deeply felt" and that "it was a melancholy fate to be cut off when victory seemed hastening to perch upon his standard."[54] The usually reserved Hardee was the most impassioned of all. According to the Georgia soldier-scholar, "It is . . . the candid belief of intelligent men that, but for this calamity, we would have achieved before sunset a triumph signal not only in the annals of this war, but memorable in future history."[55]

William Preston Johnston, of course, joined in this assessment of the impact of his father's death. To him, the general's death was a "decorous and becoming end" to his career. He also maintained that "many of the wisest and ablest leaders"

52. Connelly, *The Marble Man*, 24.
53. *The War of the Rebellion: A Compilation of the Official Records of the Union and Confederate Armies* (130 vols.; Washington, D.C.: Government Printing Office, 1880–1901), Ser. 1, Vol. X, Pt. 1, p. 469 (hereinafter cited as *Official Records*).
54. *Ibid.*, 405.
55. *Ibid.*, 569.

of the Confederacy looked upon Johnston's death as the watershed of Confederate fortunes, after which they "declined toward . . . final catastrophe."[56] Writing in *Battles and Leaders of the Civil War*, the son proudly quoted Confederate General Randall Gibson as saying, "The West perished with Albert Sidney Johnston, and the Southern country followed."[57] In 1882, by which time some of Beauregard's supporters had begun to downplay the impact of Johnston's death, the general's son made an emotional address to the Army of Tennessee Association meeting in New Orleans. Johnston noted that some had "questioned whether on Sunday evening at Shiloh . . . you [the army] were able to grasp the results of victory." In what surely was a dramatic moment, he intoned, "I appeal to the men who were at the front, and on this issue I challenge all comers to abide by your verdict."[58]

Other of Johnston's wartime friends and associates also bore the martyr's banner. General Richard Taylor argued that if Johnston had lived only one more hour he "would have completed Grant's destruction." The former president's son even asserted that, had Johnston lived, "there would have been no Vicksburg, no Missionary Ridge, no Atlanta," for the Confederacy would have been victorious long before. If it were possible, said Taylor, "for one heart, one mind, and one arm to save her [the Confederacy] . . . she lost them when Albert Sidney Johnston fell on the field of Shiloh."[59] General Basil Duke believed that Johnston was on the verge of "complete triumph" and that his survival at Shiloh might have made eventual Confederate success certain.[60]

None of Johnston's contemporaries was more fulsome in his defense than his lifelong friend Jefferson Davis. To Davis,

56. Johnston, *Life of Albert Sidney Johnston*, viii.
57. Johnston, "Albert Sidney Johnston at Shiloh," *Battles and Leaders*, I, 568.
58. William Preston Johnston, "The Army of Tennessee," *Southern Historical Society Papers*, XI (Jan., 1883), 41.
59. Richard Taylor, "Advance Sheets of 'Reminiscences of Secession, War, and Reconstruction,' " *Southern Historical Society Papers*, V (March, 1878), 139–40.
60. Basil W. Duke, "The Confederate Career of General Albert Sidney Johnston," *Southern Historical Society Papers*, V (Sept., 1878), 140–41.

Johnston's death constituted the "fall of the great pillar of the Southern Confederacy." He maintained that, had Johnston lived, "General Grant and his army would before the setting of the sun have been fugitives or prisoners." In a final tribute, Davis said that "the fortune of a country hung by a single thread of the life that was yielded on the field of Shiloh."[61] The first quarter of the twentieth century saw others, chiefly Confederate veterans and amateur historians, rise to extol Johnston. D. W. Reed noted that Johnston's death "caused a relaxation of effort" in the Confederate assault, which likely resulted in defeat.[62] J. B. Ulmer maintained that Grant "would have been relegated to the shades" had not Johnston perished when he did.[63] *Confederate Veteran* published several articles and reminiscenses defending the view that Johnston's martyrdom came at the instant of victory. For example, Mrs. A. M. Herald observed that Johnston's death "changed the result at Shiloh and prevented the capture of Grant's army."[64] Jasper Kelsey said that Johnston was killed just when the "victory seemed complete."[65]

Only a few recent historians, however, have embraced the view that Johnston's death cost the Confederates ultimate victory. Charles P. Roland, his biographer and clearly an admirer, praises his ability to motivate troops and asserts that Johnston, had he lived, "would have been an incalculable asset to the Confederacy in the trying years to come." Admitting that the supposition of victory had Johnston lived is speculation, Roland nevertheless observes that "a great captain can in moments of supreme crisis lift his troops to superhuman

61. Jefferson Davis, *The Rise and Fall of the Confederate Government* (2 vols.; New York: D. Appleton and Company, 1881), II, 67–69.
62. D. W. Reed, *The Battle of Shiloh* (Washington, D.C.: Government Printing Office, 1909), 18.
63. J. B. Ulmer, "A Glimpse of Albert Sidney Johnston Through the Smoke of Shiloh," *Texas Historical Association Quarterly*, X (April, 1907), 287.
64. Mrs. A. M. Herald, "Shiloh—The First Great Battle," *Confederate Veteran*, XXVI (Sept., 1928), 335.
65. Jasper Kelsey, "The Battle of Shiloh," *Confederate Veteran*, XXV (Feb., 1917), 73.

effort." Yet he finally concedes, "Johnston's death did not alter the outcome of the battle."[66] Johnston's most recent ardent defender is Wiley Sword, whose *Shiloh: Bloody April* is certainly the longest study of the battle. Maintaining that Johnston "evidenced the very qualities that Grant later applied to achieve final victory . . . strong determination and a driving will to win," Sword also claims that a "great void" was left by Johnston's death, which was never filled by any of the Army of Tennessee's subsequent commanders. Sword builds his strongest case for the decisive impact of Johnston's death when he says, "Like Johnston's lifeblood, the Southern Confederacy's hopes also began to ebb rapidly following the momentous events of Shiloh."[67] Led by T. Harry Williams and Thomas L. Connelly, most recent historians of Shiloh have concluded that Johnston's death had little if any impact on the outcome. Long removed in time from the maudlin romanticism of the late nineteenth and early twentieth centuries, this generation of scholars has come reasonably close to removing Sidney Johnston from his pedestal of martyrdom.

In both a biography of Beauregard and an article on the Creole's role at Shiloh, Williams boldly affirmed that at the time of Johnston's death the Confederates were nowhere near victory at any point along the front. All Johnston was doing, said Williams, was "going from unit to unit . . . performing more like a corps or division general than a commander." To Williams, Johnston "was not exerting much control over the battle" at all.[68] In an intriguing article on the Johnston mystique, which presaged a similar book-length study on the Robert E. Lee syndrome, Connelly heartily endorses Williams' interpretation, crediting him with being "the first modern

---

66. Roland, *Soldier of Three Republics*, 340, 350–51; Roland, "Johnston and the Shiloh Campaign," 378.
67. Sword, *Bloody April*, 274, 443, 446.
68. Williams, "Beauregard at Shiloh," 27; T. Harry Williams, *P. G. T. Beauregard: Napoleon in Gray* (Baton Rouge: Louisiana State University Press, 1955), 139.

historian flatly to advance the theory, bolstered by impressive evidence, that Johnston's death had little to do with the outcome of the battle."[69]

Yet a few writers, surely lesser known than Williams, had earlier taken steps toward this interpretation. In 1946, Otto Eisenschiml bluntly stated, "It was difficult to agree with . . . [the] view" that Johnston's death resulted in defeat for the Confederates.[70] Many years earlier, Y. R. Le Monnier, one of Beauregard's fellow Louisianians, sniped at William Preston Johnston for his deification of his father. Le Monnier noted that the younger Johnston "wanted his father, though dead, to have won the battle of Shiloh; he brooded over it, and with a foregone conclusion, wrote his book and declared . . . that had General Beauregard not ordered the retreat, the victory won by his father would not have been lost." Le Monnier went on to suggest that some of the more significant Confederate successes during the first day's fighting occurred hours after Johnston's death.[71]

Others who wrote both before and after Williams expressed similar views. Nathaniel C. Hughes, Hardee's biographer, hedges somewhat by calling the effect of Johnston's death "disputable."[72] In 1909, Matthew Forney Steele maintained that Johnston "exerted very little influence upon the character of . . . this great battle."[73] John Barron Deaderick flatly stated in 1942 that Johnston died "too early in the war for a fair conclusion to be formed as to his real ability."[74] Peter J. Parish, a Scottish historian, wrote in 1975 that Johnston's loss, though considered a blow at the time, "may be more soberly assessed" from hindsight. Parish argues that Johnston was an officer "of

69. Connelly, "The Johnston Mystique," 17.

70. Eisenschiml, *Story of Shiloh*, 39.

71. Y. R. Le Monnier, "General Beauregard at Shiloh, Sunday, April 6, '62," *Neale's*, III (Feb., 1914), 153.

72. Hughes, *Reliable*, 107.

73. Matthew Forney Steele, *American Campaigns* (Washington, D.C.: B. S. Adams, 1909), 187.

74. John Barron Deaderick, *The Truth about Shiloh* (Memphis: Press of S. C. Toof, 1942), 54.

the old school who would almost certainly have been outdated by the rapid changes of the Civil War."[75] James McDonough maintains that there is no evidence to support the contention that things would have gone better for the Confederates had Johnston lived.[76] Even Charles Roland, Johnston's biographer, concurs.[77]

It is Thomas Connelly, however, who comes nearest to delivering the coup de grace to the if-Johnston-had-not-been-killed theory. Maintaining that the Confederates were beaten at Shiloh "almost from the outset" because of poor command structure, he asserts that Johnston's reputation as a commander "might have been completely destroyed" had he lived through Shiloh. To Connelly, the result would have been the same—Confederate defeat—and Johnston could not have maintained his command position with another reversal on his record. He plainly implies that, for the sake of his reputation, Sidney Johnston could not have chosen a more appropriate time or way to die.[78]

DID BEAUREGARD ERR IN CALLING OFF THE BATTLE WHEN HE DID?

No other single decision in the American Civil War has been more widely discussed than P. G. T. Beauregard's order halting the Confederate effort in the late afternoon of April 6, 1862. Scarcely had the guns of Shiloh fallen silent, said Hamilton Basso, when "whispering began, and the whispers became murmurs, and finally there was shouting" against Beauregard for this decision.[79] In her famous diary, Mary Boykin Chesnut lashed out at Beauregard, saying that he "was too slow to

---

75. Peter J. Parish, *The American Civil War* (New York: Holmes and Meier, Publishers, 1975), 171.
76. McDonough, *In Hell before Night*, 153–54.
77. Roland, *Soldier of Three Republics*, 341.
78. Connelly, *Army of the Heartland*, 158; Connelly, *The Marble Man*, 24.
79. Basso, *The Great Creole*, 188.

move, and lost us all the advantage gained by our dead hero."[80]
Criticism came early also from some of Beauregard's subordinates. Corps commander Leonidas Polk asserted in his battle report that when Beauregard called off the assault "the field was clear; the rest of the forces of the enemy were driven to the river. . . . We had one hour or more of daylight still left. . . . nothing seemed wanting to complete the most brilliant victory of the war but . . . to make a vigorous assault on . . . [the federal] forces."[81] William J. Hardee, less definite than Polk, merely observed that the battle was terminated "near sunset," at which time "the enemy were huddled in confusion: near Pittsburg Landing."[82] Patrick Cleburne, the storied Irishman who commanded a division in Hardee's corps, was reported to have said that Shiloh "was a battle gallantly won and as stupidly lost," referring to Beauregard's decision. Cleburne's biographers agree, adding that "Beauregard should have ordered the attack. No one knows what the outcome would have been."[83] Braxton Bragg's chief engineer, S. H. Lockett, plainly stated, *"The victory was lost"* because of the Creole's order.[84]

William Preston Johnston, needless to say, was in the vanguard of those hanging the guilt of Shiloh on Beauregard. Johnston, arguing that his father had intended to "push the contest to a final decision" in one day, faulted Beauregard for his "policy of withdrawal and delay which led to defeat instead of victory."[85]

Perhaps Beauregard's severest contemporary critic was Florida Augusta Evans Inge. Mrs. Inge, a young woman living in Corinth at the time of Shiloh, was hostess to Albert Sidney Johnston at her home prior to the battle and helped prepare his body for burial when it was brought back to Corinth.

80. Mary Boykin Chesnut, *A Diary from Dixie*, ed. Ben Ames Williams (Boston: Houghton Mifflin Company, 1961), 211.
81. *Official Records*, Ser. 1, Vol. X, Pt. 1, p. 410.
82. *Ibid.*, 569–70.
83. Howell and Elizabeth Purdue, *Pat Cleburne, Confederate General* (Hillsboro, Texas: Hill Junior College Press, 1973), 119–20.
84. S. H. Lockett, "Surprise and Withdrawal at Shiloh," *Battles and Leaders*, I, 605.
85. Johnston, "Albert Sidney Johnston at Shiloh," I, 554.

Interviewed in her old age by Eisenschiml, she bitterly denounced Beauregard's "vanity and selfish ambition which
cost us the battle." Clearly pro-Johnston because of his
kindnesses to her as her guest, Mrs. Inge said that Beauregard
had "to hide his face in shame to the end of time, for he
betrayed the hopes of his country."[86]
     In the second decade of the twentieth century, the pages of
Confederate Veteran became a veritable battleground hosting
Beauregard's foes against Y. R. Le Monnier. L. R. Burress and
W. B. Ellis were among those denouncing Beauregard's action,
with Ellis acidly observing that Beauregard lost the battle
"when he issued his fatal order" to make camp for the night.[87]
J. B. Ulmer, another early twentieth-century critic of the
Creole, also used the word *fatal* to describe Beauregard's
cessation directive.[88] John Barron Deaderick, in his 1942
study, agreed that the criticism of Beauregard seemed justified.[89]
     In the 1930s and 1940s, historians who criticized
Beauregard's decision included Otto Eisenschiml, Robert
Selph Henry, and—strangely enough—Hamilton Basso.
Eisenschiml, who saw little to praise in either Johnston or
Beauregard, said that the Creole should "have made the supreme effort to break through [the federal lines] even with the
odds against him. . . . There was too much at stake to do
otherwise."[90] In his *The Story of the Confederacy*, Henry concurred with Bragg and others that the Louisianian's decision
lost the battle.[91] Basso maintained that, if Beauregard had
continued the attack, "Grant would have either been driven
into the river, annihilated, or forced to surrender." Admitting
that Beauregard could be defended, Basso nevertheless be-

86. Quoted in Eisenschiml, *Story of Shiloh*, 61–62.
87. W. B. Ellis, "Who Lost Shiloh to the Confederacy?" *Confederate Veteran*,
XXII (July, 1914), 314. See also L. R. Burress, "Who Lost Shiloh to the
Confederacy?" *Confederate Veteran*, XXI (Sept., 1913), 443.
88. Ulmer, "A Glimpse of Albert Sidney Johnston," 296.
89. Deaderick, *Truth about Shiloh*, 29.
90. Eisenschiml, *Story of Shiloh*, 46–47.
91. Robert Selph Henry, *The Story of the Confederacy* (New York: Bobbs-
Merrill Company, 1964), 121–22.

lieved that the Creole "in his own mind . . . thought he had made a mistake."[92]

Some of the most competent recent scholars also condemn Beauregard. Frank E. Vandiver calls the Creole's decision "the most fateful order of his life" and claims that "one final charge might have won the battle."[93] Grady McWhiney, perhaps the best modern authority on Braxton Bragg, faults Beauregard's entire role at Shiloh. According to McWhiney, Beauregard totally "misunderstood the situation at the front," accounting for his fateful decision, and he agrees generally with Bragg's postwar assessment of Beauregard's Shiloh shortcomings.[94] Wiley Sword blames Beauregard for his failure "to obtain accurate information on front-line conditions following Johnston's death," claiming that this was one of the "factors contributing to the Confederate defeat on Monday."[95] Beauregard's severest recent critic, as might be expected, is Charles P. Roland, who calls the withdrawal order "a grave mistake." Beauregard, says Roland, should have either mounted a full-scale attack or fallen back to Corinth, for to "await attack the next day by Grant's strengthened army was to invite disaster."[96]

Among the first writers to defend Beauregard's decision was the general himself. In his Shiloh battle report, he maintained that it was after six o'clock "when the enemy's last position was carried" and that nightfall was consequently "close at hand." Calling his troops "exhausted" and "jaded," Beauregard claimed that fire from the Federal gunboats on the Tennessee River effectively mitigated against any additional offensive thrust.[97] Years later, in *Battles and Leaders of the Civil War*, Beauregard maintained that none of his corps or division commanders questioned the decision at the time and that "no

92. Basso, *The Great Creole*, 183.
93. Frank E. Vandiver, *Their Tattered Flags: The Epic of the Confederacy* (New York: Harper's Magazine Press, 1970), 124–25.
94. Grady McWhiney, "Braxton Bragg at Shiloh," *Tennessee Historical Quarterly*, XXI (March, 1962), 28.
95. Sword, *Bloody April*, 107.
96. Roland, *Soldier of Three Republics*, 339.
97. *Officials Records*, Ser. 1, Vol. X, Pt. 1, p. 387.

one was heard to express or suggest that more might have been
achieved had the battle been prolonged."[98] Employing
Beauregard's "jaded" as an apt description of the psychological condition of the Confederate forces, Thomas Jordan maintained that the additional exertion of an offensive by the
Rebels would have succeeded only in tiring them to the point
where little or no resistance could have been offered the next
day. Jordan implied that Beauregard may thus have saved the
remnant of the army from total disaster.[99] Alfred Roman, the
Creole's mouthpiece, corroborated this version of the
events.[100]

In the early twentieth century, a few more writers, most
notably Y. R. Le Monnier, came to Beauregard's defense.
Bitterly critical of the accounts of William Preston Johnston,
Le Monnier called "puerile" the accusation that Beauregard
had lost the battle or that he had called off his legions while
any substantial daylight remained. Le Monnier quoted one
veteran of the Army of Tennessee as saying that it was so dark
when the order to cease the attack was received that "we could
trace the passage in the air of the enemy's gunboat shells by the
burning of its [sic] fuse."[101] Joseph W. Rich, an Iowa Federal
veteran, called "absurd" any claim that Beauregard's withdrawal order prevented a Confederate victory.[102] In 1923,
Anne Bachman Hyde wrote in *Confederate Veteran* that the
long hours of fighting, plus Beauregard's lack of knowledge of
actual conditions at the front, caused him to fear "to further
expose his troops."[103] Matthew Forney Steele affirmed that "it
is not at all likely" that Beauregard could have won the battle

98. Beauregard, "Campaign of Shiloh," I, 591.
99. Jordan, "Recollections of General Beauregard's Service," 417.
100. Roman, *Military Operations of General Beauregard*, I, 304, 306–307, 345, 351.
101. Y. R. Le Monnier, "Who Lost Shiloh to the Confederacy?" *Confederate Veteran*, XXII (Sept., 1914), 415; Le Monnier, "Beauregard at Shiloh," 147; Y. R. Le Monnier, "Who Lost Shiloh to the Confederacy?" *Confederate Veteran*, XXI (Nov., 1913), 533.
102. Joseph W. Rich, *The Battle of Shiloh* (Iowa City: State Historical Society of Iowa, 1911), 77.
103. Anne Bachman Hyde, "The Battle of Shiloh," *Confederate Veteran*, XXXI (April, 1923), 132.

with a last desperate assault, and he even asserted that
Beauregard's real failure at Shiloh was staying around to
renew the battle on April 7, which day's action Steele called "a
useless sacrifice of life."[104]

More modern defenders of Beauregard basically echo these
earlier views. Shelby Foote says that Beauregard's order to
halt the battle merely made "official" what darkness had
already done.[105] Lloyd Lewis, analyzing Bragg's assessment of
the situation, claimed that "in view of losses and demoraliza-
tion" the decision of Beauregard was correct.[106]

T. Harry Williams, the Creole's best biographer, claimed
that Beauregard's decision "seems as right" to modern historians "as it did to him [Beauregard] in the evening of that
hard-fought Sunday." Williams accused Bragg of developing
an accusatory posture toward Beauregard after Shiloh; this, to
Williams, vitiates much of Bragg's criticism of the Louisianian. [107] James McDonough, whose reasoned tome may be the
best of the studies exclusively of Shiloh, maintains that the
Confederates were "fought out" at the time of Beauregard's
order, and he asserts that Bragg's postwar criticism was collu-
sion with William Preston Johnston to enhance the reputation
of his dead father.[108] Thomas Connelly concurs with Williams
about Bragg's postwar account, defending both Beauregard's
withdrawal order and his knowledge of what was occurring on
all parts of the battlefield. As Steele had done fifty-eight years
earlier, Connelly claims that Beauregard's "real mistake . . .
was not in merely halting the action but in not retreating to
Corinth."[109]

COMMENTS AND OBSERVATIONS

Any historiographical study of Shiloh's controversies is
necessarily highly selective and incomplete, for drops of

104. Steele, *American Campaigns,* 189.
105. Foote, *Fort Sumter to Perryville,* 341.
106. Lewis, "Rivers of Blood," 71.
107. Williams, "Beauregard at Shiloh," 29; Williams, *Napoleon in Gray,*
141–42.
108. McDonough, *In Hell before Night, 169.*
109. Connelly, *Army of the Heartland,* 167–69.

Shiloh opinion can be milked from almost every study of the
Civil War in the West. From the foregoing, however, it is
apparent that a majority of modern Shiloh scholars believes
that neither Johnston's death nor any action of Beauregard
significantly altered the outcome either of the battle of Shiloh
or of the Civil War in the West.

At the risk of delving into the taboo areas of metahistory and
psychohistory, a few other questions might be offered about
Shiloh that have not been fully explored. The command situation between Johnston and Beauregard was so confused and
uncertain that "anomalous" is an understated description of
it. Indeed, considering all that has been written about the
battle, including Beauregard's account and that of William
Preston Johnston, it is safe to say that neither officer ever fully
understood their relationship. If the two commanders themselves never grasped the intricacies of their command problem, it is little wonder that historians have disagreed so
sharply concerning it. Albert Sidney Johnston probably
viewed P. G. T. Beauregard as something of a usurper;
Beauregard probably saw Johnston as a vacillating officer on a
downward slide who was badly in need of his Napoleonic
genius.

As the time for attack drew nigh, Johnston's personality
changed dramatically. With uncharacteristic bravado,
Johnston intoned such phrases as "I would fight them tonight
if they were a million" and "Tonight we will water our horses
in the Tennessee River." Perhaps Johnston tried to redeem his
reputation by going to the front of the battle with something of
a death wish; if so, it would not be the only time during the
Civil War when a Confederate full general would contemplate
such action.[110]

Beauregard's actions were equally curious. Did the Creole
sense defeat on April 5 and urge withdrawal because he knew
the loss would be blamed on him since he had composed the
battle plan? Did he pout and sulk on the first day at Shiloh
because his counsel had not been taken? Did he, in fact,

110. Douglas Southall Freeman, *R. E. Lee: A Biography* (4 vols.; New York
and London: Charles Scribner's Sons, 1934–35), IV, 121.

consider it best for his military reputation that the army lose the battle, since he believed that the defeat would be blamed on Johnston, who had ordered the attack against Beauregard's advice? Was he thus chagrined and surprised in later years when the blame was laid at his feet? Instead of being proved correct by the Confederate defeat, Beauregard found himself wearing the albatross of both the tragedy at Shiloh and the loss of substantial portions of middle and west Tennessee, north Mississippi, and north Alabama.

Perhaps the fact needs to be faced that all military commanders have not necessarily had the good of their armies or of their nations at heart at all times. Pattons, MacArthurs—and perhaps Johnstons and Beauregards—may have often been too deeply concerned about personal reputations and glory.

Modern civilization has scarcely touched the fields and forests near Pittsburg Landing. Shiloh is certainly one of the best-kept battlefield parks in the nation. On a mild day in early April, the site looks much today as it did nearly twelve decades ago. One can almost hear the cursing of the surprised federal troops, see the crimson in Bloody Pond, and smell the smoke of battle. And the old-timers still say that the wind in the oak and hickory forests can sometimes be heard to whisper softly, "If Sidney Johnston had only lived. . . ."

Such is the continuing mystique of Shiloh.

Western Rebels, Eastern War: Mississippi Troops in the Army of Northern Virginia, 1861–1865

Fabian Val Husley

At the time of the critical Gettysburg campaign, June–July, 1863, eleven Mississippi infantry regiments formed into three brigades were active within the Army of Northern Virginia. Although this number is not high compared with the forty Virginia regiments serving with that army, it is sizable for a state called upon to service the multiple fronts of 1863. As the record indicates, Mississippi was represented by the brigades of Brigadier Generals William Barksdale, Carnot Posey, and Joseph Davis in the three-day combat at Gettysburg. The statistics of the losses of the Confederate army reflect the Mississippians' gallantry in every phase of the three-day encounter. Among the ten Confederate regiments sustaining the heaviest losses in the battle, four were the 2nd, 11th, 17th, and 42nd Mississippi. Three of these four were from one Mississippi brigade alone, Davis' of Henry Heth's division.[1]

1. William F. Fox, *Regimental Losses in the American Civil War, 1861–1865: A Treatise on the Extent and Nature of the Mortuary Losses in the Union Regiments, with Full and Exhaustive Statistics Compiled from the Official Records on File in the State Military Bureau and at Washington* (Albany, 1889), 569; William A. Love, "Mississippi at Gettysburg," *Publications of the Mississippi Historical*

From their initial organization in scattered Mississippi counties to their arrival upon the field at Gettysburg, these regiments had not had a tranquil existence. They had, in most cases, served together or with units from other southern states and had already received accolades for their service in virtually every major combat in which the Army of Northern Virginia had participated since the battle of First Manassas. A survey of the regiments composing the three Mississippi brigades during the various stages of the Civil War will illustrate the tribulations not only of the field soldiers of these commands but also of field level command, as well as the effects of political management by authorities in both Jackson and Richmond.

Attesting the martial ardor in the state of Mississippi immediately following Abraham Lincoln's election, the adjutant general's office in Jackson estimated that militia companies began organizing at the rate of seven to eight per week. By January 16, 1861, fifty-five rifle companies had been formed. The office also noted that the "impossibility of procuring the Mississippi rifle with saber bayonet has produced much dissatisfaction among the companies, and . . . has caused the disbandment of some, and prevented the organization of others." From this number and a greater number organized after the report came those regiments that were early forwarded to Virginia.[2]

Society, IX (1906), 25–51; Dunbar Rowland, *The Official and Statistical Register of the State of Mississippi* (Nashville, 1908), 426–523, all contain brief sketches of all Mississippi infantry, cavalry and artillery units that served in the Army of Northern Virginia. See also Charles E. Hooker, "Mississippi," *Confederate Military History*, ed. Clement A. Evans (12 vols.; Atlanta, 1900), VII, 184–85, 235–78. See Ezra J. Warner, *Generals in Gray: Lives of the Confederate Commanders* (Baton Rouge, 1959), 16–17, 68–69, 244–45 for brief biographical sketches of William Barksdale, Carnot Posey, and Joseph Davis.

2. *The War of the Rebellion: A Compilation of the Official Records of Union and Confederate Armies* (Washington, D.C., 1880–1901), Ser. 4, Vol. I, pp. 61–62, hereinafter cited as *Official Records*; Thomas L. Livermore, *Numbers and Losses in the Civil War in America, 1861–65* (Bloomington, 1957), 25; Hooker, "Mississippi," 10–11; Fox, *Regimental Losses*, 70, 295. Original muster rolls and/or records for the 2nd, 11th, 12th, 13th, 16th, 17th, 18th, 19th, 21st, 26th, 42nd, and 48th Mississippi infantry are in the Mississippi State Department of Archives and History, Jackson. See also the papers of Edward Fontaine, Mississippi State University Library.

Anxious demands for troops were issued almost simultaneously with the conception of the provisional Confederate government in Montgomery, Alabama, and were echoed emphatically once the seat of authority was moved to Richmond in the spring of 1861. Governor John J. Pettus attempted to meet these demands by appealing to the male population of his state for volunteers to serve in the Army of Mississippi and the Provisional Army of the Confederate States. Many of the companies that were formed in answer to these pleas were quickly sent by rail to Pensacola at the urging of the provisional government. Those units not sent to the coast were ordered into the rapidly growing camp of instruction at Corinth, Mississippi, at the strategic junction of the Memphis & Charleston and Mobile & Ohio railroads. From this location they could be transported in whatever direction military exigency necessitated.[3]

With martial spirit running high, colorful companies of state volunteers—comprising men from every walk of life and bearing names such as Rough and Readies, Oktibbeha Rescue, Crystal Springs Southern Rights, and Minute Men of Attala—assembled at Corinth to be mustered into the army as twelve-month volunteers. By May 10, two regiments of ten companies each, the 12th and 13th Mississippi, destined for the Virginia front, had assembled there only to be rushed initially to Union City, Tennessee, to bolster Confederate strength in the West. By late May a total of forty-nine Mississippi volunteer infantry companies had been ordered into camp there, together with companies from surrounding states. Many of these were formed immediately into regiments and shipped by rail to Virginia.[4]

There were other companies, however, that independently tendered their services to the provisional Confederate government for the duration of the conflict. These companies were

3. *Official Records*, Ser. 1, Vol. IV, p. 388, Ser. 4, Vol. I, p. 334; Robert C. Black, *The Railroads of the Confederacy* (Chapel Hill, 1952), 60; Hooker, "Mississippi," 14–16; Dunbar Rowland, *History of Mississippi, the Heart of the South* (4 vols.; Chicago, Jackson, 1925), I, 767.
4. *Official Records*, Ser. 1, Vol. LII, Pt. 2, pp. 94, 103, 105–106; Hooker, "Mississippi," 15–16.

more highly sought by Richmond authorities than others. Of
the Mississippi regiments that would eventually serve in the
Army of Northern Virginia, the 2nd Battalion and the 19th,
21st, and 26th Volunteer Infantry regiments were composed of
companies that mustered for the duration either in Mississippi
or in Virginia.[5]

By summer's end, ten regiments of Mississippi volunteer
infantry were in Virginia, transported via Corinth—the 2nd,
11th, 12th, 13th, 16th, 17th, 18th, 19th, 20th, and 21st. There
had been little concert or pattern to the movement and placement of these units, however. The 2nd and 11th Mississippi,
organized early in May, were transported to Lynchburg, Virginia, and from there to Harpers Ferry to join General Joseph
Johnston's Army of the Shenandoah. The 12th and 13th Mississippi, formed at Corinth in mid-May, were initially sent to
Union City, Tennessee, at the urging of General Leonidas Polk.
In mid-July, however, they received orders to move rapidly to
Lynchburg, arriving in Virginia in time to take part in the
battle of Manassas. By mid-June, three other infantry regiments recently formed at Corinth—the 16th, 17th, and 18th
Mississippi—were tapped for service on the Virginia front. The
17th and 18th regiments, moving via Lynchburg, arrived at
Manassas Junction on June 17 and 18, respectively, in time to
participate in the battle. The 16th Mississippi, however, did
not entrain until July 26 and upon reaching Lynchburg was
detained there until August 8. The 19th Mississippi infantry
meanwhile rendezvoused at Oxford, Mississippi, and moved
independently to Richmond, where it enlisted for the duration
of the war and was assigned to General Johnston's army on
July 4. Arriving in Lynchburg in mid-August, the 20th Mississippi was ordered to join the Army of the Kanawha near
Lewisburg.[6]

During the organization of these early regiments, the home

5. Rowland, *Statistical Register,* 516–18, 484–94, 492–507.
6. *Ibid.,* 461, 471, 479, 487; W. J. Tancig, *Confederate Military Land Units*
(New York, 1959), 54, 56, 57, 58, 61; Robert White, "West Virginia," *Confederate Military History,* 11, 45.

location of contingent companies apparently was of little
significance to the Mississippians. A close scrutiny of the many
companies in the regiments going to Virginia reveals little. In
some cases the majority of the companies in a regiment came
from the same geographic region of the state. The composition
of individual companies was of course completely heteroge-
geneous. Also apparent is the fact that the first Mississippi
troops assigned to Virginia were disposed as military demands
dictated. When each unit reached Lynchburg—the junction of
the Virginia & Tennessee with the Orange & Alexandria and
the Petersburg & Lynchburg railroads—it was rapidly ushered
to one of the points of pressure in northern or western Virginia.
Thus the 2nd Mississippi, Under Colonel W. C. Falkner, and the
11th Mississippi, under Colonel William H. Moore, moved to
Harpers Ferry to join forces under General Joseph Johnston,
while the 13th, 17th, and 18th regiments, under Colonels
William Barksdale, W. S. Featherston, and E. R. Burt respectively, moved to join General P. G. T. Beauregard at Manassas.
These five regiments therefore played roles in the martial
drama that unfolded across northern Virginia in the summer
of 1861.[7]

The emergency caused by the movement of General Irvin
McDowell's Federal force into northern Virginia in July, 1861,
left little time for political considerations and brigading of
regiments by states. Therefore, during the Manassas campaign
the troops of the 17th and 18th Mississippi found themselves
brigaded with the 5th South Carolina under General D. R.
Jones. The 13th Mississippi, which had arrived only the night
before, early on the morning of the battle became part of a
brigade composed of the 4th South Carolina, 7th Virginia, and
24th Virginia under the command of General Jubal Early. The
2nd and 11th Mississippi, previously assigned to Johnston's
Army of the Shenandoah at Harpers Ferry, entered the fray

7. Black, *Railroads of the Confederacy*, 60–62; *Official Records*, Ser. 1, Vol. II,
pp. 469–70, 869; John B. Gordon, *Reminiscences of the Civil War* (New York,
1903), 27–28.

brigaded with the 4th Alabama and 1st Tennessee under General Barnard E. Bee.[8]

During the battle on July 21, the 17th and 18th Mississippi were deployed on the right of the Confederate line and were to have been part of Beauregard's planned assault on Federal positions abreast of that quarter, had it not been for the earlier Federal attack against the Confederate left. On the left, however, the 2nd Mississippi and two companies of the 11th bore the brunt of the grand Federal thrust momentarily as they rushed forward to assist the command of General N. G. Evans. The action of these Mississippians allowed the brigade of Thomas Jonathan Jackson to form for its famous stand. The total losses among Mississippi regiments during the battle was 191. The 11th Mississippi alone sustained 108 casualties.[9]

Immediately following the battle at Manassas, the Confederate army there was organized into eight brigades. An attempt was made at this time to maintain state integrity. Barksdale's 13th Mississippi regiment, Featherston's 17th, and Burt's 18th became the Seventh Brigade of the Confederate Army of the Potomac. The 12th Mississippi under Colonel Thomas M. Griffith became part of the Second Brigade, together with the 5th, 6th, and 12th Alabama infantry regiments, all under General Richard S. Ewell.[10] The 11th and 19th Mississippi regiments remained attached to the Army of the Shenandoah during this period. Posey's late-arriving 16th Mississippi, detained at Lynchburg, received orders on August 8 to move to Manassas Junction. The 20th Mississippi, commanded by Colonel D. R. Russell, reaching Virginia only in late August, was ordered in September to join the Army of the Kanawha in the mountains of western Virginia at Lewisburg. The regiment was shortly moved west with the command of

8. *Official Records*, Ser. 1, Vol. II, pp. 869–70; *The Official Atlas of the Civil War* (New York, 1958), Plates III, No. 1, 2, V, No. 7; James W. Moorehead Diary, July 18–25, 1861, in John K. Bettersworth (ed.), *Mississippi in the Confederacy: As They Saw It* (Baton Rouge, 1961), pp. 60–61.

9. *Official Records*, Ser. 1, Vol. II, pp. 473, 486, 538–41, 570; Hooker, "Mississippi," 23–24.

10. *Official Records*, Ser. 1, Vol. II, pp. 999–1000.

General John B. Floyd, where it participated in the Fort Donelson debacle and, though it performed gallantly, was surrendered in February, 1862.[11]

During the weeks following the battle at Manassas, the brigades of the Confederate Army of the Potomac were posted defensively along the Virginia shore of the Potomac River. In the middle of what promised to be a lengthy respite from combat in northern Virginia, a Federal force of several regiments under the command of General Charles P. Stone and Colonel Edward Baker attempted to make a lodgment on the Virginia side of the Potomac near Leesburg. Stationed in that area was the Mississippi brigade of General Evans composed of the 13th, 17th, and 18th Mississippi regiments; the 8th Virginia infantry regiment; and Jenifer's Cavalry. In an engagement that lasted the entire day of October 21, the 17th and 18th Mississippi and 8th Virginia drove a force of Federal regiments under the command of Colonel Baker into the Potomac at Balls Bluff. Meanwhile, the 13th Mississippi held Stone's units in check at Edwards Ferry. This stunning Federal defeat not only had a signal effect in boosting Confederate morale, but it also forced the Lincoln administration to convene immediately a court of inquiry.[12]

Shortly after the Leesburg encounter, Mississippi units in northern Virginia again were reorganized into part of the military districting of the state by the adjutant general's office. Accordingly, for command purposes, northern Virginia was divided into three districts—Potomac, Valley, and Aquia. With every attempt made to allow brigades to be organized along state lines, the nine regiments of Mississippians found themselves among the First and Second brigades of the First Divi-

---

11. *Official Records*, Ser. 1, Vol. V, 900–902; White, "West Virginia," 45; Jacob Cox, "McCellan in West Virginia," in R. U. Johnson and C. C. Buel, *Battles and Leaders of the Civil War* 4 (4 vols; New York 1884–87), I, 147.

12. *Official Records*, Ser. 1, Vol.348–72; Edward Porter Alexander *Military Memoirs of a Confederate* (Bloomington, 1962), pp. 57–58; Hooker, "Mississippi," 14–29; Richard B. Irwin, "Ball's Bluff and the Arrest of General Stone," *Battles and Leaders*, Vol. I, pp. 123–134; N. G. Evans in Warner, *Generals in Gray*, pp. 83–84.

sion, Potomac District, under General Earl Van Dorn. A paper reorganization with political overtones under General Order No. 15 kept the regiments involved scattered for weeks to come. On December 3 another order, Special Order No. 252, was directed from the adjutant general's office to General Johnston, listing the nine Mississippi regiments and their commanders by name and enjoining that general to allow these units to "join their respective brigades without delay." Johnston, however, asked for a postponement, questioning the feasibility of shuffling nine regiments in the face of the enemy.[13]

At this time, the 2nd and 11th Mississippi were located near Dumfries; the 13th, 17th, 18th, and 21st Mississippi, near Leesburg; and the 12th, 16th, and 19th Mississippi, near Centreville, Virginia. On December 9, Secretary of War Judah P. Benjamin, speaking for President Jefferson Davis, again ordered Johnston to effect the move. The general only reiterated his appeal. At this point the troops became concerned, uppermost in their minds the thought of having to vacate recently constructed winter quarters. As a result their commanders requested the president to rescind the order. Davis refused. As the year closed, however, no locations had changed. When Johnston reported troop dispositions in the Potomac District on January 14, 1862, the 12th Mississippi was still with R. E. Rodes' Alabama brigade, the 16th Mississippi a part of Isaac Trimble's brigade, the 2nd and 11th Mississippi in W. H. C. Whiting's brigade, and the 13th, 17th, 18th, and 21st in Griffith's.[14]

Federal attention shifted to the Virginia peninsula as the second year of the war began. Located with the undermanned forces of General John B. Magruder near Yorktown was the 2nd Mississippi infantry battalion, which had moved onto the peninsula in December. The sole Mississippi unit in that quar-

13. *Official Records*, Ser. 1, Vol. II, Pt. 3, pp. 505, 546–57; Vol. V, pp. 913–14, 979.
14. *Ibid.*, Vol. V, pp. 985, 987, 993, 1012, 1029–30; Douglas S. Freeman, *Lee's Lieutenants: A Study in Command* (3 vols; New York, 1946), I, 207.

ter, it would be joined by a host of other state units in the spring of 1862.[15]

A general withdrawal of all Confederate forces from the Centreville area began March 9. By March 11 these forces had taken up positions below the Rappahannock River. As Federal pressure began to mount, various Confederate units from Johnston's army were shifted to the peninsula. Among the first to join Magruder in late March was C. M. Wilcox's brigade of James Longstreet's division, which included the 19th Mississippi of Colonel Christopher Mott, and Rode's brigade of A. P. Hill's division, which included the 12th Mississippi under Colonel W. H. Taylor. The 17th Mississippi was added to the command of General Lafayette McLaws in April. Each of these regiments acquitted itself well in the fighting of late April as Magruder's force retired slowly before the Federal army of General George B. McClellan. During the spirited contest at Williamsburg on May 5, the 19th Mississippi sustained heavy casualties, and its commander Mott was mortally wounded. Equally heavily engaged were the companies composing the ubiquitous 2nd Mississippi battalion.[16]

When on May 21 Confederate forces ceased their retrograde from the peninsula and turned to grapple with McClellan's army at Seven Pines, Mississippi troops were again heavily engaged. Finding that McClellan's force had straddled the flooded Chickahominy River east of Richmond, Johnston determined to attack. A planned, coordinated thrust, however, became a series of piecemeal lunges by the Confederate army. The Federal drive was stymied nevertheless. During the engagement the 2nd Mississippi battalion, three hundred strong, acting as skirmishers for Samuel Garland's brigade of Hill's

15. *Official Records*, Ser. 1, Vol. IX, p. 37; James Longstreet, *From Manassas to Appomattox: Memoirs of the Civil War in America* (Bloomington, 1962), p. 64; Joseph Eggleston Johnston, *Narrative of Military Operations, Directed, During the Late War Between the States* (New York, 1874), pp. 119–22.

16. *Official Records*, Ser. 1, Vol. XI, Pt. 1, pp. 403–404, 415–18, 564–79, 589–93, 597–600, 601–606; LI, Pt. 1, pp. 90–95; Hooker, "Mississippi," pp. 114–115.

division, sustained eighty-seven casualties. The 12th Mississippi participated in the fray as the lead regiment in the attack of Rodes' brigade on the Federal line. Together with the 5th and 6th Alabama regiments, the Mississippians sustained the highest casualty rate among all Confederate troops engaged in the battle. Although not as heavily engaged, the 19th Mississippi of Wilcox's brigade and the 2nd and 11th Mississippi with General Whiting performed well under fire.[17]

The Confederate army in Virginia underwent still another organizational modification following the confusing engagement at Seven Pines. The wounding of Johnston saw General Robert E. Lee thrust suddenly into command. Under his direction a host of transfers and promotions occurred amid a general reorganization of the entire army. For the most part, General Order No. 15 was adhered to when the Mississippians were concerned. Two solidly Mississippi brigades did appear in Lee's army, but they were not structured according to the earlier dictates of President Davis. The two were Griffith's brigade of Magruder's division, composed of the 13th, 17th, 18th, and 21st Mississippi regiments, and Featherston's brigade of Longstreet's division, composed of the 12th and 19th regiments and the 2nd battalion of Mississippi infantry. The 2nd and 11th Mississippi infantry remained with E. M. Law's brigade of Whiting's division.[18]

Rejoining the main army after a successful stint in the Shenandoah with Jackson's small army was the 16th Mississippi led by Carnot Posey. Part of General Trimble's brigade of Ewell's division, it was the only Mississippi regiment to participate in the famous valley campaign. After playing only a passive role during the battles of Front Royal and Winchester, the regiment saw heavy fighting during the encounters at Cross Keys and Port Republic, June 8–9. Together with the

17. *Official Records*, Ser. 1, Vol. XI, Pt. 1, pp. 961–67, 970–76; Johnston, *Narrative of Military Operations*, pp. 126–39.
18. *Official Records*, Ser. 1, Vol. XI, Pt. 2, pp. 483–89, Pt. 3, pp. 546–47; W. S. Featherston in Warner, *Generals in Gray*, pp. 86–87.

remainder of Jackson's army, it joined Lee's army outside Richmond in late June.[19] During the bloody Seven Days' Battles, which took place from June 26 to July 1, 1862, Mississippi regiments were again conspicuously engaged, sustaining a combined total of 1,496 casualties. In that almost continuous encounter, each regiment was an active participant during at least one phase of the battles of Mechanicsville, Gaines Mill, Savage Station, and Malvern Hill. Serving with Jackson's division, the 2nd, 11th, and 16th Mississippi were heavily engaged at Mechanicsville and Gaines Mill and won the praise of their brigade commander. At Savage Station Griffith's brigade contended heavily with McClellan's rear guard, and General Griffith was mortally wounded. Command of this Mississippi brigade then devolved upon Colonel Barksdale of the 13th Mississippi, who skillfully led the brigade through the fighting at Malvern Hill. Featherston's brigade meanwhile saw severe service with Longstreet's division, which grappled with strong federal forces at Gaines Mill and Fraziers Farm. With the wounding of Colonel Featherston, Posey assumed command. At Malvern Hill fully one-third of Barksdale's brigade were casualties, the highest rate of any on that field.[20]

19. William Allen, *Stonewall Jackson's Campaign in the Shenandoah Valley of Virginia, from November 4, 1861, to June 17, 1862* (London, 1912), pp. 152–53; William C. Oates, *The War Between the Union and the Confederacy and Its Lost Opportunities with a History of the 15th Alabama Regiment and the Forty-eight Battles in Which It was Engaged* (New York, 1905), pp. 92–106, 172–173; Official Records, Ser. 1, Vol. XII, Pt. 1, pp. 717, 778–780, 795–99; Archie P. MacDonald, ed., *Make Me A Map of the Valley: The Civil War Journal of Jackson's Topographer* (Dallas, 1973), p. 34.
20. Fox, *Regimental Losses*, pp. 558–561, Featherston's brigade entered this action with 1350 men of whom 115 were killed, 542 wounded, and 9 missing for a 49.3 percent casualty rate; *Official Records*, Ser. 1, Vol. XI, Pt. 2, pp. 483–86, 503–507, Pt. 3, pp. 479–84 shows the relative strengths of Mississippi units of the Peninsula as of April 30, 1862 as:

2nd Mississippi—477	13th Mississippi—640	19th Mississippi—800
11th Mississippi—504	17th Mississippi—692	21st Mississippi—792
12th Mississippi—650	18th Mississippi—684	2nd battalion—360

Ibid., Pt. 2, 562–65, 605–607, 614, 660–74, 750–55, 756–61, 781–86, 973, 997; Longstreet, *Manassas to Appomattox*, 120–40, Hooker, "Mississippi," 116–18; Warner, *Generals in Gray*, 120.

In the subsequent reorganization of the Army of Northern Virginia that followed the carnage of the Seven Days, all Mississippi regiments in the army were placed in Longstreet's corps. Barksdale's brigade, composed of the 13th, 17th, 18th, and 21st Mississippi, was assigned to the division of Lafayette McLaws; Featherston's brigade, containing the 12th, 16th, and 19th regiments and the 2nd Mississippi battalion, was assigned to General Richard H. Anderson's division; and the 2nd and 11th Mississippi continued with Law's brigade in John Bell Hood's division.[21]

Jefferson Davis had from the outset of hostilities demonstrated his interest in the brigading of Mississippi regiments. During the fall of 1861, he proposed the organization of a brigade of five Mississippi regiments and selected General W. H. C. Whiting as its commander. The general, however, rejected the post in what the president considered an insubordinate manner. Late in May 1862, Davis began to insist that the brigading of Mississippians would produce highly effective fighting organizations. He communicated this desire to General Johnston and noted specifically that the 17th and 19th Mississippi regiments, assigned to T. R. R. Cobb's and Wilcox's brigades respectively, should be detached and reassigned in such a state brigade. The proximity of McClellan's army to Richmond, however, in addition to tactical demands of the moment, would not allow any transfers to be effected.[22]

In July, 1862, the new commander of the Army of Northern Virginia, General Robert E. Lee, became involved in this brigading effort. Colonel P. F. Liddell had applied directly to President Davis for the transfer of his regiment, the 11th Mississippi infantry, along with the 2nd Mississippi, into one of the two Mississippi brigades in the army. Davis referred the matter to Lee, who in turn advised the president that the two regiments were already part of a Mississippi brigade. He explained his intentions of substituting the 42nd Mississippi,

21. Freeman, *Lee's Lieutenants*, I, 670–75; *Official Records*, Ser. 1, Vol. XI, Pt. 2, pp. 803–805.
22. *Official Records*, Ser. 1, Vol. XI, Pt. 3, pp. 546–47; W. H. C. Whiting, in Warner, *Generals in Gray*, 334–35.

recently arrived at Richmond, for the 6th North Carolina and of eventually replacing the 4th Alabama with another Mississippi regiment. However, the 42nd Mississippi, which had detrained in the capital July 3, remained there until November 15. Whiting's brigade did not undergo the expected transformation. In December the 42nd Mississippi became part of a new Mississippi brigade under command of the president's nephew, General Joseph R. Davis.[23]

The weeks following the bloody Seven Days' battles were weeks of respite for the Mississippians in Lee's army. On August 5, however, in response to a feint carried out by a Federal corps under General Joseph Hooker near the old Malvern Hill positions, Longstreet's corps was activated by Lee as a precautionary measure. Satisfied that McClellan's army at Harrisons Landing had ceased its stirring, Lee dispatched Jackson's corps northward toward the young Federal Army of Virginia gathering under General John Pope. Longstreet's corps followed in mid-August, moving first to Gordonsville via the Virginia Central Railroad and marching from that point to the Rappahannock River. Not all of the Mississippi units in Longstreet's corps participated in this movement. While Featherston's brigade under command of General Posey moved directly with Longstreet to Gordonsville, the 2nd and 11th Mississippi remained temporarily with Law's brigade of Hood's division at Hanover Junction. Barksdale's four regiments remained near Richmond with McLaw's division. As a result of these dispositions, the entire Mississippi contingent in the Army of Northern Virginia did not engage in the August 29–30 battle of Second Manassas. The brigades of Featherston and Law were much in evidence on that field, however, and became involved in the heavy fighting on the Confederate right, where the 2nd Mississippi alone lost twenty-two killed and eighty-seven wounded.[24]

The role played by the Mississippians in Featherston's

---

23. *Official Records*, Ser. 1, Vol. XI, Pt. 3, pp. 585, 654.

24. Longstreet, *Manassas to Appomattox*, 154, 158; *Official Records*, Ser. 1, Vol. XII, Pt. 2, pp. 560–61, 595–601, 602–604, 622–25; Hooker, "Mississippi," 119.

command at Manassas is exemplified by the colorful exchange between a barefoot sergeant from the 16th Mississippi and General Lee on the day following the battle. The general, who had ridden up with his staff as the sergeant was relieving a dead Union soldier of his shoes, accused him of straggling. Bridling at the accusation by one he assumed was a Confederate cavalryman, the sergeant severely criticized Lee for not effectively participating in the engagement in which he and his compatriots had carried the entire day. At a loss for further comment, General Lee had a good laugh and moved on.[25]

Following the engagement, Longstreet's corps was given the task of policing the field, while Jackson moved off with his corps in a fruitless attempt to cut Pope's army off from Washington. During the invasion of Maryland, which preceded this activity, the Mississippians of Longstreet's command were again united when McLaws' division joined Longstreet at Frederick, Maryland, on September 7. On September 9, however, Lee issued his famous Special Order No. 191, which dictated his plan of operation for the Maryland campaign. According to the order, McLaws' and R. H. Anderson's divisions containing Barksdale's and Featherston's Mississippi brigades were directed to move via Crampton's Gap and occupy Maryland Heights overlooking Harpers Ferry. Accomplishing this, they were to cooperate with Jackson in capturing the Federal garrison at Harpers Ferry. Later, they would rejoin the main army at Boonesboro or Hagerstown. The other Mississippi regiments, the 2nd and 11th, were to move with Hood's division directly to Boonesboro.[26]

McLaws' division moved into Pleasant Valley through Brownsville Pass on September 11 and by September 12, the same day an errant copy of Special Order No. 191 fell into Union hands, had pushed on to Maryland Heights. During this effort Barksdale's regiments suffered only a few casualties in skirmishing. At Crampton's Gap on September 14, however,

25. Douglas S. Freeman, *R. E. Lee: A Biography* (4 vols.; New York, 1934–35), II, 339–40.
26. *Official Records*, Ser. 1, Vol. XIX, Pt. 1, pp. 852–57, 860; Longstreet, *Manassas to Appomattox*, 203; Hooker, "Mississippi," 120–21.

McLaws' division was handled severely by Union forces under General William R. Franklin that were attempting to take advantage of the discovery of the disposition of Lee's army. McLaws was able to maintain his position and by September 15 joined the victorious Jackson at Harpers Ferry.[27] The disclosure of Lee's plan of operation forced the Army of Northern Virginia to assemble at Sharpsburg, Maryland. The first Mississippi units to arrive there were the 2nd and 11th regiments with Hood. At noon on September 15 they took up positions on the Confederate left flank near Dunker Church. Here under a constant and punishing fire of small arms and artillery they fought throughout September 16 and 17, losing heavily.[28]

Detained by the securing of Harpers Ferry, the brigades of Barksdale and Featherston remained absent from the major conflict at Sharpsburg until the morning of September 17 with their parent divisions. The absence of the divisions of McLaws, Anderson, and A. P. Hill particularly concerned Lee, who desperately needed reinforcements to bolster his sagging and oft-penetrated line of battle.

Having marched directly from Harpers Ferry to the field of battle, the Mississippians in the absentee divisions, diminished by straggling, were near exhaustion when they were deployed into the thickest of the fighting. Barksdale's regiments, the 13th, 17th, 18th, and 21st Mississippi, entered the fray with McLaws through the West Wood on the Confederate left. Featherston's regiments, the 12th, 16th, and 19th, and the 2nd battalion moved to support D. H. Hill in the center. Although only briefly engaged, these commands suffered losses that exhibit the severity of fighting in this battle. The relative sizes of these regiments as they entered the contest likewise indicates the straggling and difficulties of the campaign at that point. In Barksdale's brigade the 13th Mississippi, which took 202 men into action, lost 62 killed, wounded,

27. *Official Records*, Ser. 1, Vol. XIX, Pt. 1, p. 860.
28. *Ibid.*, pp. 922–24, 937–38, 1056; Francis W. Palfrey, *The Antietam and Fredericksburg*, in *Campaigns of the Civil War* (10 vols; New York, 1883), V, 104–105.

and missing; the 17th Mississippi, with 270 engaged, lost 88; the 18th Mississippi with 186 lost 80; and the 21st Mississippi with 200 lost 62.[29]

On September 18 and 19, a much disorganized Army of Northern Virginia crossed the Potomac back into Virginia and took up positions near Culpeper. Here the Mississippians in Longstreet's corps together with the remainder of Lee's army received almost five weeks of rest due to the passivity of the Federal army. During this period of refitting, stragglers poured in by the thousands as the Army of Northern Virginia underwent yet another reorganization. By the time the Union army crossed the Potomac on October 26 and began inching its way toward its new target Fredericksburg, Lee was ready.[30]

Two additional Mississippi regiments appeared in Virginia during the latter part of 1862. The 42nd Mississippi, organized at Oxford in May and initially assigned to Beauregard's Army of Tennessee, was ordered to Richmond in June. Although remaining in a camp of instruction on the outskirts of Richmond, it was included in the returns of General G. W. Smith's command that guarded the approaches to the city. Four companies of the regiment were sent to Fredericksburg on November 15 to guard that city from Federal incursions from the direction of Aquia Creek. Together with a single battery of artillery and the 15th Virginia cavalry, they successfully turned back the first Federal attempt to cross the Rappahannock on November 17. The Mississippians were ordered back to Richmond on November 24. With the transfer of the 2nd and 11th Mississippi from Hood's division to Smith's command, a new Mississippi brigade, which included the 42nd Mississippi, was formed under the command of General Joseph R. Davis.[31]

The second new Mississippi regiment to appear in Virginia during this period comprised both veteran and newly recruited companies. Several companies arrived in Richmond

29. *Official Records*, Ser. 1, Vol. XIX, Pt. 1, pp. 812, 861.
30. *Ibid.*, p. 1016, Vol. XXI, p. 1016.
31. Rowland, *Statistical Register*, 510; *Official Records*, Ser. 1, Vol. XVIII, pp. 751, 759, Vol. XIX, Pt. 2, pp. 695–97, 705, Vol. XXI, pp. 551, 1017.

from the state during the late summer and were added to the extant 2nd Mississippi battalion. As a result the unit was redesignated the 48th Mississippi regiment. As a regiment, it remained in Featherston's brigade, however. On October 27 a major organizational change surfaced when Lee listed the component divisions of Longstreet's corps for Secretary of War George Randolph. Both Mississippi brigades, Barksdale's and Featherston's, were shown in Anderson's division. Because of the quickening tempo of combat at the time, however, the indicated changes occurred only on paper. In the same communication Lee recommended that Carnot Posey be promoted to command Featherston's brigade during the protracted illness of its commander.[32]

On November 19 McLaws' division of Longstreet's corps began arriving on the heights above Fredericksburg. The remaining divisions of the corps and the remainder of Lee's army closed shortly. During the prelude to the contest that ensued in mid-December 1862, Barksdale's regiments played a conspicuous role. Placed on picket duty in and below the city covering over a two-mile stretch of river, they were on duty December 11 when Federal engineers began extending pontoon bridges toward the south bank of the Rappahannock. From early morning until late evening Barksdale's Mississippians, performing before Longstreet's entire corps, resisted the Federal crossing while being subjected to a galling artillery fire. Faced with growing numbers of Union troops ferried across the river below the city, Barksdale retired late in the day, fighting through the streets. On December 12 the Mississippians assumed supporting positions on the heights above the town, from which they observed the carnage that followed. Featherston's brigade meanwhile played only a passive role in the contest, positioned with Anderson's division to support the left of the main Confederate line on the heights directly behind the city.[33]

32. *Official Records*, Ser. 1, Vol. XIX, Pt. 2, pp. 683, 697, Vol. XXI, p. 1100.
33. *Ibid.*, Vol. XXI, pp. 578–83, 600–607, 615–16; *Official Records Atlas*, Plate XXV, No. 14; James Longstreet, "The Battle of Fredericksburg," in *Battles and Leaders*, III, 73–78; Lafayette McLaws, "The Confederate Left at Fredericks-

The retirement of General Ambrose E. Burnside's bludgeoned Federal army from Fredericksburg on December 16 marked the beginning of a long winter of inactivity, except for the self-inflicted pains of the infamous "mud march" by the Union army late in January, 1863. The major portion of the Army of Northern Virginia was extended east and west along the south bank of the Rappahannock River during this period and remained so disposed until April, 1863. General Posey, who succeeded Featherston as brigade commander upon the latter's transfer to the Army of Mississippi in January, was stationed with his brigade near the United States Mine Ford at this time. Barksdale's brigade remained with McLaws' division at Fredericksburg.[34]

Meanwhile, the newly formed Mississippi brigade of Joseph Davis joined the command of G. W. Smith at Goldsboro, North Carolina, on December 17 and immediately set to work with other Confederate brigades curbing federal incursions toward the important rail junction at New Bern. Davis' brigade remained active in that quarter until March, when it joined Longstreet's force on the Blackwater line opposite Suffolk, Virginia. It continued to serve on that line until ordered to join Heth's division in northern Virginia prior to Lee's invasion of Pennsylvania.[35]

Along the Rappahannock line the winter respite of the Mississippians in Lee's army ceased when two divisions of the reorganized Army of the Potomac under the command of General Hooker crossed the river below Fredericksburg at dawn on April 28. The following day two other crossings were effected farther upriver. Both Barksdale's and Posey's brigades were to play extremely significant roles in Lee's counterthrusts to these moves. The brigades of Posey and William Mahone were the first units to react to the upriver

burg," in *Battles and Leaders*, III, 86–89, 91; Longstreet, *Manassas to Appomattox*, 300–303; Freeman, *Lee*, II, 444–48.
    34. *Official Records*, Ser. 1, Vol. XXI, pp. 1099–1100, Vol. XXV, Pt. 1, p. 795.
    35. *Ibid.*, Vol. XVIII, pp. 109–10, 190–91, 565–66, 800, 830, 832–33, 878, 1084–85, Vol. XXV, Pt. 2, pp. 841–43, 848; Longstreet, *Manassas to Appomattox*, 324–25.

crossings, marching rapidly on the night of April 29 to block a federal movement upon Chancellorsville.[36]

Once General Lee determined that the main Union thrust was coming from above, Barksdale's brigade was detached from McLaws' division and together with Early's division remained posted behind Fredericksburg to contain two Federal corps under John Sedgwick. Meanwhile, Lee concentrated upon Chancellorsville.

During the three-day combat at Chancellorsville Posey's Mississippians found themselves in the thickest of the fighting. Except for five companies of the 19th Mississippi left to guard United States Ford, the brigade led the initial Confederate drive upon the Federal masses that had crossed the Rappahannock on April 30. The Mississippians remained in almost continuous contact even after being shifted on May 4 with Anderson's division toward Fredericksburg to counter Sedgwick's belated drive.[37]

Although not in the combat around Chancellorsville, Barksdale's brigade was nevertheless subsequently heavily engaged. On May 3 Barksdale's men found themselves occupying three miles of entrenchments formerly held by fully one-half of Lee's army. One lone regiment, the 18th Mississippi, manned the famous stone wall at the foot of Maryes Heights. Assailed by 20,000 Union soldiers, Barksdale's Mississippians turned back two assaults before being driven from their position with considerable loss. This was only accomplished, however, after Colonel Thomas M. Griffith of the 18th Mississippi fell prey to a Federal ruse to ascertain the strength of his line under the guise of retrieving wounded combatants. The 18th Mississippi subsequently lost its colors in the contest. The combined losses for the Mississippi brigades during the cam-

36. *Official Records*, Ser. 1, Vol. XVIII, p. 1088, Vol. XXV, Pt. 1, pp. 796–97; Lee to McLaws, April 30, 1863, in Clifford Dowdey and Louis H. Manarin (eds.), *The Wartime Papers of R. E. Lee* (Boston, 1961), 447–48.

37. *Official Records*, Ser. 1, Vol. XXV, Pt. 1, pp. 870–73; Freeman, *Lee*, II, 528–29; Hooker, "Mississippi," 178–79. The losses sustained by the color guard of the 16th Mississippi suggest the severity of the contest—four bearers were felled, the flagstaff was shot in two, and the colors themselves were retired to the rear wrapped around the last bearer.

paign totaled 438, Posey's regiments losing 212 and
Barksdale's 226.[38]

After the Union army under Hooker retired back across the
Rappahannock River on May 5, both armies engaged in a
month-long period of mending and reorganization. The Army
of Northern Virginia underwent another major change when it
was divided into three corps—the First Army Corps under
Lieutenant General Longstreet, the Second under Lieutenant
General Ewell, and the Third under Lieutenant General A. P.
Hill. The Mississippians, however, were little affected by the
shuffle. Barksdale's four regiments, the 13th, 17th, 18th, and
21st Mississippi, remained in McLaws' division within
Longstreet's corps. Posey's regiments, the 12th, 16th, 19th, and
48th Mississippi, remained with Anderson's division, which
became part of Hill's Third Corps. Called up from the Suffolk
area, the brigade of Joseph R. Davis, the 2nd, 11th, and 42nd
Mississippi and the 55th North Carolina, joined Heth's division of Hill's corps just in time to participate in the coming
Gettysburg campaign.[39]

On Wednesday, June 3, 1863, McLaws' division in the van of
the Army of Northern Virginia moved from its position along
the Rapidan River toward Culpeper Courthouse, thus signal-
ing the beginning of the renowned Gettysburg campaign. By
June 14 the entire Army of Northern Virginia was on the move.
After crossing the Potomac on June 24 near Shepherdstown,
the three Mississippi brigades marched to the Chambers-
burg-Cashtown area with the corps of Longstreet and Hill and
rested there for three days. On July 1, after the brigade of J. J.
Pettigrew encountered strong resistance in an attempt to
secure supplies at Gettysburg, Davis' Mississippi and J. J.
Archer's Tennessee brigades were rushed to its support. This
effort began an intense combat in which the Mississippians
fought gallantly. The 42nd Mississippi, receiving its baptism
of fire, suffered severe losses.[40]

38. *Official Records*, Ser. 1, Vol. XXV, Pt. 1, pp. 806, 839–41.
    39. *Ibid.*, Vol. XXVII, Pt. 2, pp. 283–90; Diary of G. W. Bynum, in Love,
"Mississippi at Gettysburg," 27.
    40. *Official Records*, Ser. 1, Vol. XXVII, Pt. 2, pp. 637–39, 648–51, Vol. XLIV,

At the time Davis' brigade was heavily engaged in a railroad cut west of Gettysburg, Barksdale's brigade was sixteen miles away on the Chambersburg Pike. By forced march, over the most direct route possible, it closed on the outskirts of the hamlet after midnight July 2. Just after dawn it formed in line of battle but remained idle until midmorning, when it marched forward to take up a position on the edge of the soon-to-be-famous Peach Orchard. Ordered into combat, the brigade drove back successive lines of federal infantry and artillery with three successful bayonet charges. As a result of this virtually unsupported effort, every field officer in the brigade was either killed or wounded except for Colonel Benjamin G. Humphreys, who assumed command after Barksdale was mortally wounded. Brigade losses were placed at 747 killed, wounded, or missing.[41]

Carnot Posey's brigade meanwhile marched from Chambersburg with Anderson's division on the second day of the battle and after reaching the field in the afternoon was advanced against the Federal division of General Andrew Humphreys. After driving in the Union skirmishers, the brigade was retired behind the artillery in the center of the Confederate line. Here it played a support role throughout the third day. Upon Lee's retirement, it formed part of the rear guard for the Army of Northern Virginia.[42]

On the third day of the Gettysburg combat a dubious honor befell one of the Mississippi brigades when that of General Davis was selected as part of Heth's division to participate in "Pickett's charge." Rejoined by the 11th Mississippi following its guard duty with the division trains on the night of July 2, all of the brigade's regiments participated in the attack. Still

p. 649; Edwin B. Coddington, *The Gettysburg Campaign: A Study in Command* (New York, 1968), 51; Warren W. Hassler, *Crisis at the Crossroads: The First Day at Gettysburg,*" (Tuscaloosa 1970), 43–49; Love, "Mississippi at Gettysburg," 29–31; Hooker, "Mississippi," 181–82.

41. Longstreet, *Manassas to Appomattox,* 370; *Official Records,* Ser. 1, Vol. XXVII, Pt. 2, pp. 228, 363; Coddington, *Gettysburg,* 405–17; Hooker, "Mississippi," 180–81; B. G. Humphreys, in Warner, *Generals in Gray,* 145–46.

42. Rowland, *Statistical Register,* 490, 512–13; Coddington, *Gettysburg,* 420.

exhausted and worn from the first day's fighting, the brigade used its last ounce of energy in the assault and suffered dearly. Many of the companies in its regiments were reduced to as few as three or four men.[43]

Following its demise at Gettysburg, the Army of Northern Virginia retired via Hagerstown, Maryland, to the Potomac River, which it crossed near Williamsport on July 13 after an anxious three-day delay caused by high water. By July 24 the Mississippians in Longstreet's corps began arriving at Culpeper Courthouse. They later took up positions along the Rappahannock River and passed the entire month of August in relative quiet, nursing wounds and regrouping. The only command change during this juncture was the official confirmation of General Humphreys' command of Barksdale's brigade. Although much desertion occurred in the army following the heavy losses in Pennsylvania, among the Mississippians the problem was minor.[44]

On September 19, 1863, after an intense military conference in Richmond, the decision was reached to detach Longstreet's First Corps from the Army of Northern Virginia and send it by rail to support the Army of Tennessee under Braxton Bragg in north Georgia. During this movement, which took ten days to complete, Humphrey's brigade of Mississippians as part of McLaws' division left its position along the Rapidan River and moved by rail to Atlanta. From Atlanta the brigade moved toward Chattanooga and a rendezvous with Bragg's forces. On the afternoon of September 18 it arrived at Catoosa Station and from there marched to Ringgold and thence toward Chickamauga, where it joined Bragg on September 19. Because of its late arrival, Humphreys' brigade did not participate in the early phases of the battle of Chickamauga. It did, however, as

43. Love, "Mississippi at Gettysburg," 42–46; *Official Records*, Ser. 1, Vol. XXVII, Pt. 2, pp. 338–45; Jesse Bowman Young, *The Battle of Gettysburg: A Comprehensive Narrative* (New York, 1913), 304–305; Hooker, "Mississippi," 182–83.

44. *Official Records*, Ser. 1, Vol. XXVII, Pt. 3, pp. 238, 1048, 1065, Vol. XXIX, Pt. 2, p. 682; Lee to Davis, July 20, 1863, in Dowdey and Manarin, *Lee's Wartime Papers*, 563–64.

part of Hood's division, participate in the successful thrust on September 20 that drove the Union army of General William S. Rosecrans back upon Chattanooga.[45]

Following the engagement at Chickamauga, Humphreys' brigade took part briefly in the siege of Chattanooga. It later moved off with Longstreet's corps in what proved to be an unsuccessful attempt to dislodge the federal forces of General Burnside from Knoxville. Two of the brigade's regiments, the 13th and 17th, participated in the costly assault on Fort Loudon on November 29. On December 4 Humphreys' brigade retired northward from Knoxville with Longstreet's detached command and after a brief period of tactical maneuvering took up winter quarters near Russellville, Tennessee, in the bountiful valley of the French Broad River. The brigade remained there until orders recalling Longstreet to Charlottesville, Virginia, were received April 11.[46]

The two Mississippi brigades that had remained with the Army of Northern Virginia—Posey's in Anderson's division and Davis' in Heth's division—had not been inactive during this time. On October 14 both participated with their parent divisions in an engagement at Bristoe Station as Lee attempted to curb the encroachments of the Army of the Potomac beyond the Rapidan. Although losses within the Mississippi commands proved light, among the wounded was General Posey, who, taken to Charlottesville to recover, died in

45. *Official Records*, Ser. 1, Vol. XXIX, Pt. 2, pp. 693–94, Vol. XXX, Pt. 2, pp. 26, 287–90, 502–506, Vol. LI, Pt. 2, p. 761; Longstreet, *Manassas to Appomattox*, 435, 448; Glen Tucker, *Chickamauga: Bloody Battle in the West* (Indianapolis, 1961), 212, 261–62, 334–35; Thomas L. Connelly, *Autumn of Glory: The Army of Tennessee, 1862–1865* (Baton Rouge, 1971), 160, 191, 208–209. Battle flags carried by Humphreys' regiments are re-created in Howard M. Madaus and Robert D. Needham, *The Battle Flags of the Confederate Army of Tennessee* (Milwaukee, 1976), 59–60.

46. Alexander, *Military Memoirs*, 488–89; *Official Records*, Ser. 1, Vol. XXXIII, pp. 1054, 1286; Longstreet, *Manassas to Appomattox*, 451, 455–56, 503; Oates, *War Between the Union and the Confederacy*, 334–37, Orlando M. Poe, "The Defense of Knoxville," in *Battles and Leaders*, III, 741–43; H. J. Eckenrode and Bryan Conrad, *James Longstreet: Lee's War Horse* (Chapel Hill, 1936), 260–64, 274.

November. Colonel Nathaniel Harris of the 19th Mississippi assumed command of the brigade.[47]

The return of Longstreet's corps to Lee's army coincided with the opening of the spring campaign along the Rapidan by the Army of the Potomac. In what came to be known as the Wilderness campaign, the Mississippi brigades as well as those from every southern state were reduced in most cases to the sizes regiments had been in 1861–1862. Humphreys' Mississippians made a grand reentry into the Virginia hostilities when in the first major battle of 1864, in the van of J. B. Kershaw's division, they spearheaded Longstreet's timely attack in the Wilderness. The thrust not only checked the Federal advance but saved Davis' brigade of Mississippians at that time defending the right sector of the Confederate line with Hill's corps. Both Davis' and Harris' brigades had been heavily engaged since participating in the repulse of the Union army on May 5.[48]

Following Longstreet's timely thrusts, the Army of the Potomac, temporarily stymied, slipped eastward toward Spotsylvania on May 9–12. There on May 12 both armies became entangled again. At the famous Bloody Angle at Spotsylvania both Harris' and Humphreys' Mississippi brigades fought well in the face of overwhelming odds. To the former brigade, however, were delivered most of the laurels of that day, its regiments bearing a major portion of the lengthy combat in the Angle.[49]

Yet another regiment joined the flagging ranks of Mississippians when the 26th Mississippi under the command of Colonel Arthur E. Reynolds arrived in Virginia in April to join Davis' brigade. A veteran regiment with several western cam-

47. *Official Records*, Ser. 1, Vol. XXIX, Pt. 1, pp. 412–13, 426, 429, 430–32, Vol. XXXIII, p. 1207; Hooker, "Mississippi," 265; Nathaniel Harris, in Warner, *Generals in Gray*, 125–26.
48. E. M. Law, "From the Wilderness to Cold Harbor," in *Battles and Leaders*, IV, 124–26; Freeman, *Lee*, III, 288–89; Freeman, *Lee's Lieutenants*, III, 356–57.
49. *Official Records*, Ser. 1, Vol. XXXVI, Pt. 1, pp. 1057, 1061–63, 1092; Freeman, *Lee's Lieutenants*, III, 382–84, 448–49; Rowland, *Mississippi, Heart of the South*, II, 63–66; Hooker, "Mississippi," 221.

paigns to its credit, it stood firm with the brigade as part of Heth's division in the Wilderness on May 5–6, gaining time for Longstreet's corps to make its dramatic and saving appearance.[50]

Each of the three Mississippi brigades participated in the almost daily combat between the Army of the Potomac and the Army of Northern Virginia as the Federal army slipped east and south around the extended right flank of the Confederates in its movement toward the James River. The final maneuver of U. S. Grant's campaign from the Rapidan to the James, which began on the last day of May, 1864, with a race to Cold Harbor, found Anderson's division with its complement of Mississippians in the van of the Confederate army. During the sanguinary, one-sided combat that took place at Cold Harbor on June 2–3, all three Mississippi brigades—Davis', Harris', and Humphreys'—participated with few losses. After Grant's successful evasion of the Army of Northern Virginia following the battle, the Mississippians proceeded with their parent divisions across the James River to assume positions in the Petersburg trenches, the scene of the final and protracted confrontation between the two major eastern armies.[51]

While both Davis' and Harris' brigades continued to amass combat laurels at Petersburg during the late summer and fall of 1864, Humphreys' brigade as part of Kershaw's division was ordered to the Shenandoah Valley to reinforce General Early's small army then operating against Union forces near Strasburg. Kershaw's division, performing gallantly with Early, was recalled to Petersburg on September 14. The division, however, had only reached Culpeper Courthouse when it was ordered to rejoin Early. Upon their return to Richmond on November 20, the remnants of Humphreys' brigade were posted with Kershaw's troops within the defenses of the city at Garnetts Farm on the New Market and Darbytown roads.

50. *Official Records*, Ser. 1, Vol. XXXII, Pt. 3, pp. 604, 672, Vol. XLII, Pt. 2, pp. 1273, 1278; Rowland, *Statistical Register*, 506–507.
51. *Official Records*, Ser. 1, Vol. XLIII, Pt. 1, pp. 557, 576; Law, "Wilderness to Cold Harbor," 138–39.

Ordered to join Lee on April 1, 1865, the Mississippians vacated their trenches and started the trek toward Appomattox.[52]

On the Petersburg line, Harris' and Davis' brigades, attached to Mahone's and Heth's divisions respectively, participated in virtually every major contest on the Confederate right during the nine-month confrontation. Numerous battles were fought during the months of trench warfare occasioned by the siege of Petersburg from June, 1864, until April, 1865. Harris' regiments fought in the battles over the Weldon Railroad, June 22–24; Darbytown Road, August 18; Reams's Station, August 21; Hatcher's Run Bridge, October 27; and Burgess Mill, February 6. Davis' regiments fought at the Weldon Railroad, August 18–19; Reams's Station, August 21; Fort McRae, October 1; Jones Farm, October 2–3; and Hatcher's Run Bridge, October 27.[53]

The final combat of consequence involving the Mississippians occurred April 2, 1865, as the Federal army completed its encirclement of Petersburg by crushing the right of the Confederate line and driving to the Appomattox River west of the City. As the Confederate outer defenses folded, the unmanned inner works lay open to the rapidly moving Union onslaught. To buy time for his troops to occupy the defensive line closest to the city, Lee called for two forts in advance of the line—Gregg and Whitworth—to be held for two hours at all costs. Fort Gregg contained only two guns and the remnants of the 12th and 16th Mississippi, a total of 214 men. In Fort Whitworth were three guns of the Washington Artillery and 200 men of the 19th and 48th Mississippi.[54]

Both Lee and Longstreet watched as a force of more than two

52. Jubal A. Early, *Autobiographical Sketch and Narrative of the War Between the States* (Philadelphia, 1912), 56–114; Jubal Early, "Winchester, Fisher's Hill, and Cedar Creek," in *Battles and Leaders*, IV, 524–30; MacDonald, *Make Me a Map of the Valley*, 223, 224, 232–44.

53. *Official Records*, Ser. 1, Vol. XLII, Pt. 1, pp. 430–31, Pt. 3, pp. 615–18, 625, 630, 667, 675, Vol. XLVI, Pt. 1, pp. 1277–78, 1283–84; Horace Porter, "Five Forks and the Pursuit of Lee," in *Battles and Leaders*, IV, 717; G. T. Beauregard, "Four Days of Battle at Petersburg," in *Battles and Leaders*, IV, 543–44.

54. Alexander, *Military Memoirs*, 592–93; Rowland, *Statistical Register*, 493–94, 514.

federal divisions assaulted the small forts for two full hours. Although the Homeric defense by the Mississippians and artillerists provided time for the inner defense to be manned, the cost was dear—86 percent of the defenders of Fort Gregg became casualties. The losses to the assaulting units, however, numbered more than three times the size of the Fort Gregg garrison.

One week after this gallant stand, all three Mississippi brigades were surrendered at Appomattox. Of approximately 16,000 Mississippians who served in the Army of Northern Virginia, few remained to lay down their arms. At the final roll Harris' brigade numbered 382, Humphreys' 257, and Davis' only 75.[55]

Although the exploits of the three Mississippi brigades in the Army of Northern Virginia border on the heroic, they are not unlike those of countless sister brigades from other Confederate states or their counterparts in Union armies during the Civil War. By tracing the activities of state units from organization to disbandment, one may appreciate the efforts of both northern and southern states, even though the result of this focus is often an overemphasis on combat. Nevertheless, studying the effects of countless command changes, unit transfers, marches and countermarches, casualties, and political forces on the rank and file yields a more complete understanding of the major commands and commanders.

55. Love, "Mississippi at Gettysburg," 50; Hooker, "Mississippi," 226–27.

The Charleston, South Carolina, Riot of 1919

Lee E. Williams II

When the colored man said that nobody could make him fight, his colored brother in the service said: "That's right, Sam, nobody kin make yo' fight and nobody's goin' to try. All they's goin' to do is put yo' in the front-line trench and let yo' use yo' own judgment!"[1]

Disregarding the historical, economic, and psychological instability and the racial upheavals that lay at the foundation of the town, Charleston, according to the travelogue mystique of Ruth Batchelder, is "the most charming, the most enchanting city of America ... a quaint dream with its rows of galleried houses." The place existed as a city of contrasts, however. In 1920 blacks made up more than half of Charleston's population of 80,000, and they lent a "tropic touch" to the city. Persons docking at the wharf received greetings from a "multitude of dilapidated darky hack drivers" speaking in the Gullah dialect.[2] Nonetheless, blacks had long occupied a place of significance in South Carolina.

Causes for and demonstrations of racial rioting and economic ill will had been present in Charleston for a long

1. Memphis *Commercial Appeal*, May 13, 1919, p. 14.
2. Ruth Batchelder, "Enchantment of Old Charleston," *Travel*, XXXIV (March, 1920), 32.

time. Although the vast majority of blacks labored as field
hands in the antebellum period, a select few received training
in domestic arts, cabinetmaking, blacksmithing, carpentry,
shipbuilding, and other crafts. As one author has noted, "The
fact that Negro artisans outnumbered the white, and that their
masters were eager to convert Negro labor into money, led
first to a deep antagonism between the groups and then to
legal measures for the benefit of white artisans."[3] This situation compounded other problems.

Because of social, economic, and psychological maladjustment, city whites pioneered in both customary and de jure
discrimination and segregation. Blacks were not allowed in
public parks. De facto segregation in jails, hospitals, theaters,
and cemeteries became common.[4] Whites associating with
blacks on any basis that suggested equality received harsh
treatment. Several such persons were murdered in South
Carolina for the "crime" of mixing with blacks in public.
Racial antagonism further developed as widespread racial
intermixture occurred in Charleston.[5]

After Reconstruction a wave of lynchings had taken place in
South Carolina. The situation became so bad that in 1895 a
state law provided cash payment to the victims' families, to be
paid by the county in which the atrocity occurred. With the
demise of the plantation regime, development of a plantation-
type system increased antagonism between blacks and poor
whites. Blacks were confined to largely menial and unskilled
jobs.[6]

In 1900 blacks outnumbered whites in Charleston, and by
1903 blacks had made a little progress. Nonetheless, numerous
whites actively worked to have all blacks removed from of-
ficeholding in the South. Following the Norfolk, Virginia,

3. Writers' Program of the Works Projects Administration, *South Carolina: A
Guide to the Palmetto State* (New York: Oxford University Press, 1941), 46.
    4. John Hope Franklin, *From Slavery to Freedom* (New York: Alfred A. Knopf,
1971), 208, 212, 227. See also Jack T. Kirby, *Darkness at the Dawning: Race and
Reform in the Progressive South* (Philadelphia: J. B. Lippincott Company,
1972), 18, 24.
    5. Franklin, *From Slavery to Freedom*, 204, 264.
    6. Writers' Program, *South Carolina*, 51–52.

plan, complicated segregation codes arose in Charleston around 1913.[7] In 1915, with the rebirth of the Ku Klux Klan and the intensification of "legal" control of black people, matters got worse. After World War I, a black Charleston newspaper, referring to a postwar wave of lynching and racial rioting throughout the United States, noted that "there is scarcely a day that passes that newspapers don't tell about a Negro soldier lynched in his uniform. Why do they lynch Negroes anyhow? With a white judge, a white jury, white public sentiment, white officers of the law, it is just as impossible for a Negro accused of crime, or even suspected of crime, to escape the white man's vengeance or his justice as it would be for a fawn to escape that wanders accidentally into a den of hungry lions. So why not give him the semblance of a trial."[8]

Further denoting the imbalance of social relations is the following quotation, which appeared in the Charleston *News and Courier* on its editorial page taken from *Everybody's* magazine:

> A Negro private had spent long tiresome months in camp near New York and wanted to go off on leave. He had a pass, but not the password, and when he came to the sentry the sentry refused to let him go. The negro pulled out his little pass and offered it.
> 'That isn't enough,' said the sentry. 'You must have the word.'
> 'You mean that piece o' paper won't let me out?' demanded the darky. 'Have to have the word.'
> The negro reflected, then he pulled out a razor and began stropping it on his sleeve. 'Man,' he said, impressively, 'I gotta father in hell, a mother in Heaven, an' a girl in Harlem, an' I'se gwine to see one of 'em tonight.[9]

For many southern and northern whites the only "good nigger" was a dead one; and what fun it was to hunt him down, gun him down, castrate him, or string him up as due execution for "the beast."

Charleston was divided residentially into two sections, to

7. Franklin, *From Slavery to Freedom*, 306. See also Kirby, *Darkness at the Dawning*, 24.
8. Franklin, *From Slavery to Freedom*, 480.
9. Charleston *News and Courier*, May 11, 1919, p. 4.

say nothing of the mudsill area, with Broad Street serving as the dividing line. Socially it proved better to have a small house below Broad Street than a large mansion above. A true Charlestonian, it was said, had to do three things in order to enter the Kingdom of Heaven: live below Broad Street; go to the St. Cecilia balls; and attend St. Michael's Church. Likewise, it was "the epitome of a Carolinian's existence to spend the season" in Charleston. For the elite, Charleston architecture had "a charm indefinably its own" with Georgian period structures having wrought iron gateways and surrounded by "countless old-fashioned" flower gardens. The home of the Colonial Dames was the powder magazine on Cumberland Street, which happened to be the oldest building in town.[10]

To the romantic, despite present and historical harbingers of unrest, the "other half" seemed to possess "a peculiarly carefree and happy disposition," living for the day only, and working two days a week to obtain enough "hog and hominy to eke out the rest of the five days." Blacks secured fish and crabs from the surrounding waters. Many who worked as vendors of berries, vegetables, and fish wandered through the streets in the mornings "filling the air with their musical but inarticulate cries." Batchelder saw one "picturesque old darky" driving a dilapidated ox fastened "by some strange means" to a "still more dilapidated cart past the stately mansion of Charleston's Most Distinguished Citizen."[11]

Most black people lived in huts of one or two rooms with a big open fireplace over which they cooked, but they hardly ever owned their crude shelters. Secret societies of this "lesser sort" existed in great profusion throughout Charleston, such as "The Sons And Daughters of The Rising House Of Ruth."[12] A private school for black children conducted classes on Tradd

10. Batchelder, "Enchantment of Old Charleston," 33–34.
11. *Ibid.*, 34. For information on the psychosis of fear in South Carolina, see William W. Freehling, *Prelude to Civil War: The Nullification Controversy in South Carolina, 1816–1836* (New York: Harper and Row, 1966).
12. Batchelder, "Enchantment of Old Charleston," 34.

Street before it had to move to other quarters when the street underwent restoration.[13]

According to Batchelder, "the two races lived together in perfect harmony" because they understood each other. For generations blacks endured slavery, and much of the old "feudal feeling" still remained. In many families descendants of former slaves continued as the paid employees of "those to whom their forefathers belonged." Thus the city by the sea exercised a "peculiar fascination" over the stranger within its gates. Tradition maintained that Charleston possessed an enchanted well and that any one who drank from it would "never be able to remain away very long."[14]

Amid all of Charleston's tranquillity, tradition, and heritage a racial riot occurred May 10, 1919, primarily between white sailors from the naval yard and black civilians. Reports relating the origin of the riot varied. According to the New Orleans *Times-Picayune*, the trouble grew out of the shooting of a white sailor by a black man in a downtown poolroom; in a short while more sailors from the naval training station and civilians joined the fight.[15] The Memphis *Commercial Appeal* said the rioting started when fighting followed a quarrel between a white sailor and a black man in which the black man reportedly threatened the sailor's life. Other sailors rushed to their comrade's rescue, and several blacks joined the melee.[16] In the view of the Chicago *Defender*, trouble began when a white sailor, drunk and unruly, entered a poolroom on King Street and abused the proprietor and several of his black customers. The sailor pulled a revolver from his pocket, but was overpowered and in the scuffle shot through the stomach. When the news reached the bluejackets (sailors), many of them hurried to the scene.[17]

The New York *Times* reported that trouble began with the

13. Dwight J. Baum, "Glimpses of Charleston," *House Beautiful*, XLIX (April, 1921), 304.
14. Batchelder, "Enchantment of Old Charleston," 34, 44,
15. New Orleans *Times-Picayune*, May 13, 1919, p. 1.
16. Memphis *Commercial Appeal*, May 11, 1919, p. 29.
17. Chicago *Defender*, May 17, 1919, p. 1.

"shooting of a sailor by a negro in a downtown pool room."[18] Even the Birmingham News held that rioting was precipitated when a black man named Isaac Doctor fell mortally wounded after he shot a sailor.[19] The Chicago Tribune briefly noted the Charleston riot with the following: "Sailors from the naval training station here [Charleston] and civilians clashed with a crowd of colored men tonight [May 10] and a number of shots were fired in the downtown streets. Reports to the police were that several persons had been wounded. Marines were ordered out to patrol the streets and round up the sailors."[20]

Conversely, historian Robert Brisbane maintained that the rioting started when "two white sailors for no apparent reason shot and killed an Afro-American civilian."[21] Another historian, William Tuttle, said there had been an argument between a white sailor and black civilian and the civilian was fatally wounded.[22]

In light of these assessments, the Charleston riot began, according to the Charleston News and Courier and the navy yard inquiry, after a black man was accused of shooting a white sailor, whereupon military personnel assisted by civilians attacked many blacks Saturday night, May 10, 1919, and early Sunday morning, May 11.[23] There commenced a fierce street fight in what was formerly the "tenderloin" (or black) section of the city near Market and West streets.[24]

When rioting broke out, soldiers, sailors, and marines on shore leave, inspired by Alexander Lanneau, a white civilian, made a looting raid on two shooting galleries, one at 310 King

18. New York Times, May 11, 1919, p. 3.
19. Birmingham News, May 12, 1919, p. 2.
20. Chicago Tribune, May 11, 1919, p. 1.
21. Robert Brisbane, The Black Vanguard: Origins of the Negro Revolution, 1900–1960 (Valley Forge: Judson Press, 1970), 76–77.
22. William M. Tuttle, Jr., " 'Red Summer':1919," in Readings in American History (Guilford, Conn.: Dushkin Publishing Group, 1973), II, 130.
23. Charleston News and Courier, May 11, 1919, p. 1; "Record of Proceedings of a Court of Inquiry Convened at the Navy Yard, Charleston, S.C.," May 27–June 19, 1919, p. 264, National Archives and Records Service, Record Group 125.
24. Birmingham News, May 11, 1919, p. 17.

Street, operated by Fred Faress, and the other at 129½ Market
Street, managed by H. B. Morris. The looters took rifles and
ammunition and began shooting.[25] Later two shooting galleries on Beaufain Street were also raided by sailors. The
small-caliber rifles removed from the galleries were also used
by members of the civilian mob against black people. The
sailors ran amok. The police were powerless, and even whites
in the downtown section at first hurried to safety.[26]

Hundreds of sailors were on liberty Saturday night. Hearing
rumors of a racial altercation involving a navy man, they
began to swarm angrily into the city's black district. Augustus
Bonaparte, a black man, was having his hair cut at the time at
the barbershop on King Street. Startled by shots, he looked out
of the window and saw a mob of bluejackets dash by into a
nearby shooting gallery. Soon afterward the barbershop was
attacked. An army officer and a navy officer who happened
along took an active hand in compelling the bluejackets to
leave.[27]

Automobiles filled with sailors soon crowded the streets;
"Get a nigger!" was their angry cry. James Freyer, a black
cobbler, saw black men and boys running toward his shop,
shouting that the sailors were coming. One entered and
quickly closed and latched the door; "Open the door," yelled a
voice. When nobody moved, a sailor outside fired a shot
through the door, wounding Freyer's apprentice Peter Irving
(or Irwin) in the back.[28]

In a short time more bluejackets and civilians joined the
initial melee. For several hours the rioters had almost complete possession of the downtown streets. Trolley cars were
stopped and black passengers removed, several getting shot as

25. "Record of Proceedings," 235–48. See also Birmingham *News*, May 11,
1919, p. 17; Charleston *News and Courier*, May 11, 1919, p. 3.
26. Charleston *News and Courier*, May 11, 1919, p. 1. See also New York
Times, May 11, 1919, p. 3; "Record of Proceedings," 264.
27. Tuttle, " 'Red Summer': 1919," 130. See also Charleston *News and
Courier*, May 11, 1919, p. 1; Chicago *Defender*, May 17, 1919, p. 1; New York
Times, May 11, 1919, p. 3.
28. "Record of Proceedings," 168–70. See also Tuttle, " 'Red Summer':
1919," 130.

they were pulled from the streetcars. A Broad Street streetcar operator refused to stop at Marion Square. The sailors "jerked off the trolley," entered the car, seized a black man, dragged him out, beat him, and shot him down in the street. Persons in a fashionable restaurant witnessed this shooting.[29]

Some of the bluejackets went up King Street to Columbus, searching for black people. At King and John streets they spotted a black man on a streetcar with his wife. A sailor boarded the car with a stick and ordered the man off. As he descended to the ground the mobsmen jumped him. Marines appeared with fixed bayonets and held the crowd back while the man escaped down John Street, heading toward Meeting Street.[30]

The rioting continued at a fast and furious pace. Hundreds of sailors paraded in the streets and ransacked black businesses. Police estimated that at one time almost a thousand sailors took part in the rioting. Sailors moved through the black housing areas capturing, beating, and robbing black people. When news of the rioting was broadcast, a considerable portion of the city became a battleground between white sailors, soldiers, and civilians and black civilians. Just how word spread so rapidly among the military men could not be explained, but in a short time around two thousand more sailors joined the mob shouting, "Get the negroes," and similar, more derisive phrases.[31]

One of the most dangerous pieces of work during the excitement and confusion of the early rioting was done by Police Chief Joseph A. Black, who arrested the two alleged slayers of a black man named Isaac Doctor. Because no police wagon was available, Chief Black took his prisoners and began to walk

29. New York *Times*, May 11, 1919, p. 3. See also Chicago *Defender*, May 17, 1919, p. 1; Charleston *News and Courier*, May 11, 1919, p. 1.

30. Charleston *News and Courier*, May 11, 1919, p. 3.

31. Memphis *Commercial Appeal*, May 11, 1919, p. 29. See also New Orleans *Times-Picayune*, May 12, 1919, p. 1; Brisbane, *The Black Vanguard*, 76–77; Arthur I. Waskow, *From Race Riot to Sit-in, 1919 and the 1960's: A Study in the Connections Between Conflict and Violence* (New York: Doubleday, 1966), 12–16; Columbia (S.C.) *State*, May 12, 1919, p. 1.

them to the police station. Followed by ten to twenty sailors continually threatening him, he took his time, disarming everyone with a gun whom he saw and was able to reach. At the police station, besides the two prisoners, Black turned over three rifles and several small arms. The guns recovered by the police chief turned out to be part of the loot taken from shooting galleries.[32]

At 11:00 P.M. sailors, soldiers, and civilians continued to run wild. A black hackman, William Randall, underwent attack by the mob. A number of sailors took the hack after beating Randall and drove it down King Street. Randall died two weeks later. Persons in a car going south on Columbus Street saw the mobsmen on Meeting Street but hid under the seats until they were out of danger.[33]

A few blacks fought back with varying results. Shortly after 11:00 P.M. May 10, reports reached military authorities that blacks along the streets steadily sniped at all who wore service hats or rode in automobiles. Also blacks in a touring car had fired at provost guards in front of the police station. Those riding in cabs or other vehicles were cautioned to sit on the floor and keep their hats off. At Line and Meeting streets a black man was caught with a pistol in hand. Marines rushed to the area to save the man from a mounting mob, who "would have killed him had not he run into the arms of the approaching marines." One of his pursuers hit him with a club, and he was sent to the hospital with a gash over his eye.[34]

Police and provost guards were unable to stop the sailors from the naval training camp even with the aid of marines. Naval officers dispatched additional provost guards by motor car, while another detachment of marines hurried into Charleston to serve as a patrol. At midnight Saturday, May 10, a mob attacked Fridie's Central Shaving Parlor at 305 King Street. The shop, run by blacks, catered to white patrons. A

32. Charleston *News and Courier*, May 12, 1919, p. 8.
33. *Ibid.*, May 11, 1919, p. 3. See also "Record of Proceedings," 258–61.
34. Charleston *News and Courier*, May 11, 1919, p. 3. See also Brisbane, *The Black Vanguard*, 76–77; Waskow, *From Race Riot to Sit-in*, 12–16; "Record of Proceedings," 226–227.

black man was spotted entering the place. The lights went out, and the man could not be seen. Mobsmen attacked the shop, breaking windows and destroying property. Finally a provost guard went in and turned on the lights. They searched but could find no one; the black men had escaped by a rear door.

A little after midnight policemen and marines instructed all persons in the streets to go home and stay there. Rear Admiral Benjamin C. Bryan, commandant of the Charleston Navy Yard, kept in close touch with the turmoil and ordered that all bluejackets be sent by motor cars and trucks as rapidly as possible back to the navy yard and the naval training station.[35]

About 1:00 A.M. May 11, city police asked the navy to order more marines with fixed bayonets into the streets. Although the presence of troops helped restore calm, certain of these men continued the terrorizing that the bluejackets began. T. B. Nelson, for example, darted from his house upon hearing moaning in the street. Lying there wounded was William Brown, a black youth, who pleaded with the marines hovering over him, saying, "What are you shooting me for, I was not doing anything." One of the marines demanded, "Why didn't you halt when we told you to?" The youth gasped that he had not been ordered to stop. Another marine replied, "Hush your mouth or we'll give you some more." Brown later died. Also, when Isaac Moses told marines that he had not heard their command to halt, they responded by calling him a "damned liar," knocking him on the head, stealing five dollars, and stabbing him through the leg with a bayonet.[36]

Navy men sent into Charleston as additional provost guards were armed with riot guns by the city police department. They began their duty about midnight, and most worked diligently to halt the rioting. Lieutenants John R. Petersen, Jr., John R. Sandford, and John G. Nicklas strove to break up the rioters. At considerable risk to themselves these men forced

35. "Record of Proceedings," 103–106. See also Charleston *News and Courier*, May 11, 1919, pp. 1, 3.
36. "Record of Proceedings," 123–26, 157–59, 251–52. See also Tuttle," 'Red Summer': 1919," 130.

many bluejackets into line. Other naval officers arrived later and took a hand in subduing the rioters.[37]

Meanwhile, around midnight, sailors and civilians attacked Edward Boston, a black deliveryman who worked for Nick Peters' Grocery Company. Boston was stopped at King and Calhoun streets, where sailors jumped on his truck and beat him. Civilians and sailors broke all the glass and the crank in the engine. Escaping, Boston sought refuge in the police station.[38]

After midnight marines entered King Street and marched behind the raging mob. At John Street they deployed to control the situation there. In the next block, however, a black man was found in a restaurant and evicted by the mob, who began to assault him. Marines came to the rescue. At Radcliffe Street the marines blocked the intersection to protect the man. When the mob dissipated he was released, whereupon he ran "for his life."[39]

Following the Radcliffe Street encounter over three hundred civilians joined the gob rioters. Following this demonstration by the white citizenry, Admiral Bryan gave orders to rush all sailors to the navy yard posthaste. Marines received instructions to patrol the town and to stop and search all suspects, especially black people. They distributed themselves over the entire city, held up all pedestrians, stopped all vehicles, and thoroughly searched blacks for concealed weapons.[40]

Marines also received orders to search all black chauffeurs because of reported sniping by blacks from automobiles. Several chauffeurs remained on duty out of the "danger zone." A few minutes past 1:00 A.M. May 11, a black man drove across the street from the Charleston Hotel. When a marine tried to search him, the driver sharply stepped on the gas pedal in an effort to escape. The marine jumped onto the running board,

37. Charleston *News and Courier*, May 11, 1919, p. 3.
38. "Record of Proceedings," 250–52. See also Charleston *News and Courier*, May 11, 1919, p. 1.
39. "Record of Proceedings," 123–26, 157–59, 251–52.
40. Chicago *Defender*, May 17, 1919, p. 1. See also Charleston *News and Courier*, May 11, 1919, p. 3.

pulled his revolver, and forced the chauffeur to stop. Searching the man he found a loaded .32-caliber pistol. The chauffeur was thereupon forced to drive to the police station, where he was placed in the custody of the local authorities.[41]

About the same time, one hundred marines left their barracks and stationed themselves in groups of three around the city to stop all persons "for an accounting." They remained so posted the rest of the night. Authorities expected these men to stay on duty most of the next day as well. Meanwhile Mayor T. T. Hyde stayed in constant communication with the police department and also contacted Admiral Bryan. The mayor said the naval authorities cooperated fully with the police in the effort to suppress the rioting. Admiral Bryan asked that military men be kept in the police station overnight because of insufficient trucks to transport them back to the navy yard and the naval training station. No charges were made against any of these men.[42]

After 1:00 a.m. blacks received orders to abandon the city streets under penalty of arrest. The police station became crowded with military men and suspects of all kinds, especially those accused of carrying concealed weapons. All sailors were apprehended and first sent to Meeting and Columbus streets, where they boarded trucks for the navy yard. Late arrivals wound up at the police station. After a postmidnight tour of inspection, Rear Admiral F. E. Beatty ordered all sailors henceforth sent to the navy yard. From that time on, all bluejackets found on the streets, in streetcars, and in automobiles were taken into custody. When a truckload was rounded up, it went out of the city under marine escort.[43]

Meanwhile, the remaining mob proceeded up King Street to Columbus Street, where it paused. Some of the men wanted to go on, saying that "all kinds of negroes could be found further up," but the marines made every man in uniform enter the middle of the street and march toward Meeting Street. Wait-

41. Charleston *News and Courier*, May 11, 1919, p. 3.
42. *Ibid.*
43. *Ibid.*

ing at Meeting and Columbus streets stood a number of streetcars and trucks. Government cars, loaded to capacity, helped
in the transportation operation.[44]

While several thousand sailors and civilians controlled
Charleston, excitement ran high. Wild rumors circulated
quickly. All witnesses agreed that the bluejackets were after
black people only. No white civilians were attacked by the
rampaging sailors.

At 3:30 A.M. Sunday, May 11, it was impossible to get
accurate casualty figures. Police and hospital authorities continued efforts to locate wounded persons. Police believed that
some of the wounded blacks were carried home by friends and
that those cases would not be immediately known. The military men and white civilians refused to say what they knew
about the riot situation. According to police, black prisoners
and patients confessed ignorance of Isaac Doctor's death or
any other fatalities. All that was known was that after the
initial disturbance a "clean up" was implemented by the
bluejackets in the black residential and commercial districts.[45]

Preliminary casualty lists varied sharply. According to Chief
Black's statement to the press about the rioting, one person
died, one person was expected to die as a result of wounds
received, and seven people sustained injuries. The chief also
stated that as of 1:00 A.M. Sunday, May 11, the police and
provost guard had the situation under control.[46] Despite what
Chief Black said, the Memphis *Commercial Appeal* reported
two blacks dead and seventeen wounded and one sailor dead
and seven wounded.[47] The New York *Times* listed "two sailors
and four negroes" killed and "a number of persons wounded,
eight severely."[48] The Chicago *Defender* noted the deaths of
two sailors and four civilians with a number of persons

44. *Ibid.*
45. *Ibid.*, 1. See also Birmingham *News*, May 12, 1919, p. 2.
46. Charleston *News and Courier*, May 11, 1919, p. 3.
47. Memphis *Commercial Appeal*, May 11, 1919, p. 29, May 12, 1919, p. 1.
48. New York *Times*, May 11, 1919, p. 3.

wounded, eight seriously.[49] The Columbia (S.C.) *State* cited the deaths of two bluejackets and four blacks.[50] The Charleston *News and Courier* initially listed "at least one man believed killed" with seven sailors and eight blacks severely wounded.[51] Furthermore, William Tuttle reported two black men dead and seventeen wounded, seven sailors wounded, and a white police officer wounded.[52]

Out of the confusion it later became known that four black men, Isaac Doctor, James Talbert, William Brown, and William Randall, died as a result of the rioting.[53] At least seventeen black men, seven bluejackets, and one policeman sustained injuries. No extensive information on the wounded sailors could be ascertained on Sunday because medical cases among them requiring extensive attention went, in most instances, directly to the navy yard, though a naval surgeon was at Roper Hospital to render services to bluejackets as necessary.

At Roper the accommodations of the emergency room and wards were taxed to the utmost by the constant influx of wounded persons demanding instant treatment. So rapid became the flow of patients that hospital authorities were unable to keep accurate records of the admissions. The closest thing to a permanent record at Roper Hospital early Sunday morning was the list of those cases serious enough to require further treatment and confinement to a ward. The first case to be registered entered the hospital around 9:30 P.M. Saturday. Thereafter the interns and a number of surgeons found their services in constant demand. The police patrol was equally busy "plying its grim trade between the posts of call and the hospital."[54]

Amid the constant coming and going of wounded, eight

49. Chicago *Defender*, May 17, 1919, p. 1.
50. Columbia *State*, May 11, 1919, p. 1.
51. Charleston *News and Courier*, May 11, 1919, p. 1.
52. Tuttle, " 'Red Summer': 1919," 130.
53. "Record of Proceedings," 268–69. See also Charleston *News and Courier*, May 11, 1919, p. 3, May 12, 1919, p. 8.
54. Charleston *News and Courier*, May 11, 1919, p. 3.

cases were registered at Roper Hospital. Nick Arnold George, United States Navy, was hit by a brick; J. L. Wright had a heel lacerated when struck by a bottle; Ed Dubin, United States Navy, was hit in the jaw; Clifford Singleton, black, suffered lacerations about the head and shoulders; Ed Mitchell, black, had scalp wounds and contusions of the abdomen, right arm, and both hands; Gus Campbell, black, suffered a gunshot wound in the hip; William Brown, black, received a bullet wound in the right knee; and Nathan Flowers, black, was shot through the right thigh.[55]

The navy yard hospitalized the following persons. Special Policeman Bollman, white, was "struck in the head and painfully wounded"; Moses Gadsden, black, was shot in the leg; Peter Irving (or Irwin), black, was shot in the back; Edward Campbell, black, was cut about the head and face; James Wilson, black, got shot in the back; Charles Burton, black, received cuts about the body; and Isaac Moses, black, was bayoneted in the leg. Peter Irving, aged thirteen, became paralyzed from the waist down and was not expected to walk again. Yet, according to the Charleston *News and Courier*, "none of the wounded negroes is considered to be desperately hurt." Officially, twenty-four persons were known to have been hospitalized.[56]

A stray bullet Saturday night wounded a young black female walking on an uptown street. She and her companion were a considerable distance from the racial rioting, and officials supposed the wound was inflicted by a bullet fired into the air. Her name was not recorded "as the wound was not serious."[57]

From the beginning of trouble around 8:30 P.M. Saturday, May 10, police and provost guards began bringing men into the police station. Records showed that forty-nine arrests were made as follows: carrying concealed weapons, fifteen; detained without specific charge, twenty-seven; assaults on policemen, two; killing Isaac Doctor, two; and public drunk-

55. *Ibid.*
56. *Ibid.*, May 12, 1919, p. 8. See also "Record of Proceedings," 264–68.
57. Columbia *State*, May 12, 1919, p. 1.

enness, three. Scores of men were taken into custody and then turned over to naval authorities. Their names and offenses did not enter the police blotter.[58]

Because of the rioting, bluejackets at the navy yard and the naval training camp were denied leave. Only those carrying special permits got to leave the reservation and enter Charleston. Married sailors whose wives lived in Charleston received exemptions from the "operations of the drastic order." All "liberties" remained canceled by order of the naval commandant until further notice. A guard of thirty sailors was stationed on the streets to order all gobs back to their ships or wherever they might be stationed. The "no-leaves order" caused the War Camp Community Service to postpone its Sunday evening exercises.[59]

Sunday night tension in the streets ran high. Police and provost guards kept close watch on the situation and prepared to act vigorously in case the disorders recurred. However, police reported only minor conflicts. Someone supposedly fired five pistol shots into the air in the vicinity of Tradd and Legare streets at 9:30 P.M. When this incident gave rise to exaggerated rumors, Admiral Bryan, in a statement issued Sunday night, said, "No more sailors will be permitted to leave the Navy Yard unless they are married men living in Charleston until we make a full investigation of the cause or causes of the riotings. We will do everything in our power to come to the bottom of the regrettable affair and to make impossible the recurrence of another such night."[60]

Every sort of weapon had found some usage during the series of melees, from pistols and rifles to ordinary brickbats. At the police station rested a "remarkable collection" of missiles taken from men brought into custody, some under specific charges and others for detention. It was determined that the only serious property damage occurred at Fridie's Central Shaving Parlor. Damage proved slight at the looted shooting

58. Charleston *News and Courier*, May 12, 1919, p. 8.
59. *Ibid.*, May 12, 1919, p. 8, May 13, 1919, p. 12.
60. *Ibid.*, May 12, 1919, p. 8.

galleries. Nearly all the firearms taken from the rifle ranges were recovered. This small arsenal consisted of eighteen rifles and seven revolvers. Supposedly the pistols saw action as clubs because, when examined by police, they turned out to be fully loaded.[61]

Rumors floated all day Monday, May 12. One grew out of the fact that some blacks in an automobile on Vanderhorst Street fired upon a group of marines standing near the police station. In anticipation of renewed hostilities a score of provost guards was held in reserve on the receiving ship *Hartford*. Although no trouble occurred, police officials took no chances. "We haven't the slightest conception how long the naval officers will continue their order to return all sailors to their posts," said Lieutenant Conrad Stender after assigning the guard to beats, "but in the circumstances it is an essential thing to avoid further trouble between negroes and bluejackets."[62]

Monday afternoon, assurances of a thorough investigation of the causes of the rioting persisted. The navy yard reported that no sailors were killed and that none of the injured remained on the "serious" list. It was announced that Mayor Hyde, Admiral Beatty, Solicitor Thomas P. Stoney, County Coroner John G. Mansfield, Police Chief Black, and several naval officers had held a conference Sunday at the police station in which the riot situation underwent free canvassing. Immediately after leaving the conference Mayor Hyde had issued the following statement:

There will be an investigation into the cause of the riot and steps will be taken to guard against future occurrences of the same order. Monday morning I will ask W. G. Fridie, whose barber shop on King Street was demolished by the sailors, to draw up a bill of damages to be presented to the city government. This might set a precedent, but the negroes of Charleston must be protected. We are hoping that this morning saw the end of the disturbances, but if the action is taken by the negroes against whites, or vice versa, I will ask that martial law be established.[63]

61. *Ibid.* See also "Record of Proceedings," 103–107, 250–51.
62. Charleston *News and Courier*, May 12, 1919, p. 8.
63. *Ibid.*, May 12, 1919, p. 8, May 13, 1919, p. 12.

An agreement concurred in by city, state, and federal officials gave the latter custody of prisoners until a full investigation revealed the extent of their participation in Isaac Doctor's
death. County Coroner Mansfield announced that an inquest
into the deaths of Doctor and Talbert would be held in the
Fireproof Building on Thursday, May 15, at noon. Jacob Cohen
and Frank Holliday, sailors, who stood accused of killing
Doctor, were placed in the custody of naval authorities.[64]

In police court Monday the blotter was disposed of by
Recorder Theodore D. Jervey, Jonah Middleton, Daniel Poin-
sette, Arthur McCall, S. Lee, Clarence Johnson, Isaac Giles,
Thomas Reed, and Peter Williams were fined fifty dollars each
for carrying concealed weapons. Fred Hendricks forfeited his
hundred-dollar bond by failing to appear for trial. All others,
except for those charged with inciting to riot, received dismis-
sals with a cautionary talk from the recorder. Isaac Williams
and John Simmons (both black) and George Moran (a white
sailor) had to appear before Magistrate B. R. Burnet charged
with inciting to riot; however, all three were acquitted. A third
black man, Henry Williams, remained incarcerated for further
investigation.[65]

Various reports continued to circulate regarding the street
disorders. One rumor persisted that Roper Hospital had been
attacked by blacks. It was declared untrue Monday evening,
since "no one had fired on the hospital." Another rumor said
that blacks had fired on the police station, but it too proved
false. All sorts of fanciful tales gained currency, but none could
be substantiated.[66]

Meanwhile, Chief Black especially commended Lieutenant
Edward R. McDonald, who had been with him at the height of
the rioting, for his "splendid performance of duty" Saturday
night. Chief Black also directed public attention to the policemen who voluntarily had returned to their duty stations upon
learning of the seriousness of the rioting. The chief said he felt

64. *Ibid.*, May 12, 1919, p. 8.
65. *Ibid.*, May 13, 1919, p. 12.
66. *Ibid.*

"the police had done all in their power in consideration of the circumstances."[67]

Because "conditions with which the civil officials cannot cope may arise, at any time," namely renewed and more intense racial rioting based on recollections from slavery and Reconstruction days, the reorganization of the South Carolina National Guard proved "imperatively necessary," said Governor Robert A. Cooper. He made these remarks Monday in connection with a call from Adjutant General William W. Moore for a convention of national guardsmen to be held at Columbia on Tuesday, May 20, when plans for such a reorganization would be discussed. Both the governor and the adjutant general wanted full representation from every part of the state at the proposed convention, because they felt that a well-trained national guard was one of the "primary essentials now facing the State." The recent racial rioting in Charleston, "which could break out in any section of South Carolina," had vividly emphasized the need. The governor decided that the convention would be held in the senate chamber of the state legislative library at the capital.[68] Governor Cooper, in another press release, said, "There are many reasons why the National Guard should be immediately reorganized.... There would be great potential danger in such a situation. The welfare of the nation also demands the reestablishment of the National Guard.... We cannot afford to be without a citizen soldiery."[69]

Adjutant General Moore, who had just returned from a meeting of the National Guard of the United States, held in St. Louis May 5, 6, and 7, issued a statement at the behest of Governor Cooper. Each state was urged to immediately reorganize its national guard. Moore noted, "It is especially desired that all former officers and enlisted men of the National Guard be represented [at the Columbia meeting]. All officers of the reserve militia and enlisted personnel, as well as all citi-

67. *Ibid.*
68. *Ibid.*, 1.
69. *Ibid.*

zens who are interested in the future organization and development of a strong and efficient National Guard be present on this occasion, and they are cordially invited to take part in this reorganization."[70]

In the meantime, all riot patients in Roper Hospital showed marked improvement, although none were discharged. All riot victims had improved enough to merit placement on the "fair" list.[71]

Although the Charleston *News and Courier* chose not to editorialize the rioting, the Columbia *State* printed an article on its editorial page under the heading "Not a Charlestonians' Row." It read:

> In the city of Charleston the relationship between the white and negro race have been as good as they have been in any other American city, North or South, the last forty years. While race conflicts have not been infrequent in New York and Philadelphia, and many other smaller cities, no violent clash between negroes and whites has taken place in Charleston. Even Boston newspapers have in the last ten years reported at least one incident of this kind of conflict, but not since the political riots about the close of the Reconstruction period has Charleston had them.
>
> The affair Saturday night, perhaps not so serious as reported yesterday, between sailors and negroes was not a Charleston riot, so far as the white citizenry of Charleston is concerned. After the trouble some Charlestonians may have participated in it, but it may be set down that they were in no sense representative of the community.
>
> For the maintenance of kindly relations between the races, due to the uniformly considerate and good behavior of both blacks and whites, Charleston's record is excellent. What happened Saturday night, with sailors and negroes as parties, might have happened anywhere.
>
> The investigation of the riot should be thorough and prompt and the guilty should be punished.[72]

All was quiet Tuesday, May 13, in Charleston. However, reports of shooting in the upper part of the city and in the

70. *Ibid.*
71. *Ibid.*, 12.
72. Columbia *State*, May 12, 1919, p. 4.

immediate suburbs late Wednesday night caused various rumors to circulate. Especially detailed policemen thoroughly investigated, and according to their report the shooting came from the back of a truck on which bluejackets traveled up the Meeting Street Road. Chief Black, who said no reports of injury to any person had been received, mentioned that his information showed shooting had occurred and that the naval yard authorities knew of the incident and planned to take action. County Sheriff J. Elmore Martin said rural police heard the shooting and reported it to him. Martin also said no injuries had been reported. Many people telephoned the police station saying they heard gunfire.[73]

On Thursday, May 15, County Coroner Mansfield held an inquest into the deaths of Isaac Doctor and James Talbert. Testimony came from Police Chief Black; Police Lieutenant McDonald; Harry Police, who ran the pool hall at Market and Charles streets; Senior Detective Charles Levy; Policeman Chris Redell; and Senior Lieutenant W. W. Thompson, who with Junior Lieutenant A. G. Sanford of the naval yard acted as counsel for the accused sailors, Jacob Cohen and George Holliday. Others present were Solicitor Thomas P. Stoney and Sheriff Martin.[74]

During the proceedings the defendants, who sat in the custody of three marines, did not testify. Speaking of the investigation by naval officials, Lieutenant Thompson said that the work done so far tried to ascertain whether the outbreak Saturday, May 10, arose from a series of incidents or hard feeling between enlisted men and black people. The result of the investigation, he said, "was the reassuring conviction of all officials that the disturbance was a spontaneous outburst, the like of which has occurred throughout the country. The exact cause of the outbreak is still unrevealed."[75]

The first witness was Harry Police. He testified that around 9:30 Saturday night several sailors came into his poolroom,

73. Charleston *News and Courier*, May 15, 1919, p. 2.
74. *Ibid.*, May 16, 1919, p. 10.
75. *Ibid.*

grabbed cues and billiard balls, and ran out into the street followed by black men in the place who also took out cues and balls. He immediately closed his establishment. Contradicting him, Officer Chris Redell quoted Police in his report to his superiors as saying "that negroes entered the pool room, grabbed cues and balls and attacked the sailors outside of the store." Redell also said that about 8:50 p.m. Saturday while stationed at King and Wentworth streets he heard shooting that seemed to come from the direction of Market and Charles streets. When he arrived at the pool hall he heard that "several sailors had been taken away wounded." When Redell reached 55 Charles Street bystanders told him the "gobs had been attacked from that house, and while there the bluejackets had attempted to surround the house and gain entrance." Redell rounded up the sailors and put them in charge of several provost guards. He added, "They did not resist arrest."[76]

Lieutenant McDonald described the scene when he and Detective Levy arrived after the first call to the police station related to the racial disturbance. He testified that when he and Levy reached Beaufain Street, between Charles and Wilson streets, a sailor came out of an alley with his hands clasped to his side saying that "a negro had shot him." The sailor was immediately rushed to Roper Hospital in a police patrol car. McDonald then heard that a man had been killed at 155 Market Street and rushed to the scene accompanied by Levy and Chief Black. While standing in front of the house McDonald heard someone say that the two men who had shot the black man were "the two standing nearby." He placed them under arrest, took from them two .22-caliber rifles, and turned the men over to Chief Black. The body of the black man was placed in the police wagon. McDonald later charged the sailors Jacob Cohen and George Holliday with "shooting to kill."[77]

Next, Chief Black took the stand to relate the following account:

76. Ibid.
77. Ibid.

Upon reaching the rear of 155 Market Street I found the lot
crowded with enlisted men and negroes. . . . I examined the negro
and could find no trace of any weapon, nor was there any signs
that a scuffle had taken place. ... It was here that Lieut.
McDonald gave me the prisoners. I marched them to the police
station, enroute to which they made the following statement to
me, repeating it upon arrival at the station house. "We each shot
him twice. He was throwing rocks, and an army officer with two
gold bars told us that if, when he told a negro to halt and he didn't
do it we were to shoot him." It seems that after Holliday fired his
second shot the negro fell. . . .
    Later in the day . . . R. O. Coleman ran into the station house all
out of breath, and asked me to take him in charge, saying that he
was implicated in the shooting scrape with the other two sailors
and that the walls looked better to him than the mob outside.[78]

Coleman also sat in court with Cohen and Holliday.

The verdict in the inquest for Isaac Doctor read that he came
to his death May 11, 1919, at Roper Hospital, from a gunshot
wound in the chest inflicted by "unknown enlisted men during
a riot in this City between enlisted men and negroes." The
verdict concerning James Talbert's death was similar, except
that it read "inflicted by party or parties unknown to this
jury." Talbert died of gunshot wounds in the abdomen. Both
men "came to their death[s] from wounds inflicted with a rifle
or pistol, in the opinion of the jury, in the hands of enlisted men
while engaged in a riot on May 10." The Court of General
Sessions Grand Jury did not investigate the Charleston riot or
mention it in its final report.[79] After the inquest verdict Cohen,
Holliday, and Coleman were turned over to naval officials,
who received responsibility "as to what course will be pursued."[80]

According to Lieutenant Thompson, who conducted the
preliminary Navy Department inquiry, Cohen, Holliday, and
Coleman would be held in custody until the case could be
disposed of by a board of inquiry. It was thought that the naval
inquiry would last several weeks. The first report was sup-

78. *Ibid.*
79. *Ibid.*, May 16, 1919, p. 10; June 13, 1919, p. 8.
80. *Ibid.*, May 16, 1919, p. 10.

posed to be given to Admiral Beatty on May 16, 1919. Meanwhile, in a statement released May 15, Beatty said it was entirely up to city officials when the bluejackets would be permitted to receive city "liberties" again. Relative to a report that army officers planned an inquiry into the part soldiers had played in the rioting, Colonel H. C. Merriam, chief of staff, Southeastern Department, said, "The reports of soldiers who were on guard from midnight of Saturday [May 10] until 4 o'clock Sunday morning [May 11], state that not a soldier was seen on the streets. When our attention is called to the fact that soldiers played an active part in the riot we will surely hold an investigation. This so far has not been done."[81]

Mayor Hyde was informed Thursday, May 15, by Admiral Bryan that the alleged shooting by bluejackets from a truck proceeding up Meeting Street Road Wednesday, May 14, came "solely by the back-firing of the gasoline engines and that none of the bluejackets had fired a shot from the vehicle." Immediately upon the truck's arrival at the naval yard, officers launched an investigation. They found that none of the sailors on the truck had guns and that the "wild reports" were due to "local tension following the street disorders Saturday night." Mayor Hyde said he felt gratified to know the reports of shooting by sailors were groundless.[82]

The mysterious gray automobile, which figured in the shooting at marines in front of the police station Saturday night, was found. The man who presumably drove the car at the time landed in jail. Leroy Jackson, a black, drew the charges of aggravated assault, firing at marines who were returning fire in the discharge of their duty, and inciting a riot at St. Philip and Vanderhorst streets. The automobile, a six-passenger Zozier, according to the newspaper account "presented a concrete example of the marksmanship of the 'soldiers of the sea.' The rear of it had a clean hole through which a bullet had passed." Two glancing shots appeared next to the driver's seat,

81. *Ibid.*
82. *Ibid.*, 3.

and two others showed up on the opposite side. Jackson's companions could not be found.[83]

It also became known that a number of black people, who had been assaulted by sailors, marines, and civilians, had received injuries although they had not entered Roper Hospital. Some investigators of this development now placed the total number wounded at more than sixty.[84] Meanwhile, the situation in Charleston Thursday night was "quiet in every way." No rumors of any shooting or other disorder gained currency. However, the police department continued its strict vigilance.

Charleston on Saturday night, May 17, was quiet, although most of the streets were darkened by an accident at the Consolidated Company producing a partial failure of the lighting system. Police reported that "excellent order prevailed in all parts of the town." Mayor Hyde said Saturday afternoon that he had been in close touch with army and navy officers regarding the riot situation. He told them the city "did not object to the presence of soldiers and bluejackets, provost guards to be on duty, of course."[85]

On Sunday, May 18, a letter written by Admiral Bryan appeared in the Charleston *News and Courier* saying that sailors had nothing to do with any shooting incidents May 14.[86] Bluejackets, who had been prohibited from entering Charleston, expressed elation at noon Tuesday, May 20, when orders stated, pending good behavior, that their usual liberties would be resumed. Wednesday morning the normal flow of sailors into the city was expected, though sixty provost guards and twenty marines established a temporary headquarters at the police station. Naval and civil officials related the opinion that tension had lessened to the point where they deemed it "proper for bluejackets to be in the streets."[87]

83. *Ibid.*, 10.
84. Columbia *State*, May 16, 1919, p. 2. See also Charleston *News and Courier*, May 16, 1919, p. 3; "Record of Proceedings," 179–183.
85. Charleston *News and Courier*, May 18, 1919, p. 1H.
86. *Ibid.*, 10H.
87. *Ibid.*, May 21, 1919, p. 10.

In the aftermath of the rioting, a committee of black ministers and laymen sent a manifesto, written May 16, to the Charleston *News and Courier.* The committee consisted of E. L. Baskervill, chairman; C. H. Uggams, secretary; J. R. Pranon; F. B. Nelson; P. J. Chavis; R. R. Madison; W. P. Jones; C. A. Harrison; W. H. Johnson, M.D.; Edward C. Mickey; and Edwin A. Harleston. The manifesto, noting the riot situation and its consequences, suggested:

1. That the naval authorities be requested to take steps to prevent the further occurrence of lawlessness by enlisted men.
2. That the police force be enlarged to a number sufficient to assure protection to all persons and property in the community.
3. That an addition of men of the negro race be placed on the police force, who will encourage respect for law and order in the minds of the negroes of this city.
4. That an appointment of a committee be made which will confer and cooperate with a like committee of negroes upon questions of interest to the community and to the negroes, and which will strive to appreciate the viewpoint of the negroes.
5. That the pulpit and press use their influence to discourage the mob spirit and race antipathy, and to advocate praiseworthy endeavors for all people.
6. That social justice and a square deal be given to all people.
7. That the housing, lighting, sanitary and educational conditions of the negroes of this city be improved.[88]

In the meantime, the navy yard began its full-scale investigation into the racial rioting of May 10 and 11, 1919.[89] After lengthy and detailed hearings by the board of inquiry, Roscoe Coleman, George T. Holliday, and Jacob Cohen were court-martialed. Coleman was acquitted, but Cohen and Holliday were sentenced to a year's imprisonment at the Parris Island, South Carolina, Naval Prison with the possibility of parole after serving one-third of their terms, after which they would be dishonorably discharged.[90]

88. *Ibid.,* May 25, 1919, p. 8H.
89. "Record of Proceedings of a Court of Inquiry Convened at the Navy Yard, Charleston, South Carolina," May 27, 1919, National Archives and Records Service, Record Group 125.
90. Letters to United States Representative William A. Ashbrook and United States Senator Atlee Pomerene from George R. Clark, Judge Advocate General,

In retrospect, the economic, social, and historical causes of interracial maladjustment, compounded by years of physical and psychological abuse on both sides, combined to produce the Charleston riot. Pushed over the edge of racial accommodation as in the Tulsa, Brownsville, Chicago, Washington, and other riots, blacks were forced to defend themselves without overtly demonstrating vengeful retaliation or retribution. However, these "soldiers," lacking training yet placed in the front lines on America's city streets, soon developed various stratagems for survival. All the while they knew the "enemy" would not only face them but also stand at their backs.

Jan. 3, 1920, *ibid.* See also letter to United States Representative Charles P. Coady from George R. Clark, Judge Advocate General, Jan. 16, 1920, *ibid.;* letter to United States Senator Kenneth D. McKellar from George R. Clark, Judge Advocate General, Jan. 16, 1920, *ibid.*

Reflections on a Murder: The Emmett Till Case

William M. Simpson

An ominous cloud hovered over white Mississippians as they readied for the state Democratic primary in August, 1955—a recent United States Supreme Court dictum that would surely shred the fabric of Mississippi society. In the state with the largest percentage of black residents proportionally, a decree ruling segregated public schools unconstitutional was tantamount, many whites feared, to endorsing miscegenation and "mongrelization."[1] Although the Warren Court later modified its momentous decision, declaring vaguely that desegregation was to commence with "all deliberate speed," an apprehensive mood prevailed among Mississippians, and the overriding concern in the governor's primary focused squarely upon the candidates' ability to circumvent federally planned desegregation.

1. Thomas P. Brady's *Black Monday* (Winona, Miss., 1955) appeared shortly after *Brown* v. *Board of Education*. Brady, at the time a member of the Mississippi Supreme Court, took as title for his tract a phrase coined by Congressman John Bell Williams, later governor of Mississippi, in reference to the day upon which the court ruling was rendered. *Black Monday* stood as a testament to those who believed that the "Brown case" was wrought by Communist forces within the judiciary and feared that school desegregation meant an end to "racial purity."

The vast majority of Mississippi's black population had not been aroused by the judicial attack upon segregation. The few who challenged the state's social and political traditions often succeeded only in illuminating the hazards of "stepping out of place." In May, 1955, the Reverend George W. Lee of Belzoni was killed by a shotgun blast from a passing car. He had been active in voter registration throughout Humphreys County.[2] Several months later Lamar Smith, another black political activist, was gunned down in broad daylight on the courthouse square in Brookhaven. These two murders underscored the strained racial atmosphere in Mississippi during the 1955 state elections.

Unaware of the grave crisis threatening Mississippi's status quo, vacationing fourteen-year-old Emmett Louis Till, a black Chicago youth, entered the state in late summer to visit relatives near Money, a placid, tiny outpost in the cotton-rich Delta of Leflore County. His violent death within a few days after arrival would bring worldwide opprobrium upon the state. The incident responsible for Till's tragic end occurred on the night of August 24, when the youngster entered a general store in Money attended by Carolyn Bryant, an attractive white woman. What transpired is veiled in controversy; later, most accounts depicted Till making lewd advances upon Mrs. Bryant before leaving the premises with a "wolf whistle" directed at her.[3] In the early morning of August 28 Till was abducted from his uncle's house, and three days later his body was discovered floating in the Tallahatchie River near Philipp,

2. For a detailed treatment of the death of George Lee, see Jack Mendelshon, *The Martyrs* (New York, 1966).

3. This version of the store incident was offered by Carolyn Bryant in the subsequent trial of the defendants, including her husband, in Till's murder. Other reports emanating from the store encounter held that the lad merely whistled at Mrs. Bryant. Recently, one interested in the case presented information obtained from a locally respected source indicating that Till's demeanor was completely unobtrusive while alone in the store with Mrs. Bryant. According to the account, playmates who accompanied Till into Money later fabricated the "store incident" as a joke to play on their visiting cousin. See David A. Shostak, "Crosby Smith: Forgotten Witness to a Mississippi Nightmare," *Negro History Bulletin,* XXXVIII (Dec., 1974–Jan., 1975), 321

another small farming community several miles northeast of Money.

Although the murder of Emmett Till appeared, in 1955, a possible climax awaiting any black male who broached the sanctum of "unsoiled" southern femininity, a serious student of the case concluded that the turbulent political situation in Mississippi stemming from awaited court-ordered desegregation was a congruent factor in the murder and trial.[4] Another chronicler of the Till murder attributed to J. J. Breland, dean of the defense that represented those accused of killing Till, the appraisal that the wanton act would not have occurred except for "Black Monday."[5]

Shortly after Till was abducted, Roy Bryant, husband of Carolyn, and his half-brother J. W. Milam were arrested on charges of kidnapping. Prior to the arrests Till's uncle, Moses Wright, told Leflore County authorities that at approximately 2:00 A.M. August 28 three white men approached his house and that two of them entered seeking his nephew. According to Wright's account Till was forced outside to an automobile, where he was identified by a fourth person, thought to be a woman. The abductors then sped away with the captive lad. Later both Bryant and Milam confessed the kidnapping to arresting officers, but claimed they released Till unharmed when Mrs. Bryant failed to recognize him as her molester.[6] The two additional figures that Wright linked to the abduction were never identified or apprehended.

4. Hugh S. Whitaker, "A Case Study in Southern Justice: The Emmett Till Case" (M.A. thesis, Florida State University, 1963), ix. Whitaker's study is to date perhaps the most exhaustive account of the kidnap-murder of Till. Another work, upon which Whitaker relies heavily, is William B. Huie's *Wolf Whistle and Other Stories* (New York, 1959). Although Huie's source material has frequently received challenge, the book nonetheless deserves attention by those who explore the Till case. Reflecting lesser merit, assorted tracts and pamphlets published soon after Till's murder depict primarily the more sordid aspects of the crime.

5. Huie, *Wolf Whistle,* 41.

6. *Ibid.,* 25; Memphis *Commercial Appeal,* Aug. 30, 1955; Greenwood *Commonwealth,* Aug. 29, 1955; Clarksdale *Press Register,* Sept. 2, 1955; Jackson *Clarion-Ledger,* Sept. 19, 1955; New Orleans *Times-Picayune,* Sept. 19, 1955; "Trial by Jury," *Time,* LXVI (Oct. 3, 1955), 18; "The Place, the Acquittal," *Newsweek,* XLVI (Oct. 3, 1955), 29.

On August 31, two days after the arrest of Bryant and Milam, Till's body was discovered in the Tallahatchie River by several young fishermen, who promptly notified the authorities. The corpse, weighed down by a cotton gin fan, was badly decomposed. A bullet hole was found in the head, and it appeared as though the grotesque figure had been "brutally beaten." Moses Wright was summoned to identify the body, after which it was taken to a nearby funeral home.[7]

After the discovery of Till's body, Bryant and Milam, already in jail at Greenwood, were charged with murder. Although the kidnapping had occurred in Leflore County, the corpse was found in adjoining Tallahatchie County. Thus, jurisdiction in the murder case fell to the latter, where there were two county seats. Because the circuit court session convened during September in the western seat, Sumner, the murder charge against Bryant and Milam would be adjudicated there.

Initial reaction across the state to the murder of Emmett Till was generally outrage and indignation. Governor Hugh White called for a "vigorous prosecution" of the responsible parties, emphasizing that "Mississippi deplores such conduct on the part of its citizens and certainly cannot condone it."[8] The Mississippi press recoiled aggressively against the crime, even the arch-conservative Jackson *Clarion Ledger* and Jackson *Daily News*. The capital's two dailies proclaimed that "everyone is in solid agreement that it was a stupid, horrible crime. Intelligent Mississippians can only suppose it came about in the sick mind[s] of men who should be removed from society by due course of law."[9] Especially outspoken in demanding retribution for the killing was the Clarksdale *Press Register:* "If conviction with maximum penalty of the law cannot be secured in this heinous crime, then Mississippi may as well burn all its law books and close its courts, for we cannot then stand before the nation and world as a self-governing

7. Whitaker, "The Emmett Till Case," 117–18; Memphis *Commercial Appeal*, Sept. 1, 1955; Greenwood *Commonwealth*, Aug. 31, 1955.
8. Memphis *Commercial Appeal*, Sept. 2, 1955; Greenville *Delta Democrat-Times*, Sept. 1, 1955.
9. Jackson *Daily News*, Sept. 2, 1955; Jackson *Clarion-Ledger*, Sept. 3, 1955.

state capable of making and enforcing its own laws and punishing [those] who most grievously offend those laws."[10]

In Tallahatchie and Leflore counties residents were more disturbed by outside attention invading their domain than by the murder. However, many did desire swift punishment of the guilty. Leflore County Deputy Sheriff John Ed Cothran offered a popular reaction to the slaying, commenting that most folks in the region were "decent" and would not allow the guilty to go unpunished. Several days after the discovery of Till's body, the local power structure refused to back the accused. Initially Bryant and Milam were unable to secure legal representation because the local lawyers demanded fees that they knew the half-brothers could not afford.[11]

Mississippi's hostile attitude toward the men charged with kidnap-murder soon tempered with a heavy influx of northern recriminations. Numerous accounts labeling the murder a lynching infuriated many within the state.[12] Particularly distressing to the locals were frequent assertions that the state as a whole was responsible for the crime. This, coupled with derogatory misquotes often found in the Jackson papers, played a significant role in bringing a sudden shift among Mississippians, especially in the region of the murder, toward support of the accused. Within less than a week after the discovery of Till's corpse, Tallahatchie County "leaders" had decided to defend Bryant and Milam.[13]

District Attorney Gerald Chatham, serving the judicial region that included Tallahatchie County, voiced concern over the "constant agitation" of the NAACP and others, warning that the interference would arouse resentment within the state

10. Clarksdale *Press Register*, Sept. 1, 1955.

11. "A Boy Goes Home," *Newsweek*, XLVI (Sept. 12, 1955), 32; Whitaker, "The Emmett Till Case," 119–21.

12. The executive secretary of the NAACP, Roy Wilkins, branded the crime a lynching and proclaimed that "it would appear that the state of Mississippi has decided to maintain white supremacy by murdering children." See Memphis *Commercial Appeal*, Sept. 1, 1955.

13. Whitaker, "The Emmett Till Case," 122–25. Whitaker provides a thorough description and analysis of state and local reevaluation of the Till murder after much adverse publicity began to emerge.

that could jeopardize prosecution of the accused. Jackson *Clarion-Ledger* scribe Tom Ethridge echoed the sentiment of legions in Mississippi when he penned that agitation by outsiders in the Till murder gave all the indications of a "communist plot" to destroy southern society. One aroused patriot from a neighboring state wrote that if Bryant and Milam were convicted of murder "it will clear the right-of-way for Communist carpetbaggers to step up their raping and murdering."[14] Projecting moderation, the Greenville *Delta Democrat-Times* editorialized that both sides—those in sympathy with and those against the accused—were guilty of overzealous reaction. Critical of Mississippians who sought to whitewash the case, the paper also maintained that the NAACP displayed "macabre exhibitionism" designed to purposely vent Mississippi indignation and bring about acquittal for the defendants. It charged that the civil rights organization would then use the acquittal as ammunition against the South.[15]

The first tangible sign of local support for Bryant and Milam came three days after Till's body was pulled from the river. At this juncture, Tallahatchie County Sheriff H. C. Strider expressed reservations regarding the identification of the corpse. He concluded that the body was much too decomposed to have been in the river only a few days. According to the sheriff's account, even Moses Wright "wasn't sure" about the identity until some of his children claimed a ring found on the deceased belonged to Till. Strider surmised that the "whole thing looks like a deal made up by the National Association for the Advancement of Colored People."[16] Shortly after Sheriff Strider's stunning revelation, Bryant and Milam were able to obtain

---

14. Memphis *Commercial Appeal*, Sept. 4, 1955, Jackson *Clarion-Ledger*, Sept. 6, 1955; Greenville *Delta Democrat-Times*, Sept. 16, 1955. Letters defending the accused found on editorial pages of newspapers often bore one of three themes: the fanfare accompanying the case was either a Communist conspiracy, another attempt by northerners to interfere in southern affairs as in Reconstruction, or an attempt to assail protection of white women against the "lustful desires" of black males.

15. Greenville *Delta Democrat-Times*, Sept. 6, 1955.

16. *Ibid.*, Sept. 4, 1955; Memphis *Commercial Appeal*, Sept. 4, 1955; Jackson *Clarion-Ledger*, Sept. 4, 1955.

defense counsel from the attorneys who recently had scorned the service.

While local support swelled for the defendants, the funeral for Emmett Till was held in Chicago. The morbid spectacle attendant with the service amassed even greater sentiment across Mississippi favoring the half-brothers. Till's body lay in state from Saturday, September 3, until the following Tuesday, when burial occurred. The corpse had been shipped from Mississippi with the understanding that a closed-casket funeral would be observed, because the deteriorated condition of the body had restricted a mortician's service. However, when the casket arrived in Chicago Till's mother, Mamie Bradley, demanded it be opened for all "to see what they did to my boy." The appalling sight triggered an "emotional explosion" from those who filed past the coffin. Over a three-day span thousands flocked to view the now-martyred Till. The occasion proved a financial bonanza for the NAACP, as contributions of "fighting dollars" poured into the organization from patrons enraged by the murder.[17] Many in Mississippi and elsewhere looked upon the funeral as a disgusting extravaganza planned for pecuniary gain and with intent to incite inflammatory reaction against the Magnolia State.

While Till's body lay subject to public view in Chicago, alarming rumors spread across Mississippi that angry blacks from Illinois were coming into the state to "tear up" Greenwood, where Bryant and Milam were thought to be detained.[18] Labor Day weekend traffic compounded the worry of state authorities guarding against the alleged "invasion." A roadblock immediately north of Clarksdale on Highway 61 netted several motorists with Illinois license plates; however, the local sheriff denied the procedure was aimed at preventing certain carloads from entering the state.[19]

17. Greenville *Delta Democrat-Times*, Sept. 4, 1955; Memphis *Commercial Appeal*, Sept. 4, 7, 1955; "A Boy Goes Home," 32; Huie, *Wolf Whistle*, 26; Whitaker, "The Emmett Till Case," 124.
18. Numerous threatening letters and telephone calls had prompted the secret transfer of Bryant and Milam to Greenville.
19. Memphis *Commercial Appeal*, Sept. 4, 1955; Jackson *Clarion-Ledger*, Sept. 4, 1955; Jackson *Advocate*, Sept. 10, 1955; Clarksdale *Press Register*, Sept. 5, 1955.

On Monday, September 5, the Tallahatchie County grand
jury convened in Sumner, among its cases the Till murder. An
eighteen-member body was quickly selected. The first day's
session recessed without a decision in the Till case. The jury
listened to testimony from Leflore County Sheriff George
Smith and his deputy John Ed Cothran, along with Tallahatchie County Sheriff Strider and his deputy Garland Mel-
ton. Strider reiterated his earlier contention that the body
recovered from the river on August 31 was not that of Till.
Deputy Cothran offered contrary testimony, convinced that
identification was beyond doubt.[20]

On Tuesday the grand jury heard testimony from Moses
Wright and one of his sons. The two reconstructed events
surrounding the kidnapping and maintained that it had been
Till's body later pulled from the Tallahatchie River near
Philipp. Dr. L. B. Otken, a Greenwood physician who had
examined the corpse, was summoned to attend the session but
was never called before the jury. Dr. Otken shared Sheriff
Strider's opinion that the body claimed as Till's was much too
deteriorated for such a brief period in the water.[21]

When all testimony had been concluded in Tuesday's hearing, the grand jury solemnly indicted Roy Bryant and J. W.
Milam with kidnapping and murder. Later in the day the two
men were arraigned before Judge Curtis L. Swango—a highly
respected jurist serving the Seventeenth Judicial District in
Mississippi—where they pleaded not guilty to both counts.[22]
Afterward Judge Swango announced that a trial date would be
set later in the week.

In light of the polarizing sentiment within the state and local
community against prosecution of the half-brothers, the grand
jury indictment came as a surprise to many.[23] The Tal-

20. Memphis *Commercial Appeal*, Sept. 6, 1955.
21. *Ibid.*, Sept. 7, 1955; Clarksdale *Press Register*, Sept. 6, 1955; Greenwood
Commonwealth, Sept. 6, 1955; Jackson *Clarion-Ledger*, Sept. 7, 1955.
22. *State of Mississippi* v. *Roy Bryant and J. W. Milam*, Tallahatchie County,
Miss., Second Circuit Court District, Case No. 1,959 (Sept., 1955); Memphis
Commercial Appeal, Sept. 7, 1955.
23. Later in September, during the murder trial in the Till case, the Lincoln
County grand jury failed to bring an indictment against the murderers of

lahatchie County prosecuting attorney Hamilton Caldwell later confided that he was opposed to indictment because the prosecution faced an impossible task in gaining conviction. Caldwell believed that a white jury would "turn loose" anyone who had murdered a Negro accused of grossly insulting a white woman.[24]

Reactions from black spokesmen across the state and elsewhere to the grand jury indictment were generally laudatory. Percy Greene, editor of the Jackson *Advocate*, commented, "The fact remains that the Tallahatchie County grand jury, made up of white men, took this step against other white men for a crime against a Negro. . . . The prompt action of the grand jury in the Till case indicates that the people of contemporary Mississippi are against this form of murder (lynching) as against other forms of murder."[25] Ed Cochran, president of the Greenwood NAACP, applauded the grand jury action and declared that he had "not lost faith in a trial by jury." Dr. J. H. Jackson of Chicago, presiding at a black Baptist convention in Memphis, secured floor approval of a resolution commending Mississippi officials for the "speedy handling of the case."[26]

Speculation that the Till murder case might be postponed until the spring term of circuit court ended when Judge Swango set the trial date for September 19. A special venire of 120 prospective jurors was drawn in addition to the regular panel, from which 12 would be selected on the initial day of the trial. Although the Tallahatchie County grand jury had charged Bryant and Milam with kidnapping and murder, the case tried in Sumner would deal only with the murder count since abduction had occurred in Leflore County.

Lamar Smith, although the crime occurred on a courthouse lawn before numerous bystanders. The Tallahatchie County grand jury indicted Bryant and Milam on far less conclusive evidence. However, the Till case attracted much more interest, and certainly greater pressures were exerted for indictment.

24. See Whitaker, "The Emmett Till Case," 130. In a recent interview with me, one of the attorneys who defended Bryant and Milam ascribed much validity to Caldwell's contention.

25. Jackson *Advocate*, Sept. 17, 1955.

26. Grenada *Daily Sentinel-Star*, Sept. 7, 1955; Memphis *Commercial Appeal*, Sept. 8, 1955; Jackson *Clarion-Ledger*, Sept. 10, 1955.

   The burden of prosecution in the murder case rested primarily upon District Attorney Gerald Chatham, who planned retirement at the end of his current term. County Prosecutor Caldwell proved to be of little assistance because of a recent heart attack. Ordinarily, prosecution received support and investigative help from the sheriff's office, but in this instance Sheriff Strider had become a willing ally of the defense. Confronted with these obstacles, Chatham appealed to State Attorney General J. P. Coleman, recent victor in the Democratic gubernatorial primary, for assistance. Coleman immediately appointed Robert B. Smith, former FBI agent, as special prosecutor in the case.[27]
   As the trial grew closer, the verbal battle continued between those demanding conviction and defensive Mississippians. Representative of the former camp, one moralist declared that unless Mississippi acted "forthrightly to avenge" the murder of Emmett Till federal troops should be dispatched into the state in order to secure justice. Typical of the outspoken seeking to clear the state's name was one who penned: "If anyone is guilty, other than the actual killer or killers, it is the United States Supreme Court. As certain as daylight and darkness, these political shysters contributed to the death of Emmett Till. The guilt is upon them because of the unfair and unconstitutional decrees that will bring nothing but trouble to both races."[28]
   More than angry recriminations and threats pervaded the sensitive atmosphere prior to the trial. In Memphis several black youths were arrested for the repeated rape of a white girl. According to the victim's boyfriend, the assailants were angered by the circumstances surrounding Till's demise.[29]

27. Memphis *Commercial Appeal*, Sept. 10, 1955; Jackson *Clarion-Ledger*, Sept. 10, 1955.
28. "Emmett Louis Till," *Nation*, CLXXXI (Sept. 24, 1955), 252; Memphis *Commercial Appeal*, Sept. 11, 1955. Sensitive to derogatory references aimed at the state after the Till murder, the Mississippi press sought to mold an image of tranquil, harmonious racial co-existence. An example of such coverage was the extensive front-page attention most newspapers in the state devoted to the "heroic" rescue of a drowning black woman by an eleven-year-old white girl, coincidentally from Money.
29. Greenville *Delta Democrat-Times*, Sept. 18, 1955.

This incident, along with others, bred hysteria and paranoia among some Mississippians and undoubtedly jarred the resolve of others who favored a vigorous prosecution of the accused in the Till murder. A "defense fund" organized in behalf of Bryant and Milam rapidly gained contributions from across the Mississippi Delta, ultimately accruing an estimated $10,000.[30]

The approach of September 19 saw Sumner residents bewildered by the buildup in attention. Population in the little town of 550 began to swell as media personnel and curious individuals converged on the normally serene community. Of the news media alone, over 70 correspondents—among them noted figures representing the nation's major newspapers and magazines and the radio and television networks—would cover the trial. Many townspeople resented the threat to their isolation and were hostile to the prospect of parading their community before the pious scrutiny of an entire nation. The publisher of the town's weekly newspaper probably echoed the sentiment of Sumner's majority in voicing his fear that the trial coverage might turn into a "Roman holiday."[31]

Finally the trial date arrived. From Monday through Friday, September 23, when the jury rendered its verdict of not guilty, people throughout the country anxiously followed the proceedings.[32] For some the outcome offered solace and the assur-

30. Memphis *Commercial Appeal*, Sept. 13, 1955; "Trial by Jury," 18.

31. Memphis *Commercial Appeal*, Sept. 18–21, 1955; Greenville *Delta Democrat-Times*, Sept. 18, 22, 1955; Whitaker, "The Emmett Till Case," 148. While wary of the "aliens" in their midst, residents often extended traditional southern courtesy to the visitors. The publisher of the local newspaper allowed the correspondents use of his printing office in preparing their accounts and often entertained the weary reporters at his home. Rob Hall, reporter for the Communist *Daily Worker*, noted that the media representatives "should have no complaint whatever for the way local folk have treated them."

32. Extensive front-page coverage saturated the major daily newspapers throughout the nation, chronicling in minute detail each day's events. Whitaker presents a thorough day-to-day narrative of the trial proceedings, and the official record of the case is found in the *Minutes of the Circuit Court*, Tallahatchie County, Miss., Second Judicial District. Whitaker cites as source material an "official transcript" of the trial. No transcript of the case is found in the court records. If a trial ends in acquittal, the court is not bound to preserve a transcript. However, the lawyers for Bryant and Milam did retain a

ance of a democracy at work; others manifested anger and
were certain that respect for law and order had succumbed, at
least in this instance, to another form of "Southern justice."[33]

All activity on the first day of the trial centered upon jury
selection. The prosecution weeded numerous candidates on
questions regarding racial prejudice and monetary contributions to the defendants. Before the session recessed, District
Attorney Chatham announced that the state would not seek
the death penalty because much of the prosecution's case
rested upon "circumstantial evidence."[34]

Jury selection concluded early Tuesday, after which the
prosecution presented to the court its summons calling thirteen witnesses for state's evidence. Excitement rippled
through the tightly packed little courtroom when Till's mother
entered about midmorning for the first time. Shortly after
Mamie Bradley's appearance, more commotion resulted with
the arrival of Congressman Charles C. Diggs, Jr., of Michigan.
After an awkward moment in the segregated courtroom, he
was directed to the small press table reserved for blacks.[35]

Immediately before calling the first witness, Chatham made
a surprising request for recess until Wednesday morning in
order that "new witnesses" might be examined. Judge Swango
agreed to the motion over protests from the defense, citing
as another reason for recess the fire hazard created by the
overflowing courtroom. He ordered a limit upon public attendance during the remaining sessions.[36]

The new witnesses sought by the prosecution were three

private transcript of the case several years afterward, probably Whitaker's
source. In an interview I conducted with one of the surviving attorneys in the
case, he indicated that the transcript had "disappeared."

33. Dan Wakefield, "Justice in Sumner," *Nation*, CLXXXI (Oct. 1, 1955),
284–85, bitterly underscores the racist aspects of the trial and mocks all
factors leading to acquittal.

34. Memphis *Commercial Appeal*, Sept. 20, 1955; Jackson *Clarion-Ledger*,
Sept. 20, 1955; Greenwood *Commonwealth*, Sept. 19, 1955; Clarksdale *Press
Register*, Sept. 19, 1955.

35. Memphis *Commercial Appeal*, Sept. 21, 1955; Clarksdale *Press Register*,
Sept. 20, 1955.

36. Memphis *Commercial Appeal*, Sept. 21, 1955; Clarksdale *Press Register*,
Sept. 21, 1955; New York *Times*, Sept. 21, 1955.

black farm tenants from neighboring Sunflower County. A local black civil rights figure, Dr. T. R. M. Howard of Mound Bayou, disclosed that the three had come to him on the night preceding the trial's opening with information "possibly" relevant to the murder of Till.[37] Such testimony could definitely buttress the state's case since no witnesses to the murder had been revealed.

The courtroom in Sumner, despite Judge Swango's admonition, was packed again for Wednesday's session. The most dramatic testimony of the day came from the prosecution's first witness, Moses Wright. The elderly black man "dramatically arose" from the witness chair and pointed out Bryant and Milam as two of the men who abducted his nephew on August 28. Wright maintained, as in his earlier accounts, that two additional accomplices were with the defendants during the kidnapping. In cross-examination the defense attempted to dilute Wright's charges by attacking his ability to positively identify the abductors. After stringent questioning the old man still confidently proclaimed that Bryant and Milam were two of the men responsible for the abduction of Till.[38]

Leflore County Sheriff George Smith and his deputy also took the stand Wednesday in behalf of the state. Over vigorous defense objection, Judge Swango permitted them to recount the defendants' confession to the kidnapping upon arrest. The law officers noted that Bryant and Milam claimed Till had been released unharmed. Among others to testify in the same session were C. F. Nelson, funeral home director in a nearby community who had examined the corpse sent to Chicago for burial, and the lads who discovered the body floating in the Tallahatchie River on August 31. Nelson indicated that he had no reason to doubt the victim as someone other than Till.[39]

37. Greenville Delta Democrat-Times, Sept. 21, 1955; Clarksdale Press Register, Sept. 21, 1955; Greenwood Commonwealth, Sept. 21, 22, 1955.
38. Memphis Commercial Appeal, Sept. 22, 1955; Clarksdale Press Register, Sept. 22, 1955; Jackson Clarion-Ledger, Sept. 22, 1955; "The Place, the Acquittal," 29.
39. Jackson Clarion-Ledger, Sept. 22, 1955; Clarksdale Press Register, Sept. 22, 1955; Greenville Delta Democrat-Times, Sept. 22, 1955.

Early in the afternoon of the third session, Judge Swango recessed court until the following morning, allowing more time for prosecution and defense to interview the three important Sunflower County witnesses.

District Attorney Chatham and Special Prosecutor Robert Smith concluded their case against the defendants Thursday at approximately 2:00 P.M. Their first witness of the day was Till's mother, who had observed the trial since her arrival from Chicago on Tuesday. Mrs. Bradley testified that the body shipped from Mississippi earlier in the month for burial was that of her son. She was certain of identification and noted that the ring found on the dead youth was his father's. By now in tears, Mrs. Bradley told the court that her first husband had died in Europe during World War II.[40]

After Till's mother retired from the witness stand, the prosecution introduced its strongest evidence linking the defendants to the actual murder of Till. Eighteen-year-old Willie Reed, one of the belated witnesses for the state, offered testimony that sent a "murmur of excitement" through the trial audience, although Bryant and Milam maintained passive expressions. Reed stated that shortly after daybreak on August 28 he saw a pickup truck with four white men and three blacks drive up to a barn located on a plantation near Drew,[41] where J. W. Milam's brother Leslie worked as manager. He added that one of the blacks resembled Emmett Till. Once the group entered the shelter, Reed heard "licks and hollering" and saw one of the white men, whom he claimed was J. W. Milam, leave and reenter with a pistol.[42]

40. Memphis *Commercial Appeal*, Sept. 23, 1955; Clarksdale *Press Register*, Sept. 22, 1955; Greenwood *Commonwealth*, Sept. 22, 1955. In an editorial blasting the outcome of the trial, *Life* magazine eulogized that Till's father had been "killed in France fighting for the American proposition that all men are equal." See "In Memoriam, Emmett Till," *Life*, XXXIX (Oct. 10, 1955), 48. In fact, it was later revealed that Private Louis Till had been executed in Italy by the U.S. Army in the summer of 1945 for a series of rape-murder convictions. Had the true fate of Emmett Till's father been known prior to the trial, acquittal of the defendants would have probably been automatic.
41. Drew is a small town approximately twenty-five miles northwest of Money.
42. Greenwood *Commonwealth*, Sept. 22, 1955; Clarksdale *Press Register*, Sept. 21, 22, 1955; Greenville *Delta Democrat-Times*, Sept. 22, 1955; "The

Despite strong objection, defense counsel failed to get Reed's remarks expunged as evidence. During cross-examination the defendants' attorneys hammered at the black youth's testimony. Reed conceded that he could not positively identify any of the men in the truck because he was a considerable distance from the scene.[43]

Two other black Sunflower County residents called by the state supported Willie Reed's account. Both lived near the site of the incident described by the lad and further maintained that they saw the white men drive away from the barn in a truck with a tarpaulin spread over the bed.[44] Prosecution closed its case after this sensational testimony.

Immediately upon conclusion of the state's case, the defense appealed for a directed verdict of not guilty. Judge Swango dismissed the pretentious motion, whereupon counsel launched its attack to secure acquittal. The first witness summoned was Carolyn Bryant. Judge Swango ruled most of her account concerning the store incident with Till inadmissible to the jury because it had occurred "too long before the abduction." With the jury closeted, Mrs. Bryant reconstructed the events that transpired after Till entered the store where she was working. She stated that the black youth grabbed her and made lewd propositions before she could finally free herself.

Place, the Acquittal," 29. If Reed's version was accurate, the two whites in the truck other than Bryant and Milam remained anonymous. The two blacks in the pickup in addition to Till were later reported to be LeRoy Collins and Henry Loggins, field workers known by the defendants. The speculation concerning their presence in the episode suggests that the white men were perhaps anxious to employ other blacks to accomplish their "dirty work." After the trial had ended, Till's mother claimed that several "eye-witnesses" to the murder, referring to Collins and Loggins, were detained in jail to prevent their testimony. A black correspondent covering the trial, Jim Hicks, brought the same accusation. See Memphis *Commercial Appeal*, Sept. 25, 1955, and Jackson *Daily News*, Nov. 18, 1955. Whitaker corroborates these charges, stating that Collins and Loggins were held in the Charleston (county seat of East Tallahatchie) jail under false names during the trial. He maintained his information came from Bryant and Milam's chief counsel, J. J. Breland. See Whitaker, "The Emmett Till Case," 150.

43. Greenwood *Commonwealth*, Sept. 22, 1955; Clarksdale *Press Register*, Sept. 22, 1955; Greenville *Delta Democrat-Times*, Sept. 22, 1955.

44. Greenwood *Commonwealth*, Sept. 22, 1955; Clarksdale *Press Register*, Sept. 21, 22, 1955; "The Place, the Acquittal," 29.

She further noted that when Till left the building he directed a loud wolf whistle at her. One of the defense attorneys acted the part of Mrs. Bryant's attacker for the court audience, embracing the pretty witness in the way she indicated that Till had done and also producing a shrill wolf whistle.[45] Although Carolyn Bryant's testimony held little direct bearing on the innocence of the defendants, the defense realized its significance in gaining "understanding" for their clients.

A major part of defense strategy lay in convincing the jury that the body recovered from the Tallahatchie River on August 31 was not that of Till. In this endeavor Sheriff Strider proved an eager witness, testifying that in his opinion the corpse had been in the river from ten to fifteen days. Defense attorneys also called upon two morticians, Dr. L. B. Otken of Greenwood and H. D. Malone of Cleveland, for their expertise regarding decomposition. Both agreed that the body in question had been much too deteriorated for only three days in the river. However, under cross-examination Dr. Otken acknowledged that the injuries found on the victim could have hastened decomposition.[46] After the state finished questioning the morticians, Judge Swango recessed court until Friday morning.

On the fifth day of trial defense rested its case at approximately 10:30 A.M., after six "character witnesses" had been brought forth in behalf of the defendants. Once again attorneys for the accused appealed unsuccessfully for a directed verdict of not guilty.[47] A short recess followed the conclusion of defense evidence, after which final summations were presented.

Prosecution and defense were given an hour and ten minutes each to summarize their cases before the jury. Both took all the

45. Memphis *Commercial Appeal*, Sept. 23, 1955; Clarksdale *Press Register*, Sept. 23, 1955; Whitaker, "The Emmett Till Case," 151. Although the jury members were not permitted to hear Mrs. Bryant's re-creation of the store incident, they were already well aware of the details and rumors surrounding the episode.

46. Clarksdale *Press Register*, Sept. 23, 1955; Greenville *Delta Democrat-Times*, Sept. 23, 1955; Whitaker, "The Emmett Till Case," 151–53; Huie, *Wolf Whistle*, 30.

47. Clarksdale *Press Register*, Sept. 23, 1955; Greenwood *Commonwealth*, Sept. 23, 1955; Memphis *Commercial Appeal*, Sept. 24, 1955. Neither Bryant nor Milam was called to testify during the course of the trial.

allotted time, during which a silent courtroom audience followed every word of the emotional pleas. District Attorney Chatham, closing a long and distinguished career, delivered such an impassioned oration for conviction that the defense could not look him in the face. Concluding his argument, Chatham expounded that the case was "dripping with the blood of Emmett Till."[48]

At approximately 2:30 p.m., the jury retired to consider its verdict. Few attending the week-long proceedings seriously doubted what the outcome would be, yet many were caught by surprise with the brevity of deliberation. After little more than an hour, the cloistered panel announced that it had arrived at a verdict—not guilty. The acquittal came so suddenly that the prosecution had to be summoned hastily into the chamber to receive the decision. Very little "commotion or excitement" from the audience accompanied the finding. Upon hearing the verdict rendered, Roy Bryant concluded, perhaps more accurately than intended, "I'm glad to get loose."[49]

After the widely heralded murder trial had ended, the jurors were besieged by reporters anxious to know the reasons for acquittal. The general consensus of the twelve-member panel was that the state had failed to prove conclusively the identification of the body. The jury foreman noted that his colleagues were "unimpressed" by the statement from Till's mother positively identifying her son and that they also had "ignored" the testimony of Willie Reed.[50]

---

48. *Ibid.*, Jackson *Clarion-Ledger*, Sept. 24, 1955.

49. Clarksdale *Press Register*, Sept. 23, 1955; Jackson *Clarion-Ledger*, Sept. 24, 1955; Memphis *Commercial Appeal*, Sept. 24, 1955; New York *Times*, Sept. 24, 1955.

50. Clarksdale *Press Register*, Sept. 24, 1955; Memphis *Commercial Appeal*, Sept. 24, 1955; New Orleans *Times-Picayune*, Sept. 24, 1955. Identity of the corpse could have been established easily enough by summoning expert medical examiners. However, Whitaker concludes that the jury never actually doubted the identity of the body. Long after the trial he interviewed the jurors, claiming only one expressed reservations regarding the corpse. Whitaker further notes that all of the jurors believed Bryant and Milam, or others with them, guilty of the murder. His conclusion, akin to that of Hamilton Caldwell, evolves to the thesis that the defendants would not be punished "simply" for the murder of a Negro who had been foolish enough to violate a long-standing southern "taboo." See Whitaker, "The Emmett Till Case," 155.

If the trial "revealed the innocence" of Bryant and Milam, many other questions had been raised. Whose body was pulled from the Tallahatchie River if not Till's, and where was Till? What about the truckload of men that Willie Reed maintained he had witnessed enter a barn—incidentally on a farm managed by one of Milam's brothers—from which he heard a brutal beating administered? Was this account simply to go "ignored" as the jury had done? Finally, Moses Wright had insisted that others besides Bryant and Milam abducted his nephew. Leflore County authorities testified during the trial that the two men admitted the kidnapping, proving Wright a sound witness. Why then would the elderly black man lie about the number involved in the crime?[51]

Outside response to the acquittal of Bryant and Milam was immediate and emotional. Congressman Diggs, who had attended most of the trial sessions, stated that he had "never witnessed such perjury and fantastic twisting of facts. . . . The one antiseptic which helped clean the bad taste of the trial from my mouth was the fairness of Judge Curtis Swango."[52] In addition to the thousands of individuals expressing outrage at the verdict, leading newspapers, magazines, and journals editorially blasted the trial outcome. The *Christian Century* noted that the "brevity of the trial and its incredible verdict piled shock upon shock." Although referring to the judge as "fair" and the prosecution "diligent," the magazine continued, "What offends common humanity was the spirit of the defense, the atmosphere in the community, and the swift certainty of the jury's decision." Displaying an even greater disgust, *Life* magazine concluded simply that justice had been trampled by the "whole mass of Mississippi prejudice." Denunciation even echoed in Europe, where the popular French

51. Newspaper columnist B. J. Skelton alluded to these questions in the Clarksdale *Press Register*, Sept. 24, 1955. If Reed's testimony was accurate regarding what he saw at dawn on August 28 and if the blacks linked to the scene were secretly jailed during the trial, as maintained by Whitaker, what later became of them remains a mystery.

52. Jackson *Advocate*, Oct. 1, 1955. Abundant praise was generally accorded Judge Swango for his conduct in the trial, even by those who scorned the verdict.

newspaper *Aurore* printed that Bryant and Milam were acquitted "to the enthusiastic cries of a racialist public, by a racialist jury."[53]

Challenging the hostility voiced in reaction to the Till case, dispatches supporting acquittal also inundated news outlets. The core of these accounts, as earlier, suggested a Communist complicity in the dramatized affair, along with the "God-given" right of white men to defend their women. One ever-vigilant American wrote, "The party member who worked on Till did not know exactly what the boy would do to stir up trouble, but he planted ideas which he knew would explode in some way that could be used by his party. . . . Did not some communist agent murder the young Negro after the white men turned him loose?"[54]

Practically the entire Mississippi press, along with neighboring state newspapers, praised the "fairness and integrity" displayed at the trial in Sumner. Most papers maintained that, in spite of earnest and vigorous prosecution, the state had failed to produce necessary evidence warranting conviction for murder. Voicing a near statewide sentiment, the Greenwood *Commonwealth* observed that "Mississippi can handle its affairs without any outside meddling and its long history of proper court procedure can never be questioned by any group. The trial at Sumner added another chapter to this fact."[55]

One of the few critical state dailies was Hodding Carter's Greenville *Delta Democrat-Times*. The paper refused to condemn the decision of the jury, "despite the logical conclusions it might have made concerning whose body was most likely found in the Tallahatchie River, and who most likely put it there." It did castigate the "law officials who attempted in such small measure to seek out evidence and to locate witnesses," especially damning the role of Sheriff Strider before and

53. "Double Murder in Mississippi," *Christian Century*, LXXII (Oct. 5, 1955), 1132; "Emmett Till's Day in Court," *Life*, XXXIX (Oct. 3, 1955), 37; Memphis *Commercial Appeal*, Sept. 25, 1955.
54. Memphis *Commercial Appeal*, Sept. 25, 1955.
55. Greenwood *Commonwealth*, Sept. 24, 1955.

during the trial. However, criticism was directed not only at local bodies; Carter chided the NAACP for its "distorted reporting" of the case, blaming such as a contributing factor to the verdict.[56]

Over the weekend following the trial, the NAACP sponsored rallies in New York, Chicago, Detroit, and Baltimore decrying the acquittal of Bryant and Milam. Congressman Diggs, Till's mother, and Dr. T. R. M. Howard were among those who addressed the audiences. During the next few months thousands of dollars poured into NAACP accounts, the result of more public appearances by those who had attended and testified at the trial, including Moses Wright and Willie Reed—no longer residents of Mississippi.[57]

Controversy surrounding the trial in Sumner continued long after the army of reporters had vacated the small community to pursue other headlines. Sheriff Strider resolutely maintained that Till was alive and well and that the entire episode had been staged in order to focus hostile national attention upon Mississippi society. At the same time, aroused black leaders repeatedly sought Justice Department intervention into the case. Finally a small delegation secured an audience with Arthur Caldwell, head of the Civil Rights Division in the department, only to be informed that no legal basis existed for federal intervention.[58]

Final legal action by the state against Bryant and Milam did not conclude until a Leflore County grand jury met in early November to consider indictment of the men on charges of kidnapping. If there had been a shred of vindictive journalism held in abeyance by forces angered at the outcome of the murder case, no doubt it was due in some degree to the

56. Greenville *Delta Democrat-Times*, Sept. 25, 1955.
57. *Ibid.*, Sept. 26, 1955; Greenwood *Commonwealth*, Sept. 26, 1955; Clarksdale *Press Register*, Sept. 26, 1955; Whitaker, "The Emmett Till Case," 169. Eventually the NAACP canceled sponsorship of speaking engagements by Till's mother because she demanded most of the proceeds from her appearances.
58. Greenwood *Commonwealth*, Sept. 29, 1955; Memphis *Commercial Appeal*, Sept. 30, Oct. 25, 1955.

assumed fact that Bryant and Milam would at least be incarcerated for abducting Till. Earlier the half-brothers had even confessed the deed to Leflore County authorities!

A week after their acquittal for murder, Bryant and Milam had secured bond release on the kidnapping charge. On November 7 a twenty-member grand jury began two days of deliberation in Greenwood to determine whether indictment should be brought against the two men. In addition to testimony from Sheriff George Smith and his deputy, officers to whom the accused had admitted the abduction, Moses Wright reentered the state to once again give his eyewitness version of the kidnapping. The grand jury failed to bring indictment.[59] The half-brothers were now freed of all charges originally filed against them in the Till case. Much of America looked on numb as the now famous duo sought a return to their former nondescript status.

Mississippians eagerly sought to forget the painful Till case as 1955 drew to a close. However, in January, 1956, a startling exposé appeared in *Look* magazine that rekindled national attention and resulted in haunting embarrassment for many who had supported Bryant and Milam. William Bradford Huie wrote the account purporting to chronicle the "actual facts" surrounding the Till murder. The article, according to Huie, was based primarily upon J. W. Milam's recollection of how he and Roy Bryant had carried out the kidnap-murder of Emmett Till![60]

Reaction to the story was instantaneous. Scores doubted the credibility of the publication. John Temple Graves, one of the era's noted southern spokesmen, described Huie as a "masterly and dastardly imaginist." Even numerous blacks attacked Huie because he had characterized young Till as an insolent molester who had provoked his tragic end. For

59. Greenville *Delta Democrat-Times*, Sept. 30, 1955; Greenwood *Commonwealth*, Nov. 7, 9, 1955; Jackson *Daily News*, Nov. 10, 1955; "Ill-Chosen Symbol," *Time*, LXVI (Nov. 21, 1955), 21.
60. William B. Huie, "Shocking Story of Approved Killing in Mississippi," *Look*, XX (Jan. 24, 1956), 46–50. Huie's story also appeared in *Reader's Digest*, LXVII (April, 1956), 57–62.

others, on the other hand, the article served only as confirmation of what they had always suspected. Congressman Diggs introduced the account into the *Congressional Record*, declaring that the "stunning revelations are so detailed and stated so positively, the magazine's journalistic integrity and knowledge of libel law is so well established there is no doubt in my mind that the information came directly from the killers themselves."[61] Finally, some fully accepted the exposé yet continued to defend the pair. Particularly adamant was one who wrote, "Roy Bryant and J. W. Milam did what had to be done. . . . To have followed any other course would have been unrealistic, cowardly and not in the best interests of their family or country."[62]

In later publications centering upon the Till case, Huie maintained that the firsthand information contained in his astonishing *Look* feature came by persuading, monetarily, Bryant and Milam to divulge their crime. Allegedly, in several nightly sessions with Huie the two men, Milam assuming the lead, reconstructed the details of their violence during the early hours of August 28. Milam stated, according to Huie, that they had intended initially only to scare Till and teach him a lesson regarding respect for white women. However, Till could not be intimidated and murder ensued.[63]

Nowhere in the account credited to Milam was there indication that others in addition to the half-brothers were involved in the crime, contradicting the testimony of Moses Wright and Willie Reed. Of course, though Bryant and Milam were relatively safe under the protective cloak of double jeopardy law from further prosecution in the murder case, any accomplices revealed could be subject to arrest. Thus, Milam's story aside,

61. Huie, *Wolf Whistle*, 44; (Jackson *Daily News*, Jan. 13, 1956; *Congressional Record* (Appendix), 84th Cong., 2nd Sess., A247–48.
62. *Look*, XX (March 6, 1956), 12.
63. Huie, *Wolf Whistle*, 33–36; Huie, "What's Happened to the Emmett Till Killers?" *Look*, XXI (Jan. 22, 1957), 63–68; "Shocking Story of Approved Killing in Mississippi," 46–50. Whitaker contends that Huie paid Bryant and Milam $3,500 for their story and that the interviews were held in the presence of two attorneys who had represented the men at the murder trial. See Whitaker, "The Emmett Till Case," 102, 106, 111.

the possibility remained that more than two took part in the kidnap-murder of Till.

Huie's article in January, 1956, completely altered the lives of Bryant, Milam, and their families. Many in Tallahatchie and Leflore counties who had remained unfalteringly behind the "home boys" resented the "sell out." Very soon afterward the two men found it increasingly difficult to earn a livelihood. The chain of country stores operated by the Bryant-Milam clan across the Delta had lost much of its vital black trade shortly after the murder of Till, and now the half-brothers were compelled to solicit a suddenly hostile white community for employment. After several years of meager income, Bryant and Milam relocated out of state seeking anonymity.[64]

More than twenty years after the murder of Emmett Till, most have forgotten the trial held in Sumner during a muggy September week in 1955. However, many local citizens still react defensively when reminded of it. Although the Till case might be lost in the abyss of later racial struggles, perhaps it should receive some recognition for nurturing what some historians term the "Second Abolitionist Crusade." From the time of Till's disappearance through the conclusion of the murder trial, spanning a month, the entire nation monitored the proceedings. The trial itself was one of the most publicized race cases of the twentieth century, polarizing public interest in the affair. Racial tensions had already been aroused by the Supreme Court decisions of 1954 and 1955 involving school desegregation, and the Till case fueled the bitterness. To the concerned black population in the country, the trial's outcome illuminated the many prejudicial obstacles yet to be hurdled by a people increasingly restive in their quest for color-blind justice.

One student of the Till case contends that the acquittal of Bryant and Milam stirred the "Negro revolt" that began "officially" with the Montgomery, Alabama, bus boycott in December, 1955.[65] Although this assessment might be lofty, it

64. "What's Happened to the Emmett Till Killers," 63–68; Whitaker, "The Emmett Till Case," 181.
65. Whitaker, "The Emmett Till Case," 181.

is worthy of note by those who study the sudden progression of black activism beginning in the mid-1950s. Certainly the Till murder alone and subsequent release of his killers did not prompt Rosa Parks's historic obstinacy in refusing to give up her seat on a Montgomery city bus—catapulting overnight an obscure twenty-seven-year-old black Baptist minister into the forefront of the civil rights movement—but the activist energies immediately triggered among southern blacks owed much to the frustrations ignited by the celebrated Emmett Till case.

Contributors

FRANK ALLEN DENNIS is Professor of History at Delta State University in Cleveland, Mississippi. He is the editor of *Kemper County Rebel: The Civil War Diary of Robert Masten Holmes, C. S. A.,* and is the author of several articles and book reviews. He is Bibliographical Editor of *The Journal of Mississippi History,* and is currently compiling the comprehensive index to the first twenty volumes of that journal.

ROY V. SCOTT is Professor of History at Mississippi State University.He is the author of *The Agrarian Movement in Illinois, 1880–1896, The Reluctant Farmer: The Rise of Agricultural Extension to 1914,* co-author of *The Public Career of Cully A. Cobb,* and more than a dozen articles in scholarly journals. He is a noted authority on agricultural history and the history of railroads, and has served as President of the Agricultural History Society.

JAMES W. McKEE, JR. is Professor of History at Eastern Tennessee State University in Johnson City, Tennessee. He is the author of several articles and book reviews, and lectures frequently on genealogical research methodology. He received the C. M. McClung Award in 1971 for the best article appearing in that year's volume of the East Tennessee Historical Society's *Publications,* and is a contributor to *The Encyclopedia of Southern History.*

RICHARD C. ETHRIDGE is Chairman of the Division of Social Science at East Central Junior College in Decatur, Mississippi. He has read papers to a number of scholarly conventions, and is a contributor to *The Encyclopedia of Southern History.*

FABIAN VAL HUSLEY is Administrative Assistant to the President for Academic Affairs at West Virginia Institute of Technology in Montgomery, West Virginia. He is the author of several articles and book reviews, and has drawn maps for such works as Thomas L. Connelly's *Autumn of Glory*. He is currently at work on a study of the Civil War in West Virginia.

LEE E. WILLIAMS, II is Assistant Professor of History at the University of Alabama in Huntsville. He is co-author (with his father, Dr. Lee E. Williams, Sr.) of *Anatomy of Four Race Riots*.

JOHN RAY SKATES, JR. is Professor of History at the University of Southern Mississippi. He is the author of *A History of the Mississippi Supreme Court, Mississippi: Present and Past*, and *Mississippi: A History*, and a number of articles and book reviews. He is a member of the editorial board of *The Journal of Mississippi History*, and is a contributor to *The Encyclopedia of Southern History*.

WILLIAM M. SIMPSON is Associate Professor of History at Louisiana College in Pineville, Louisiana. He is the author of several book reviews, and is currently editing his grandmother's memoirs which chronicle the life of a Methodist ministerial family in the North Mississippi Conference.